The Fiction of R.K. Narayan
Appeal in the 21st Century

Life fascinated him.

Love enamoured him.

Death remained an enigma for him.

Dedicated to my adorable father,

poet Sashikanta Das,

who has been the guiding spirit and

inspiration of my life.

The Fiction of R.K. Narayan
Appeal in the 21st Century

Subrata Debangana

Prestige Books International
New Delhi

Published by
Prestige Books International
New Delhi 110 060
prestigebooks@gmail.com
Phones: 9818755529; 9810323134

Associate Office
11 B, Broomwood Road
London SW11 6HU, U.K.

Associate Office
P.O. Box 2250
Sydney 2001, Australia

ISBN: 978-81-943009-9-1

Printed in India

Contents

Acknowledgements

This book has developed out of my Ph.D. dissertation. I am deeply indebted to my Supervisor Dr. Santwana Haldar (retired Professor of English from Odisha), who guided me with her insightful counsel at every step and helped me gain immensely as a research scholar. I express my heartfelt thanks to her for advising me to publish the book and introducing me to esteemed Prestige Books International for the purpose. I am thankful to Dr. R.K. Dhawan and Dr. Suman Bala (University of Delhi) for helping me to edit and update the book for publication.

I owe an appreciation to my friend and colleague Dr. Debasisha Pati, Asst. Professor of English, who has been instrumental in creating the urge in me to go ahead with the publication work and to make meaningful a time that has diffused an air of gloom and purposelessness all around due to Covid-19 pandemic. His critical comments on my work and his suggestions to improve have specially been helpful.

I am sincerely grateful to all the members of my families, especially to my mother, Sanjukta Devi, my husband, Suvendu Mohanty, my son, Pallav Parashar and my daughter-in-law, Pragyan Parimita, for their invaluable support and encouragement without which nothing would have been possible. My acknowledgement would be incomplete without expressing my deep gratitude to my elder brother, my mentor, my first and foremost teacher Sudev Rajarshee. A student of English literature himself and a passionate lover of it, he has introduced me to the vast and fascinating worlds of experience, opened my eyes and awakened my mind to the delight of seeing into the life of things. With his erudition, wit and wisdom, he has helped me grow and evolve through my literary journey with books and the language.

Last but not the least, I express my gratitude to Prestige Books International for bringing out this book so expeditiously and elegantly.

Subrata Debangana

The Fiction of R.K. Narayan
Introduction

R.K. Narayan (1906-2001) along with Mulk Raj Anand (1905-2004) and Raja Rao (1908-2006) established the foundation of Indian Novel in English, breaking new ground with unique styles and masterly touches. These three writers, known as the Great Trio of the Indian Novel in English, chose careers in creative writing during the nineteen thirties when it was unthinkable that a living in India as a man of letters might be possible. It required a stern consistency of purpose and an unshakable conviction to stick to the career of writing, particularly writing in English. Nineteen thirties were the crucial time in the political history of India; Gandhiji's Satyagraha movement of 1930 and 1932, the passing of the Government of India Act of 1935, the introduction of Provincial Autonomy in 1937 and the involvement in the World War in 1939, indicated the beginning of a new era, and the rise of a Post-Colonial India. Social changes, which had begun in the nineteenth century as a result of individual revolts, were also gathering momentum especially through Gandhiji's social reform movement. Reforms aiming at women emancipation and abolition of social evils like untouchability were shaking the roots of age-old traditions. Time was indeed The Fiction up for a novelist to start his work, though the task was Herculean.

Born in Madras to Rasipuram Krishnaswamy Iyer, R.K. Narayan was the second son and third child of the house. His full name was Rasipuram Krishnaswamy Narayanswamy Iyer. Rasipuram referred to the taluk in the district of Salem to which his family traced its ancestry and Krishnaswamy referred to his father's name, both attached to his name following a tradition of South India. Like others of his generation in his town R.K. Narayan dropped Iyer from his name which signified his Brahmin caste, and later dropped the 'Swamy' from Narayanswamy, when his *Swami and Friends* was published lest the book be taken for an autobiography. Though his mother tongue was Tamil, he had a good knowledge of Kannada from his boyhood as he spent a major part of his life in Mysore. He was also well acquainted with Sanskrit, the language of all ceremonies and rituals. Later in life he became an enthusiastic reader of Kamban, the poet of the 11th century who rendered Valmiki's *Ramayana* into a great Tamil Epic. Narayan had his education entirely in South India. His schooling started in Lutheran Mission School in Madras. Later he was shifted to C.R.C. High School. During that period he was staying with his maternal grandmother, Ammani, who brought him up in her loving care and strict discipline. After a period of time he came to stay with his parents in Mysore and read in Maharaja Collegiate High School where he completed his schooling. He got his Bachelor's Degree from Maharaja's College at Mysore. He had a natural and instinctive dislike for the conventional outlook to education and examination. But he was an avid reader of books of different types. The stories from Indian epics which he heard from his grandmother, along with his reading of *Palgrave's Golden Treasury*, Tagore's *Gitanjali*, Shakespeare, Keats, Shelley, Byron, Browning, Scott, Dickens, H.G. Wells, Arthur Conan Doyle, P.G. Wodehouse, Arnold Bennet, Shaw and many more, whetted his taste and shaped his mind. Gradually he began to read book reviews and developed a critical sense.

Narayan started creative writing mostly under the influence of events occurring around him and wrote in the style of any writer who was uppermost in his mind at that time. But when he started his literary career as a writer of fiction with *Swami and Friends,* he took care not to read too much or read anything that might influence his writing at the moment. His ordeals as a writer started with the repeated rejection of his writings by the publishers. He made some futile attempts to take up a job and even for a short period of time he served as a teacher, soon to realize that these things were not meant for him. At a time when he had been to Bangalore to stay with his grandmother who was there to recoup her health, Malgudi as a setting of fiction shaped in his mind and he began writing *Swami and Friends*. He completed it later after he was back at Mysore. At Bangalore he also wrote stories for an editor mainly on subjects other than love, because love appeared to be the sole theme for every novel, short story, poem and drama in existence. Later he went to Madras and had some free-lance efforts there. Soon he got an opportunity to review a book and had a story published in 'The Hindu.' He also had some experiences as a newspaper reporter in 'The Justice,' a modern daily. He did this to stabilize his income because by that time he was married to Rajam, the girl he fell in love with at first sight.

However, Narayan stopped his work as a newspaper reporter when he came to know that Graham Greene had taken the responsibility to have *Swami and Friends* published. Though he was satisfied that his book was published his financial condition hardly improved. Moreover, he had to face the pangs of separation. After a short and blissful married life his wife had an untimely and tragic death and before that his father had also died. He was left with his daughter, Hema, whose bringing up became a major preoccupation of his life. It took a long time for him to recover from the shock of the untimely death of his wife. He stopped writing for a few years and wandered aimlessly. In *My Days*, he describes the mystic experience of having psychic contact with his dead wife for some time, during the period. He learnt to compose himself, to calm down and then, he resumed his normal life and activities. He wrote his fourth novel, the very autobiographical *The English Teacher* and had it published by

Eyre and Spottiswoode, where Graham Greene was a director. The raging Second World War had already started disrupting the day-to-day life of common man causing shortages of every type. It had its repercussions on his career too. 'The Hindu' to which he was contributing articles was on the verge of being closed due to a financial crisis. He along with some of his friends started a journal 'Indian Thought' and gathered a good experience in journalism. At the same time, he continued to write his novels and stories and at a later period managed to publish them. In the course, a few collections of short stories and novels like *Mr. Sampath*, *The Financial Expert* and his most famous *The Guide* followed. Between 1953 and 1954 Michigan State University press published five of his novels all of which were extremely well received by American critics. After that there had been no looking back. By the time his arduous journey of life ended, he had left behind him a vast legacy of writing that tells today the story of his amazing success as a writer.

R.K. Narayan has fifteen novels to his credit: *Swami and Friends* (1935), *The Bachelor of Arts* (1937), *The Dark Room* (1938), *The English Teacher* (1945), *Mr. Sampath-The Printer of Malgudi* (1949), *The Financial Expert* (1952), *Waiting for the Mahatma* (1955), *The Guide* (1958), *The Man-eater of Malgudi* (1962), *The Vendor of Sweets* (1967), *The Painter of Signs* (1976), *A Tiger for Malgudi* (1983), *Talkative Man* (1986), *The World of Nagaraj* (1990) and *Grandmother's Tale* (1992). There are six collections of short stories: *Malgudi Days* (1943), *Dodu and other Stories* (1943), *Cyclone and other Stories* (1944), *An Astrologer's Day and other Stories* (1947), *Lawley Road* (1956), *A Horse and Two Goats* (1970). Among his non-fiction writings there are the travel books—*My Dateless Diary*, *The Emerald Route*—and five collections of essays—*Next Sunday*, *Reluctant Guru*, *A Writer's Nightmare*, *A Story Teller's World*, *Salt and Sawdust*. These are as delightful and enchanting as his fictional writings. He also has to his credit translations of Indian epics and myths from Tamil to English—*The Ramayana*, *The Mahabharata*, and *Gods, Demons and Others*. There is also his very lovable memoir—*My Days*.

A.L. McLeod, the editor of the book *R.K. Narayan-Critical Perspectives,* gives his tribute to R.K. Narayan in the preface: "Some, as Rabindranath Tagore, Mohandas Karamchand Gandhi, Jawaharlal Nehru, may have attained greater stature for a brief time or exerted greater influence on world events or national politics, but as a writer per se, none has worked with such great acclaim in so many genres for such a long period and with so great renown." Narayan has been duly honoured and awarded for his literary achievements both at national and international levels. He was invited by the Rockefeller Foundation to visit America. During his stay at Berkeley he wrote *The Guide* for which he won the Sahitya Akademi Award in 1960. He was awarded the A.C. Benson Medal by the Royal Society of Literature in 1980 and was made an Honorary Member of the American Academy and Institute of Arts and Letters. In 1989 he was made a member of the Rajya Sabha, the Upper House of Indian Parliament, and in 2000 he was conferred Padma Bhushan by the Government of India. An Honorary Degree was conferred on him by University of Leeds in 1967, and an Honorary D. Litt. by Delhi University. For his *My Days* published by Viking Press he won the 'English Speaking Union Books Abroad Award' of the American University, Washington D.C. Besides all these and many more, at the age of eighty-eight he was awarded with the newly-established Yatra Award, meant for an outstanding Lifetime Achievement by a South Asian Writer.

Narayan breathed his last in 2001. Even after his death there has been a widespread growth of interest in his writing both in India and abroad. In view of the increased attention to his writing, the flow of critical writings on his work remains undisturbed. Besides the reviews of his book in learned journals, serious study of his work is being done by critics and scholars all over the world.

The existing bulk of critical writings on R.K. Narayan is fairly significant and any additional comment necessitates an explanation and justification. There is hardly any aspect of his fictional writings that has been left untouched. Realism, myth, irony, humour, narrative art, vision of life—all these aspects have been thoroughly discussed from various perspectives by critics in India and abroad. Since the exploration of realism is ultimately subsumed in the larger question of the relationship between life and art, most critics harp on realism in Narayan's work, using the word realism from their own perspectives. A brief assessment of the major critical writings on Narayan—an assessment particularly of Narayan's rendering of 'reality' in his fictional work—is given here for instance.

Graham Greene, Narayan's earliest western admirer, wrote enthusiastically (Introduction, *The Bachelor of Arts*) with reference to his first novel that "it brought India . . . in the sense of the Indian population and the Indian way of life alive to me." William Walsh, one of the noted critics of Narayan's writings (*R.K. Narayan: A Critical Appreciation* 1992), emphasizes the autobiographical elements which, he says, are responsible for imparting a realistic touch to his portrayal of characters and places. In his early novels, Walsh says, an immediate transmission of these elements is noted. But in the next set of novels these elements are "thrown into new combinations, suffused with the colour of the novel's theme and modified to fit the particular context" (61). This change in style marks, according to Walsh, a passage from "an enclosed, contemplative personal art to a more strenuously imagined and external fiction" (62). Walsh praises the lucid, unaffected and lively style of Narayan's short stories which are packed and crammed with life, work, habits, expectations, predicament and religion of India. He appreciates the setting of Malgudi as India itself and credits Narayan for making the microcosmic world of Malgudi a real one.

Almost a similar observation that realism in Narayan's work is entirely based on the autobiographical elements has been made by R.M. Varma in his study of R.K. Narayan's fictional writings (*Major Themes in the Novels of R.K. Narayan* 1993). He finds Narayan tied down to events, people and places of real life. He also differentiates Narayan's art from that of a writer of historical romance which is set in a world of thrilling and glorious past, far removed from the world of present-day reality. Varma categorizes the major themes of Narayan's fictional work in the following way: (i) Human Relationship, (ii) Love and Marriage, (iii) Socio-cultural and political scene of the country between 1933 and 1983, and (iv) the Hindu ethos, including renunciation as an ideal of the Hindu way of life in India. These four major themes, Varma asserts, run through Narayan's fiction as recurrent and compulsive motifs, and are faithfully portrayed by the novelist against his fictional locale of Malgudi.

P.S. Sundaram, another notable critic of Narayan, (*R.K. Narayan* As a Novelist 1988), too, puts emphasis on the personal experience that goes to make the theme of his novels and on the fidelity with which Narayan presents things as they are. According to him Narayan deals only with those characters, which he had come across as they were, without exaggerating their virtues and their vices, and as a result Narayan is true to life and true to his art. The picture he draws reveals a fine picture of India.

Hillary Mantel ('Real Magicians' 1995) describes Narayan's world as one that is already familiar to the Indians and is made familiar to the non-Indian readers. Yet, she maintains that the exotic is still maintained within that familiarity. She appreciates Narayan's sharp eye and his capacity to get surprises from life. Any day, any street, any room, in an accustomed house, any face known since childhood, can suddenly be fresh, strange and new for Narayan. It is as if one reality peels away, and shows another underneath. Rather ignoring the prominence given to the autobiographical elements, Edwin Gerow ('The Quintessential Narayan' 1977) puts emphasis on the artistic elements in Narayan's novels and defines them as belonging to the 'classical art.' He finds in Narayan a happy blending of an essential Indianness, a stylistic sophistication and familiarity as well as a profound intellectual commitment to artistic modes and ideals. Meena Sodhi ('R.K. Narayan: His Life into Art' 2000), finds no photographic representation of life in Narayan's work. Rather, she finds very ordinary people being portrayed in amazingly extraordinary manners. The routine of ordinary life is transformed into a rich experience. The bits and pieces of his life do not exist in his novels as mere autobiographical statements but are turned into a kind of leitmotifs of his art. While some critics find fault with Narayan's choice of setting in his fiction, she finds Narayan's strength in the selective nature of his setting that offers a sense of proportion. According to her, Narayan selects and organizes the raw material available to him in the city of Mysore and immortalizes that material in the form of art.

Among the severe critics of Narayan, V.S. Naipaul, comes first. He (*A Wounded Civilization* 1979) criticizes Narayan's stock figures in his cosy novels, his restricted settings, his 'karmic' world view that is seen as an ideological retreat for Hindus unable to cope with quotidian realities, his non-interference and fatalism. He comes upon heavily on what he says, Narayan's refusal to break away from 'religious theatre' in order to take a serious look at what is happening in the streets. And in the process, he says, Narayan abdicates his office. According to him, Narayan simplifies reality. In contrast to the cosy and comic world of Narayan, Naipaul finds India as cruel and overwhelming.

In his reply to Naipaul's allegation, Sudesh Mishra ('Malgudisation of Reality' 1994) holds that Naipaul's is the Post-Romantic tradition of psychological realism. For Naipaul, Mishra says, novel is a form of social enquiry that narrates socio-political realism and assesses the ideological formations which govern the motives and actions of individuals, institutions and communities. He does not privilege "aestheticism over verism" (87). Narayan, on the other hand, is concerned primarily with imparting 'comic pleasure' at the expense of *le realisme.* The world he creates is a 'fantastic enclave' inhabited by characters who reflect a caricatural reality that can never, no matter how fertile the human imagination, be taken as an approximation to phenomenal reality. Mishra further argues that Narayan invents an 'aberrant microcosm' in which complex realities are displaced so that even the probable strike us as sensational transferences to the remote and the improbable. Naipaul blunders to compare Malgudi with actual India or for that matter with simplified India. Sudesh Mishra says that Narayan renders an 'insular milieu' where privation and distress are under erasure and Naipaul shows his dissatisfaction with it. John Updike ('Malgudi's Master' 1997) also dismisses the dissatisfaction as expressed by critics, the dissatisfaction at Narayan's light hearted treatment of a small field of observation and omission of the problem ridden, poverty-stricken immensity of India. He finds himself happy and content in Narayan's world, for he sees the entire humanity in it, if not the whole continent. In his opinion the details of life in Narayan's fictional works has a resonance, 'a branching truth,' which has no match anywhere. Critics are often vocal about Narayan's faith in Hinduism which, they say, turns his fiction to fable. Naipaul's view (*A Wounded Civilization* 1979) in this regard is that "Narayan's novels are less the purely social comedies I had once taken them to be than religious books, at times religious fables, and intensely Hindu" (22). For Shyam S. Agarwalla, however, Narayan's quiet and gentle Hindu identity does not come in conflict with his art.

K.R. Srinivas Iyengar, an acknowledged authority on Narayan, and Meenakshi Mukherjee, another noted critic, do not take into account the autobiographical elements that go into his fictional writings. Iyengar (*Indian writing in English* 1983) and Meenakshi Mukherjee (*Twice Born Fiction* 2001) focus on Narayan's fictional world as being small, confined, uncomplicated but Indian in spirit. They show how Narayan has made the best use of his limitations. They show him as a detached observer, dealing with his observations with wit, humour and irony. Drawing a comparison of Narayan's art with that of Jane Austen, Iyengar observes that he is satisfied like Jane Austen, in his small precocious world. He is a detached observer who likes to concentrate on a narrow scene, sense the atmosphere of the place, to capture a small group of characters in their oddities and angularities. He is also credited with the capacities of exposing the mind, heart and soul of his characters and catching the uniqueness in the ordinary, the tragic in the prosaic. Iyengar observes that in thoughts and feelings, in the stirrings of the soul, the wayward movements of the consciousness, Narayan in every bit belongs to the soil of India. Meenakshi Mukherjee (*The Perishable Empire* 2002) also draws attention to the "even-toned minimalist representation" in Narayan that avoids any kind of intricacies which only insiders can decipher. She observes that Narayan's readership is spreading far and wide, India and abroad, and he converts his constraints to his advantage by using humour and irony as weapons. According to her, he portrays "distillable Indian reality" (170) through particularized situations but remains uninvolved in them.

H.M. Williams (*Precarious Innocence: Patterns in the Novels of R.K. Narayan.* 1981) perceives Narayan as essentially a comic writer. According to him, Narayan's comedy benefits from the relatively fixed and traditional nature of South Indian Society in much the same way as Jonson's 'humours' comedy did from the fixity of Elizabethan medieval society. Shyam S. Agarwalla ('The Achievement of R.K. Narayan-A Perspective on his Novels') quotes E.M. Forster's comment on Narayan—

Narayan's writing is "high-class comedy free of all isms," Forster said—to assert his point of view that Narayan's comic sense is meant for pure delight and entertainment. He also finds it unusual that living in the colonial and post-colonial period, Narayan could make his work singularly devoid of ideology or propaganda of any colour. Anita Desai ('Narayan Country' 1982) brands the particular realism found in Narayan as compassionate realism with which the author observes life in the microcosmic world. She also praises his sense of humour—fresh, sharp and wryly ironic—that prevents his writing from crumbling into the sugary crystals of sentimentality. C.V. Venugopal has a different opinion on Narayan's humour. He criticizes ('A Master of Comedy—R.K. Narayan as a short story writer' 1969) Narayan's humorous sketches (in his short stories) in which he makes us laugh heartily over silly themes. Referring to the great masters of English Short Story—H.E. Bates, D.H. Lawrence, Graham Greene, William Faulkner et al—Venugopal observes that, "the short story in the twentieth century has attained a form that is compact, concentrated, significant and even symbolic of deep significance occasionally, while maintaining the ease and familiarity of diction" (186-87). Narayan's stories, he observes, are lacking in these qualities and they are hardly significant. Venugopal alleges Narayan for being content with only those aspects of life that provide the readers with 'harmless mirth.' As a result, a fantastic range of human absurdities dominate in his writing.

A new age critic Shashi Tharoor ('Revisiting R.K. Narayan' 1994) has a mixed opinion of the treatment of reality in Narayan. He points at the banality of Narayan's concern, the narrowness of his vision, the predictability of his prose, the shallowness of the pool of experience and vocabulary from which he draws his style. He also points at the restricted setting, ordinariness of subjects, and inadequacy of language, all leading to a bathetic rendering of intense and potentially charged situations. Yet, on the other hand, he says, what makes up for these shortcomings is the precision and empathy with which he portrays the small and restricted society. Tharoor also speaks of the gentle wit, the simple sentences, the easy assumptions of inevitabilities of tolerant Hindu social and philosophical systems, and the characteristically straightforward plotting of Narayan's fiction. Blissfully free of the political clashes, social conflicts and historic upheavals that dominated Indian life during Narayan's time, his writing is authentic in reflecting faithfully the world view of a self-obsessed and complacent community (small town, upper-caste, middle-class). Shashi Tharoor further says, "Like Austen, his fiction is restricted to the concerns of a small society portrayed with precision and empathy" (22) and "unlike Austen, his prose cannot elevate those concerns beyond the ordinariness of its subjects" (22). Yet, he says, "Narayan's writing offers the simple and timeless pleasures that only straightforward depiction of the familiar can provide" (22) and there is "a charm, an aptness in the unselfconscious descriptions" (23) in his writings.

S.P. Swain ('The Novel of R.K. Narayan and Indian Reality' 1992) too, affirms that Narayan's characters dwell in the reality of our existence. According to him, the Indian myth is a reality in Narayan, and myth figures as the ultimate vision of reality. S.P. Swain finds in Narayan's fiction individuals who are deeply rooted in the Indian social matrix. Indian reality in his novels is reflected in the perpetual clash between tradition and modernity. The novelist's spatio-temporal consciousness makes his work more real and genuinely artistic. With a reference to Soyinka's famous study *Myth, Literature and the African World*, Dr. Rama Kundu observes in her article ('Myth, Ritual and Demonology' 2003) that Myths arise from man's attempt to externalize and communicate his inner intuitions. She finds Narayan's basic Indianness in his use of themes, vocabulary, proverbs, personae, place and the use of myths. According to K. Chellappan ('Indianness as a mode of perception; A. Study of R.K. Narayan,' 1994) the core of Narayan's vision and art seems to lie in an awareness in which illusion and reality, the mundane and the spiritual, the comic and the human, the tragic and the cosmic easily exchange places. It is a change in the mode of perception that matters.

Thus, critics have explored various aspects of Narayan's fictional writing: an Indianness and a universal appeal; real life elements and artistic elements; the tragic and the comic; humour, pathos and irony. Critics have agreed that realism is one major aspect of his works but they differ in their views about his approach to reality. In view of the existing critical writings on Narayan's approach to reality in his fictional writing, the present study makes a humble attempt to make a fresh appraisal of the author as a realist.

The Artist and His Art

Realism in art and literature means "portrayal of familiar things as they really are without idealizing them" (Oxford Dictionary). This brief definition hardly does any justice to the vast realm of theories on realism. Moreover, the portrayal of things as found in life is likely to be of varied nature, thanks to the different perspectives of observing the world around. Ever since Aristotle's definition of poetry as 'Imitation of life' has given rise to the 'Mimetic Theory of Art,' there has been an endless discourse on the relation between truth in life and truth in art and literature. On the basis of this theory a literary work is viewed as an imitation, or reflection, or representation of the world and human life, and the primary criterion applied to it is that of the 'truth' of its representation. It is curious to note that authors claiming to be realists indicate the nature of 'truth,' which they wish to project in literature in various ways and thereby make their own definitions of realism. These authors, sometimes belonging to opposite poles, are influenced by different philosophers who have used the term 'realism' to suit their respective purposes and judgments, and thus have given rise to concepts opposed to one another.

Any attempt to define 'realism,' therefore, is likely to be bogged down in what Mark Kinkead-Weekes and Ian Gregor say "a notoriously treacherous concept."[1] As Damian Grant points out, the "chronic instability" of the word 'realism' is revealed in its "uncontrollable tendency to attract another qualifying word, or words, to provide some kind of semantic support"[2]. Grant offers, primarily, twenty seven examples such as "psychological realism," "socialist realism" etc., and suggests that it could be better for the future critics to find a new word other than finding some permutation of the word 'realism.'[3] Yet the word 'realism' is profusely used by authors and critics, particularly by the novelists and the critics of novels. For, any definition of 'novel' as a distinct genre lays emphasis on its capacity to portray characters and events within a specific time. A characteristic trait of the Western novel from Defoe to Balzac is an apprehension of the details of the visual world including specific human action. Such an apprehension is loosely called 'reality.' 'Novel' is differentiated from the earlier forms of narrative on the basis of how a novelist apprehends this 'reality' through his/her consciousness of time and space.[4] To quote Meenakshi Mukherjee in this context, the novelist depicts situations, spatial and temporal ones, employing realism as one of the viable forms of viewing this concrete human reality (1985: 5).

As a literary movement of the 19th century, realism in prose fiction has begun with Balzac in France, George Eliot in England and William Dean Howells in America. In spite of the differences in their approaches to 'realism' these writers and their followers have followed a common pattern: they have selected the commonplace and the everyday life for their subject matter, choosing characters from the middle class or the working class people who have lived through ordinary experiences and found life rather dull and unhappy. The extreme kind of such presentation which the critics chose to label 'naturalism' is based on a world-view according to which a human being exists entirely in the world of nature and inherits compulsive instincts such as hunger and sexuality. The exposure of these instincts was taken up so enthusiastically that the trend drew severe criticism. The critics of 'naturalism' in literature could not however deny the contribution of the naturalist school to literature: it is Naturalism that has marked the deviation from 'once-upon-a-time' ambience in fictional writing. In his celebrated work '*Mimesis*,' Erich Auerbach has asserted the superiority of the 19th century French

Novelists over the earlier world literature, observing that "the serious realism of modern times cannot represent man otherwise than as embedded in a total reality, political, social and economic, which is concrete and constantly evolving."[5] He is, yet, not blind to "a realm beyond reality" when he refers to the great art of Homer. "(Homer) does not need to base his story on historical reality, his reality is powerful enough in itself; it ensnares us, weaving its web around us, and that suffices him. (And this) *real* world into which we are lured exists for itself, contains nothing but itself" (11). Auerbach's observation on Homer refers to "reality" other than historical truth, or fidelity to actuality and thereby opens the possibility of blending factuality with a realm beyond factuality. In fact, "fidelity to actuality" focuses on the immediate, the here and now, and anything beyond the immediate is ignored.

Indian literature did not have any tradition of involvement in the immediate. Even when the nineteenth century Indian writers of fiction started writing on the Western model they could not remain engaged only with the palpable sources of physical reality. The Indian writers during the late nineteenth and early twentieth century—writing both in regional languages (Bhasha Literature) and in English—sincerely tried to come out of the environment of the pre-novel tales, and yet they could not altogether deny the existence of reality beyond the physical world. The unconscious influence of the Indian tradition—of *the Ramayana, the Mahabharata* and *the Puranas*—was always there, forbidding the writers to focus on individual doubt and loneliness ignoring absolute faith and collective values.

The main trend of novel, even at its early stage of development as a distinct genre in India, however, was to adopt the mode of 'social realism' prevalent in the contemporary European novel. Mimetic representation of contemporary Indian society replaced the fairy tale atmosphere of earlier fictional writings. In his preface to *Indulekha* (1888), a Malayalam novel, the writer

O. Chandu Menon wrote, "A taste has set in for pictures, whether in oil or water colours, in which shall be delineated men, beasts, and things according to their true appearance, and the closer that a picture is to nature, the greater is the honour paid to the artist. Just in the same way, if stories composed of incidents true to natural life and attractively and gracefully written, are once introduced, then by degrees the old order of books, filled with the impossible and the supernatural, will change, yielding place to the new."[6]

The trend continued and the advent of Marxist thoughts introduced specific social problems such as exploitation and oppression, in the domain of fictional writing. Harinarayan Apte (Marathi), Bankim Chandra Chatterjee (Bengali), Fakir Mohan Senapati (Oriya) and Prem Chand (Hindi) are well known Indian novelists who modified the mode of social realism in their writings.

Though the emergence of the Indian novel in English is attributed to the colonial legacy, even the early writers of the genre sincerely chose to be Indian, accepting the Indian society as the setting for their novels. The choice of typical Indian characters and introduction of Indian issues, social, economic and political, helped the development of Indian novel in English. Among the first generation Indian novelists in English Mulk Raj Anand sought to explore the oppression inflicted on the lower class people (*Untouchable, Coolie, Two Leaves and a Bud*) and also introduced political themes (*Across the Black Waters, The Sword and the Sickle*). Anand made use of the novel as a medium to express his plea for social change. As a writer he was motivated by anger and pity. His association with the Progressive Writers' Movement in India made him a natural supporter of the leftist 'Peace' Movement, though politics claimed only a small part of his life. In his special preface to the second Indian edition of *Two Leaves and a Bud* (1951) Anand acknowledged that the characters in his novels—a waif like Munoo in *Coolie*, an untouchable like Bakha, an indentured labourer like Gangu, among others—were reflections of the real people he knew during his childhood and youth. He wrote "they were flesh of my flesh and blood of my blood, and obsessed me in the way in which certain human beings obsess an artist's soul. And I was doing no more than what a writer does when he seeks to interpret the truth from the realities of his life." Anand had no laborious psychological or ideological preoccupations and he allowed his characters to speak and act in their own ways.

While Anand concentrated on the struggles for economic and political power by the underprivileged, Raja Rao focused on the nationalist struggle and its revolutionary implications in terms of mythology, religion and culture. Raja Rao depicted the development of the Non-co-operation Movement led by Gandhiji in India (*Kanthapura*). For Raja Rao the real nature of India was to be found in 'racial self-consciousness' and therefore, he presented life as constantly reflecting the past as in the Hindu concept of successive rebirths and the arrival of the God in the form of 'Avataras' during chaos. Raja Rao's narrative art and his enchanting prose style made him quite a different sort of novelist. He revealed in his work the forces let loose by the Gandhian Revolution and also the forces of past tradition. In a brilliant passage of *The Serpent and the Rope*, Raja Rao wrote "the world is either unreal or real—the serpent or the rope. There is no in-between the two—and all that is in between is poetry, is sainthood." For him the novel was a medium to discuss the revolutionary fervour and religious consciousness.

R.K. Narayan, the third of the trio, is neither an angry protester nor a revolutionary[7]. He is interested in the life of the middle class people of South India—a life free from the privations and agonies, political conflicts and economic depression of Anand's India and also from the magic and mystery of Raja Rao's. But like theirs, life rendered in Narayan is remarkably faithful and real. He draws an imaginary, but credible locale called Malgudi in South India. Raja Rao's "Kanthapura" is in South India too, set in the province of Kara. It is an ancient slow-moving village that symbolizes Hindu India. He shows how this remote village is stirred to life by the impact of Mahatma Gandhi, a social and political messiah. For Raja Rao, this small, insignificant village of common and ordinary people gained in immense significance from time to time, over the ages having gone through such ecstatic experiences as Gandhi's pilgrimage to it[8]. Narayan's Malgudi however gains little significance from any outside source. It is a growing and developing town, teeming with humanity and drawing its sustenance from the human drama that is enacted in it. In return it gives the personages a local habitation and name. Like Thomas Hardy, William Faulkner and Arnold Bennet, Narayan achieves great success in the localization of life, a factor essential to realistic novels.

Critics have tried to locate the locale of Narayan's fiction, Malgudi, in various ways. But the answer so far has remained elusive and inconclusive. Trying to ascertain the real identity of Malgudi K.R. Srinivasa lyengar poses a few questions as his answer—"Can it be that Lalgudi, in Trichinopoly District, and fringing the River Cauvery, is the original of 'Malgudi'?" (1983: 361) and "Has Lalgudi merged with Yadavagiri to become Malgudi?" (1983: 363). According to William Walsh, Malgudi is the imaginative version of his beloved Mysore[9] (1992: 6). According to M.K. Naik, "It must be remembered that Malgudi is situated in Tamil Nadu, as is clear from Raju's description of the newly started Malgudi railway station in *The Guide*. He clearly refers to two whole trains each day, the noon train from Madras and the evening one from 'Trichy' (38). The local language is obviously Tamil, as is evidenced by several references in the novels beginning with the one to the Tamil Pundit (40) in the school *in Swami and Friends*''[10]. However, all these views can only be regarded as mere conjectures and not as facts.

In this context Narayan's own version of the genesis of Malgudi is more reliable. According to him, "On a certain day in September, selected by my grandmother for its auspiciousness, I bought an exercise book and wrote the first line of a novel; as I sat in a room nibbling my pen and wondering what to write, Malgudi with its little railway station swam into view, all ready-made, with a character called Swaminathan running down the platform peering into the faces of passengers, and grimacing at a bearded face; This seemed to take me on the right track of writing." (*My days* 2006: 87)

Earlier in an interview with Ved Mehta, Narayan had thrown light on the conception of the place: "I remember waking up with the name Malgudi on Vijaya Dashami, the day on which the initiation of learning is celebrated. It was in September 1930 that the name of the town was vouchsafed to me by the divine patrons of knowledge. Malgudi was an earth-shaking discovery for me, because I had no mind for facts and things like that, which would be necessary in writing about Malgudi or any real place. I first pictured not my town but just the railway station, which was a small platform with a banyan tree, a station master, and two trains a day, one coming and one going. On Vijaya Dashami, I sat down and wrote the first sentence about my town: 'The train had just arrived at Malgudi station.'"[11]

In an interview he says to Susan E. Croft, that the idea for this famous place "just happened" in his head: "An imaginary town like that has great possibilities. You can make anything of it, whereas if you set your town in a real place you are bound by the geography and its existing structure. But in a place like Malgudi, though the heart of the city may be fixed, it can expand."[12]

Narayan sounds, in fact, hesitant about giving Malgudi a specific location: "Malgudi has been only a concept but has proved good enough for my purposes. I can't make it more concrete however much I might be interrogated. When an enthusiastic television producer in London asked me recently if I would cooperate by showing him around Malgudi and introducing him to the characters in my novels for the purpose of producing an hour-long feature, I felt shaken for a moment and said out of politeness, I am going to be busy working on a new novel . . . about a tiger possessing a human soul" (Author's Introduction, *Malgudi Days*).

Taking a cue from Narayan's words in *My Days* that "Finally I did break out of the triangular boundary of Madras, Mysore and Coimbatore[13] and left for the United States in October 1956" (2006: 188), R.M. Varma concludes that it is this 'triangular boundary' of the novelist which is shaped by his imagination as Malgudi: "Malgudi is no single place—not even an imaginative version of any single place; it is a happy blend of three major South Indian cities in which the novelist has breathed, moved about, and lived all his life." (1993: 74)

Arguing against M.K. Naik's propositions that Malgudi is situated in Tamil Nadu because the local language in Malgudi is Tamil as evidenced by several references in the novels, R.M. Varma observes that Narayan's mother tongue being Tamil he is more at ease with his mother tongue than with any other language; and that language spoken by the characters can hardly establish the identity of Malgudi, "just as the nationality of a person cannot be determined by the language he speaks, unless he knows only one language—his native language." Moreover, "Tamil is not spoken exclusively in Tamil Nadu" and "Tamil is still spoken by some people, at least beyond the geographical and political boundary of Tamil Nadu at present, in the adjoining states, including Mysore, which used to be a part of the greater Modern State not very long ago" (1993: 73). This, according to Varma, makes it inconclusive to say that Malgudi is in Tamil Nadu.

Irrespective of all these debates and controversies critics are unanimous in the point that this local habitation of Narayan has an Indianness as well as a ring of the universal around it. It is not that this local habitation does not face strong criticism for being narrow and circumscribed[14]. But as Meenakshi Mukherjee says, nothing could be "more provincial and localized than the life of Malgudi town, yet R.K. Narayan successfully achieves a universal vision through it" (2001: 35). Iyengar finds Malgudi to be 'the real hero' of Narayan's novels (1983: 363). According to C.D. Narasimhaiah, "Malgudi is the microcosm of traditional Indian society."[15] Though confined to the geographical boundary of South India, life in Malgudi brings profound resonances of the real Indian experiences—experiences of school children and college boys, men at work, family life and human relationships, marital harmony and disharmony, relationship beyond marriage, religious ethos and activities, blind faith and superstitions, disease and death, social evils like caste system and corruption, freedom struggle and its impact on the masses, a cross current of the East and the West, and the like—experiences that every Indian is well acquainted with. But the delineation of these Indian experiences immediately strikes a chord in readers beyond the national boundary. There is a universal appeal in them for there is a 'humane face' to the rendering of the story of man. Walsh rightly says, "What happens in India happens in Malgudi, and whatever happens in Malgudi happens everywhere" (1992: 59).In the words of Iyengar, "Malgudi is Narayan's 'Casterbridge,' but the inhabitants of Malgudi—although they may have their recognizable local trappings—are essentially human and hence, have their kinship with all humanity. In this sense, 'Malgudi' is everywhere" (1983; 360). Each of Narayan's novels thus opens a new door into human existence.

A keen observer of life, Narayan has gathered his materials from his varied experiences of life and knowledge of the physical world in which he spent his life. The places among which he moved at different phases of his life have had a strong impact on his conception and creation of Malgudi as well as in picturing its growth and development. This is justified when he says in *My*

Days, "I found in the life around me plenty of material. The atmosphere and mood were all important. Life offered enough material to keep me continuously busy." (105)

Narayan has had the map of Malgudi conceived by him in his mind and had no confusion about it. He has also been fascinated by the map of Malgudi drawn by an American professor visiting Mysore.

Like any village or town of the world, Malgudi is a land of river, hill, temple, forest, roads and the like. Malgudi goes through different phases of growth and development. At the beginning in *Swami and Friends* it is neither a village nor a city, but a town of modest size. As time passes, it grows with extensions from all sides and develops rapidly as a modern town. However, the major landmarks remain intact—the river Sarayu flowing by its side, Nallappa's Mango Grove and the Mempi forest surrounding it, the Forest Road leading to the Grave and the Trunk Road leading to Trichinopoly. There are the streets—Kabir Street, Vinayak Mudali Street—and the lanes—Kabir Lane, Abu Lane etc.—which also remain the same. In the early thirties Malgudi even has a Municipality, Town Hall, a club, the Albert Mission School, the Board School and the Albert mission College. New landmarks like the Palace Talkies, Anand Bhawan, and Modern Lodge are added to the old ones. There are the Lawley Statue, Lawley Extension, Temple street, the small shops and business establishments, the houses with their 'pyols' in front and many other things. These places recur in all his novels achieving a sort of transmigration, novel after novel, stories after stories and give out a sense of continuity and familiarity. The main streets and residential places are given their character and distinctiveness through the people who live there and who are the main characters in the novels. Lawley Extension is described in the early novels as a place where mainly the rich, respectable Brahmin families live with a certain code of behaviour prescribed for them. The New Extension has enormous showy houses such as Neel Bagh, where important people live. Similarly Kabir Street, another part of the town, is marked by the conservatism of the people who reside there. Kabir Street and Ellamman Street are the two spots where village landlords settle and build houses in order to seek the comforts of urban life and educate their children in Albert Mission. Their descendants are comfortably placed, occupied mainly in eating, breeding, celebrating festivals, spending the afternoons in prolonged siesta on the pyol, and playing cards. The women rarely come out as they spend their time in the kitchen or in a safe room scrutinizing their collection of diamonds and silks.

There are villages like Sukur and Mangala surrounding Malgudi. Newly discovered places of beauty and importance—the Mempi Peaks, the Mempi Peak House on the topmost cliff, and the caves with their carved doorways, wall paintings and musical notations on the wall—attract attention. The myth-steeped minds of the Malgudians associate mythical or legendary importance to the certain places like the Sarayu and the Mempi forest[16]. At the same time Malgudi is introduced with many development schemes—construction of a bridge over the river, a housing project, road development and tank building etc, under the process of rapid modernization and urbanization in the post-independent era. To the age-old values and beliefs, traditions and social systems, are added new ways of living and thinking. But in actuality Malgudi remains more economically ravaged than culturally touched. As Nivedita Ganguly says, "Life flows as gently as the Sarayu—there are no earth shaking events, no melodrama, no great conventionalities in any of the characters or events. Life is as placid and easy as Narayan's own."[17]

For his fictional works, Narayan draws no story from history or from any great historic events of the country or outside. He focuses his attention obviously on the commonplace, but not exactly on the everyday represented in minute detail. His is mundane reality, but the reality does not dwell upon the daily drudgery of man. It rather centres on the common man, mostly belonging to the Indian middle class, making sincere efforts to fit him into a world of customs and traditions and of changing values. But, unwittingly, in the process he betrays his own oddities and angularities, eccentricities and absurdities, whims and fancies, strength and weakness. He leads mostly an uneventful and peaceful life, but sometimes he has to face ups and downs, conflicts and confusion. It is his reactions to such situations that form the basis of Narayan's stories. And as Narayan often alludes to certain actual experiences of his life, the characters and events of his stories acquire a fervour that persuades the readers to believe that the entire story is taken from actual life. Narayan's characters don't possess heroic qualities and are not great achievers. They are not men of power and fortunes, but yet, they, too, try to transcend the levels of the ordinary. They, too, experience short phases of greatness and momentary glow in their lives which redeem their quiet and commonplace living. But ultimately, it is their return to and reconciliation with the bare realities which matter. According to William Walsh, "Things flow as an infinite variety of things, of men and manners, relations and women, associations and degrees, joys, disappointments and disasters. To the author this is the nature of reality; to the characters living their day to day life, it is what they will, perhaps, with a moderate kind of happiness, finally accommodate themselves to." (1992:168)

Narayan projects life as seen from various perspectives, not from the perspectives of one character. Except for the first three novels *Swami and Friends, The Bachelor of Arts, and The English Teacher*, in which the autobiographical overtone is strong and resonant, and the writer's presence is felt quite clearly, the autobiographical elements recede to the background in his later works. Leaving behind the 'sheltered existence' of 'dear old Malgudi,' in these novels we enter into "an exotic world of half-headed and half hearted dreamers, artists, financers, speculators, twisters, adventurers, eccentrics, cranks, cinema stars, sanyasis—several of them not Malgudi products, but straying or imported from 'outside.'" (Iyengar 1983: 373)

Malgudi life is seen from the perspective of these new inhabitants. Narayan tries to explore the inner recesses of the human mind from where spring man's dream, fantasy, fancy and imagination, his rare experiences of magic and mystery, which are integral and indispensable to his existence. These elements serve the purpose of showing life from various angles, of presenting a panorama, rich and varied, broad and wide. The use of the fantastic in Narayan's work may raise a doubt in regard to his concept of reality. But Narayan apprehends the fantastic as a part of reality, not as something opposed to reality. As says P.S. Sundaram, the fantastic in Narayan, is deliberate, as in Dickens. "Basically Narayan's world is our own everyday world, not Sudhin Ghose's world of magic and whimsy" (1988: 137). According to Manoj Das, "There is no clear evidence of Narayan believing in matters occult despite a character or two of his having supernatural experiences like his modest hero in *The English Teacher* who sees the apparition of his wife but which can very well be interpreted as hallucination. Nevertheless mystery of a kind abound in Narayan—the mild delectable mystery of hopes, anticipations, of things expected and unexpected, with which we go on."[18]

Narayan's writings also provide ample scope to rediscover Indian myths, exposing the beliefs, superstitions, rites and rituals contained in those myths all of which is fundamental to an average Indian's very existence. They show man's roots in his past and also create the mindset with which he has to live in the present. In them lies the power to shape his reality, to alter his perception, to hold differing perspectives and create new worlds of experiences. Reiterating his views on an average Indian's knowledge of age-old myths and legends and its impact on his mental growth, Narayan says,

> For an Indian classical training begins early in life. Epics, mythology and Vedic poetry (of Sanskrit origin and of tremendous antiquity) are narrated to everyone in childhood by the mother or the grandmother in a cosy corner of the house when the day's tasks are done and the lamps are lit. Later one reads them all through one's life with a fresh understanding at each stage. Our minds are trained to accept without surprise characters of godly or demonic proportions with actions and reactions set in limitless worlds and progressing through an incalculable time scale.
>
> With the impact of modern literature we began to look at the gods, demons, sages and kings of our mythology and epics, not as some remote concoction but as types and symbols, possessing psychological validity even when seen against the contemporary background. When writing we attempted to compress the range of our observations and subject the particle to an intense scrutiny. Passing, inevitably, through phases of symbolic, didactic, or over-dramatic writing, one arrived at the stage of valuing realism, psychological explorations, and technical virtuosity. (*The Writerly Life* 2001: 466)

Narayan's use of myths and legends, magic and mystery produces a uniquely different effect. It reveals his comic view of life. It also helps him create the necessary framework on which his story is built. Narayan shows an in-born capacity to view the everyday world with humour; like an entertainer he writes with the purpose of entertaining. Human follies and foibles, misadventures and misfortunes are exposed for the readers, to watch and enjoy. These are exposed with utmost sympathy and perfect understanding. There is no harshness in tone and no acrimony of intent. There is no despondency, no desperation either. In the Introduction to *The Bachelor of Arts* Graham Greene says, Narayan's is a different kind of humour which has an 'underlying sense of beauty and sadness.' In what are called Narayan's comedies of sadness, the serious is blended with irony, humour and satire to set the tone. His comic characters pose difficulties for themselves or for the society and build up the comic tension, which is finally solved amicably or harmlessly for all concerned, without bringing about any major change in life. These comic characters—the "motley crowd," as says Monaj Das—are ultimately "fascinating for their naiveté and oddities as well as small dreams and modest sacrifices"[19]. Satire, if directed at them, is mild. Irony and humour being integral parts of his narrative technique he could easily overwhelm the readers with the subtlety of his art. To quote H.M. Williams, "Conservative India is seen with humour and some satire as a mixture of traditional holiness, with the comfort loving sterility of the bourgeoisie. Modern India is seen as an inevitable, but on the whole inescapable phenomenon, compounded extreme political activism (nationalist and Marxist), permissive sexual morals, the breakdown of the traditional extended family system, American popular culture and rabid half-lunatic violence. The secret of Narayan's art is his ability to keep the views in a perfect balance. It makes him a subtle writer, concealing irony beneath a blandly simple exterior as a 'plain' storyteller teller."[20]

Irony and humour also project Narayan as a detached observer of reality. As a detached observer Narayan chooses to withhold his comments, and leaves it to the readers to interpret the thought and action of his characters. He does not present his own opinions through his characters or no particular character ever represents him. Irony and humour are used as camouflage; readers are misled to get at his world view. Comparing him with Raja Rao and Mulk Raj Anand, Meenakshi Mukherjee says that there are two categories of novelists, "some who carry a burden of commitment which they hardly ever lay down, while there are others who write as observers and chroniclers." She says further, "Among the non-committed again, the degree of detachment differs greatly. There is R.K. Narayan whose whole achievement depends on his capacity to remain uninvolved" (2001: 45). He is just a passive onlooker and not a citizen of the fictive town, because he never participates in its activities.

Narayan neither professes a moral truth in his novels and short stories, nor does he suggest what human nature ought to be. He does not aim at rectification or reformation or reconstitution of any aspect of life because he realizes that evil and good, vices and virtues shall remain together, side by side. Himself a religious man, he has no religion to preach. Both a religious-minded Sastri and a secular Vasu, as in *The Man-Eater of Malgudi*, have their points to make. Narayan's sensibility operates on various levels of human experiences and he does it in a style that can be called neutral"[21]. He wants his novels only to be read and enjoyed, and to be left at that[22]. Graham Greene compares Narayan's objective and dispassionate observation and his portrayal of life with that of Chekhov and Gogol. It may be pertinent in this context to refer to Chekhov's remark on his own art as quoted from one of his letters to A. Suvorin, the founder editor of *Novol Vremya*. The comment brings out the difference between his method of writing fiction and that of the authors of the great realistic period: "The best of them are realistic and paint life as it is; but because every line is permeated, as with a juice, by awareness of a purpose, you feel beside life as it is, life as it ought to be, and this captivates you. And we? We paint life as it is and beyond that no 'gee-up' nor no 'gee-down.' . . . Beyond that even if you lashed us with whips we could not go. We have neither immediate nor remote aims, and in our souls—a great emptiness."[23] Narayan, too, paints life as it is, without any purpose to show what life ought to be.

In the process of commenting on the exclusion of many aspects of life in Narayan's novels, Iyengar compares Narayan's art appreciatively, with that of Jane Austen and says that Narayan is content, like Jane Austen, in his small world (1983: 360). But most of the other critics have attacked Narayan for excluding a vast area of life, and this exclusion is seen as a weakness of his fictional writings. According to V.S. Naipaul, Narayan tells an Indian truth, but does not tell the whole truth: "Too much that is overwhelming has been left out, too much has been taken for granted. There is a contradiction in Narayan, between his form which implies concern, and his attitude which denies it."[24]

Keith Garebian criticizes Narayan for not cultivating what he says "a certain measure of unsparing brutality" and this, he says, is the cause of failure of *Waiting for the Mahatma*. Narayan is criticized for presenting the half truth, the image of Gandhi having been portrayed as sentimental Indians like to see it[25]. While Garebian finds *Waiting for the Mahatma* disappointing as a satire, A.N. Kaul finds *The Dark Room* disappointing as a tragedy.[26]

It is, in fact, true that though Narayan's writing spans the greatest period of change in modern Indian history, and also in world history, hardly does it reveal the vast Indian panorama during the declining days of the British Raj and the period after Independence. There is little impact of the Second World War on his characters. That is why Naipaul finds Narayan lacking in the spirit of rebellion[27] and observes that Narayan cannot, therefore, be called a great novelist[28]. There are some other critics who find Narayan sensitive to the plight of individuals but unable to relate their dilemmas to the social structure in which they live. P.S. Sundaram strongly opposes all such criticism: "The trouble with this kind of criticism is that we are accustomed to, or expect a particular presentation and have no patience with a writer who has his own ways and values. There is a great deal in our country that is wrong and ought to make us indignant. But who are we to prescribe that the only correct attitude is one of indignation? Rebellion is often a virtue but to say 'no rebellion, no art' is just nonsense. . . . The world presented by Narayan is commonplace only to those who have no time to go beneath the surface."[29]

However, Narayan has been aware of this alleged limitation of his writings. In his characteristic humorous and satiric tone, he records an imaginary conversation among the members of the Nobel Award Committee. One member is imagined to be arguing that Narayan's work possesses none of the elements that go to make great literature: "All great literature must echo the soul of man. The struggles, agonies and anguish in the soul of the individual must be reflected in the work, against the background of historical and social convulsions of the countries in which the individual finds himself tossed about as a helpless victim. All the grimness of existence must find a place in a writer's work. Above all, a certain degree of obscenity and difficulty of idiom in the text enhances the structure of a literary work. 'Applying these tests Narayan's work fails.'" (*The Writerly Life* 2001: 505)

In the course of this imaginary conversation, when Narayan is asked by a professor whether he has ever tried to place his finger on the pulse of the nation, he replies,

> No, because I am interested only in the individual and I am extremely suspicious of the phrase 'national aspiration.' It is pretentious and phony. Each person has a private universe and lives many lives. You will be nearer the mark if you speak of the problems, hopes, and aspirations of a person: say a doctor's hope to see more sick people coming in; the sick man hoping his doctor is a minor God capable of holding him back from the grave; the politician's jugglery to win votes; the voter's fleeting euphoria of being a king-maker; the boys' hope that his school roof would have collapsed at week-end; the politico-man's dream that the thief would walk-in with stolen property and save him all the trouble; the cobbler at the street-corner watching passing feet for worn-out soles; the house-holder's concern to keep his budget and family in proper shape; the snake charmer with his assets curled up in the bamboo baskets; the peripatetic knife-grinder's cry down the street on a hot afternoon, an infinite variety of lives overlapping and complementing one another. I am moved by such patterns of life, and not by your 'national aspiration.' What is it really? Do you visualize six hundred million to look skyward on a given day and shout their aspiration in a single voice? (*The Writerly Life*: 508)

In a reply to the charge brought against him that he never bothers to describe the details of love relationship in his novels, he says:

> Is there any need for elaboration? I find that the very mention of a darkened room with whispers coming through the bolted doors stirs your imagination to such an extent that you ask for more. I am confident that at a certain point I can safely leave it all to the reader's imagination without fettering it with wordy descriptions. Particularly after D.H. Lawrence, no writer can have anything original or fresh to say about lovers. However, to please you, I am prepared to add a footnote at the appropriate place in my novels: For further details look up *Lady Chatterley's Lover*. Even the authors of American bestsellers, which provide its readers bed scenes at regular intervals, say once every five thousand words, exhibit nervousness while seeking new phrases for an old experience, and often let their narrative degenerate into a sort of popular treatise on anatomy. (*The Writerly Life:* 509)

When Narayan is accused of skipping fundamental human experiences, he says, "Experience is vast and one is forced to be selective. If every bodily function and physical and mental activity is to be recorded without any omission, not all the world's paper supply will suffice even for a single novel. Anyway, I now have an idea of what you are looking for. Why don't you go and contemplate the sculptural masterpieces at Khajuraho to start with? There you will find exuberance, beside which Swedish films will look like the work of starched puritans?" (*The Writerly Life*: 509)

This imaginary conversation, written in a humorous way, focuses on the particular 'reality' (truth) that Narayan seeks to depict in his fictional writings and on those aspects of truth that he seeks deliberately to shun. First, it is found that his approach is different from that of the naturalist, who ends in the desert of an exact likeness to what happens in one's daily life when one is affected by, say, hunger, sexuality and such other feelings. Secondly, Narayan has little to do with national consciousness. That is why when he introduces Gandhiji as a dominant figure in *Waiting for the Mahatma*, his focus is not on the national movement but on the change in the life of the common man, thanks to Gandhiji's arrival in that place called Malgudi. Thirdly, when he uses myth (as in *The Man Eater of Malgudi*), he does it in quite a different way—different, say, from the way Raja Rao does. He adds an ironic twist to the myth that helps him render the traditional Indian viewpoint with a mildly satirical tone.

Narayan is also accused of leaving out the poor and the unprivileged from the scope of his narration. The accusation does not, in fact, hold good, because Narayan writes about what he understands best and with what he can do justice. It is his fidelity to his art that matters. The beauty and honesty with which he paints the middle class, the class he could encompass within his vision the best, makes his writings quite gratifying and his characters entertaining. It is this that makes Manoj Das remember 'the charming attitude' with which Graham Greene views Narayan. Graham Greene says, "Whom shall I meet in Malgudi? That is the thought that comes to me when I close a novel of Mr. Narayan's. I don't wait for another novel. I wait to go out of my doors into those loved and shabby streets and see with excitement and a certainty of pleasure a stranger approaching, past the bank, the cinema, the hair-cutting saloon, a stranger who would greet me I know with some unexpected and revealing phrase that will open a door in to yet another existence." (Introduction, *The Financial Expert*).

Besides his probe into the affairs of the middle class, there is also rendering of the marginalized. The kind of subtlety and mastery he shows in his insight and understanding of the poor, particularly in his short stories, is noteworthy. In this context, his stories like 'A Horse and Two Goats' and 'The Evening Gift' are worth mentioning. Though the focus of attention in these stories remains somewhere else, yet they contain vivid pictures of the harsh realities of life. Coming forward in defence of Narayan's selection and exclusion of certain aspects of life Manoj Das very appropriately comments, "Narayan was the first Indian fiction writer to be widely read abroad. That was remarkable, for he cooked no delicacies out of his country's shortcomings; he churned out no concoction of realism and erotica. He focused on the little ironies of life, exaggerated to the permissible degree of caricature and cartooning. Also he often presented authentic glimpses of South Indian scenes where God, Love and life made a smooth collage, as in *The English Teacher*."[30]

Narayan is evidently unique in his art. He blends exact realism, poetic myth, a mild ironic tone of narration and humour with melancholy. Dreams and facts are often set against each other to present a whole picture of life. His comic vision embraces an intense humanism. His art is kind but unsentimental, profoundly Indian and at the same time distinctly individual. The attractive Indian setting and the human drama enacted in it explain his success as a realist. The landscape embodies structural solidity of Indian reality. Narayan's characters take after people we meet in real life, people for whom renunciation, incarnation, rebirth and the law of Karma are very much real. Some critics ascribe the faith of his characters to the author, ignoring the humour and irony with which he creates them. In his humour lies the deepest wisdom that tells of human limitation and, quite without illusion, of human achievement.

NOTES

1. Mark Kinkead-Weekes and Ian Gregor, *William Golding*: *A Critical Study*, London: Faber & Faber, 1967: 121.
2. Damian Grant, *Realism*, London: Methuen, 1970: 1.
3. *Ibid*, p. 2. He says, "The word (realism) is in fact delinquent, and writers have indicated their mistrust of its behaviour."
4. To quote George J. Becker in this context, "Realism is a formula of art which conceives of reality in a certain way, undertakes to present a simulacrum of it." *Documents of Modern Literary Realism*, Princeton, 1963:36. Harry Levin even claims that "all great writers, insofar as they are committed to a searching and scrupulous critique of life as they know it, may be reckoned among the realists." *The Gates of Horn*, New York, 1963: 83.

5. Erich Auerbach, *Mimesis*, trans. William Trask, Princeton, 1953: 408. Auerbach also exposes the insufficiency of this definition. He acknowledges that Dante's 'realism,' projected into a changeless eternity, differs from what appears on earth and yet is evidently connected with it in a necessary relation. Again, Shakespeare embraces reality but he transcends it; his tragedies go beyond "actual realism."
6. *Indulekha* (Trans. from Malayalam by W. Dumergue), Calicut, 1965; reprint: xiv.
7. Comparing R.K. Narayan with Mulk Raj Anand in *R.K. Narayan, A Critical Appreciation*, 1992, William Walsh says that though as a writer Anand has a deep feeling for the deprived, a grasp of the social structure of his society and an extraordinary fluency of communication, he lacks 'the concrete sagacity,' the 'finesse,' 'the talent for the particular' . . . which marks everything that R.K. Narayan writes (5). Raja Rao, as Walsh says, is very different from Narayan in being 'poetic, metaphysical, Lawrentian' (5). Walsh further says, 'If Anand is the novelist as reformer, Raja Rao the novelist as metaphysical poet, Narayan is simply the novelist as novelist' (6).
8. Introducing his 'Kanthapura,' Raja Rao says, there is no village in India, however, mean, that has not a rich sthala-purana, or legendary history, of its own. Some god or god-like hero has passed by the village—Rama might have rested under the peepal tree, Sita might have dried her clothes, after her bath on this yellowstone, or the Mahatma himself, on one of his many pilgrimages through the country, might have slept in this hut, the low one, by the village gate. In this way the past mingles with the present, and the gods mingle with men to make the repertory of your grandmother always bright. One such story from the contemporary annals of my village I have tried to tell (Foreword, *Kanthapura*).
9. In *My Days* Narayan categorically speaks of the river side, forest, village, and woods, granite steps and the crumbling walls of an ancient shrine all in Mysore—which combined to make up the Malgudi of '*The Guide*,' where he wanted the film version of the novel to be shot (2006:196).

10. M.K. Naik, *The Ironic Vision: A Study of The Fiction of R.K. Narayan*, New Delhi: Sterling, 1983: 107.
11. Ved Mehta, 'The Train Had Just Arrived at Malgudi Station,' *The New Yorker, Digital Edition*, September 15, 1962: 74. Again, in an interview with the All India Radio, Narayan had said, "Malgudi is a small temple town situated on the bank of a holy river, like Nanjangud. It is also a University town, like Mysore." Qtd. N.S. Ramachandraiah, 'Review of P.S. Sundaram's *R.K. Narayan*,' *The Deccan Heralds*, 14 April, 1974.
12. Susan E. Croft, An Interview with R.K. Narayan, *R.K. Narayan: A Critical Spectrum*, Bhagwat S. Goyal, Meerut: Shalabh: 30.
13. Besides Madras and Mysore, Coimbatore is another place to which Narayan remained connected. He used to visit his sister's house at Coimbatore and it was during one of his visits to the place that he met Rajam for the first time, fell in love with her and later married her.
14. Naipaul alleges: "His comedies were of the sort that requires a restricted social setting with well-defined rules; and he was so direct, his touch so light, that, though he wrote in English of Indian manners, he had succeeded in making those exotic manners quite ordinary. The small town he had staked out as his fictional territory was, I knew, a creation of art and therefore to some extent artificial, a simplification of reality." *India: A Wounded Civilization*, 1979: 21. Referring to Narayan's fictional world of Malgudi and its underlying sense of stability and continuity, Stephen Hemenway comments, "This accounts for provincialism in novels, a trait which is simultaneously good—it provides continuity and skilled handling of local colour—and not so good—it limits his subject matter and ultimately results in a circumscribed view of life." *The Novel of India Vol.2*, Calcutta: Writer's workshop: 19.
15. C.D. Narasimhaiah, *The Swan and The Eagle*, Simla: Indian Institute of Advanced Study, 1969: 136.
16. In *The Guide* Raju describes how a tourist goes to the source of the river Sarayu and speaks all night about it: "how there was a small shrine on the peak right at the basin. 'It must be the source of Sarayu mentioned in the mythological stories of goddess Parvathi jumping into the fire; the carving on one of the pillars of the shrine

actually shows the goddess plunging into the fire and water arising from the spot' etc." (1985: 51). In *A Tiger for Malgudi*, pointing at the towering peak of the Mempi range, the ascetic says to the tiger, "I was here before, and once saw a flash of light on the very tip of that peak and felt overwhelmed by its mystery since no human being has ever set foot there. Although I realize now that it might be no more than a touch of the moon rising behind it, I will still watch for it: I have a great desire to see that flash again." (156-57).

17. Nivedita Ganguly, 'Any Town Tamilnadu,' *The Sunday Statesman, Literary*, Sunday 24 June, 2001.
18. Manoj Das, 'Tribute, Goodbye to Malgudi,' *The Sunday Statesman, Literary*, Sunday 20 May, 2001: 3.
19. *Ibid*, p. 3.
20. H.M. Williams, *Indo-Anglican Literature 1800-1970: A Survey*, Madras: Orient Longman, 1976: 50.
21. J.K. Biswal, *A Critical Study of the Novels of R.K. Narayan*, 1987: 123. Biswal says, A comic vision embraces the multifarious facets of human life. Narayan operates in a framework of traditions and social morality which is much bigger than the individual, his ego and oddities. Sooner or later, normal reality takes hold of the situation including the aspiring and erring individuals. Hence man's encounter with the world appears ludicrous. The comic vision always offers the consolation of a reconciliation. Man's small villainies, his innumerable temptations and tragedies and the frequent abysses and heights in his life—all these that form the totality of life are affectionately treated by Narayan with a humane understanding of life's complexities (1987: 75).
22. Expressed in a letter to P.S. Sundaram and also to Sujata Balsubramaniam video *Imprint*, Bombay, June 1976, as quoted in 'Malgudi to Manhattan.'
23. Qtd. Harish Raizada, *R.K. Narayan: A Critical Study of His Works*, New Delhi: Young Asia Publications, 1969: 157.
24. V.S. Naipaul, *An Area of Darkness*, 1968: 216.
25. Garebian says, "Narayan is not writing political drama of the nature of Markandaya's *Some Inner Fury* or Malgaonkar's *The Princess*. . . . Yet, we must not hesitate to find his lapses and criticize

him for his sins of omission." *The Literary Half-Yearly*, Jan. 1976: 89-90.

26. A.N. Kaul, 'R.K. Narayan and the East-West Theme,' C*onsideration*, ed. Meenakshi Mukherjee, New Delhi: Allied: 43-65.
27. In his article 'Assertiveness in R.K. Narayan,' Vinay Kirpal strongly opposes V.S. Naipaul's criticism that Narayan is a passive, other worldly writer with characters who are indifferent to the social and political tensions in Indian society. To lend authority to his argument, Naipaul quotes Camus from *The Rebel*: "It is possible to separate the literature of consent, which coincides, by and large, with ancient history and the classical period, from the literature of rebellion, which begins in modern times. . . . The (modern) novel is born at the same time as the spirit of rebellion and expresses, on the aesthetic plane, the same ambition." (*An Area of Darkness*: 216). Kirpal argues in favour of Narayan's 'aesthetics of rebellion' and observes that Narayan's characters are both 'illustrative' and 'representational.' He writes "He is a writer who exposes the wrongdoings and weaknesses of individuals and systems with a cartoonist's irony and detachment. Narayan does not have to write history and politics to be called a rebel or his characters assertive." *The Critical Endeavour*, ed. M.Q. Khan and B.K. Das, Cuttack, vol. XV, Jan., 2009: 217-227.
28. V.S. Naipaul, *An Area of Darkness*, 1968: 216.
29. P.S. Sundaram, 'Naipaul on Narayan,' *The Indian Journal of English Studies,* Vol. XVII, 1977: 131-32.
30. Manoj Das, 'Tribute, Goodbye to Malgudi,' *The Sunday Statesman, Literary*, Sunday 20 May, 2001: 3.

Short Stories: India in Microcosm

The short story is a brief narrative in prose with the usual constituents of the novel—plot, characters and setting. Like the novel the short story organizes the action, thought and interactions of its characters into the pattern of a plot with a beginning, middle and some sort of denouement at the end. The plot may be comic, or tragic, or romantic, or satiric presented in the mode of fantasy, realism or naturalism. However, the short story is never an abridged form of the novel. Nor does it possess the dimension of the novel. The short story has some restrictions while the novel enjoys the freedom of introducing unlimited characters, leisurely analysis, sustained development of characters, detailed rendering of the social milieu and the like. Edgar Allan Poe, who is often called the originator of the modern short story, emphasizes on the 'unique or single effect' of a story. All the details are subordinate to that effect. A popular definition of short story—that it can be read in an hour and remembered for a life time—focuses on this unique effect as well as the economy in management of its various components.

In its oldest form the short story appeared as the fable and the folk tale, written both in verse and prose. Its modern form has been brought to existence by writers like Washington Irving, Hawthorne and Poe in America, Sir Walter Scott in England, E.T.A. Hoffman in Germany, Balzac in France, and Gogol, Turgnev, Tolstoy and Dostoevsky in Russia. It has reached its height in the works of Guy de Maupassant and Anton Chekhov in the second part of the nineteenth century and then in the writings of the experimentalists—James Joyce, D.H. Lawrence, Katherine Mansfield, Franz Kafka as well as Herman Melville, O' Henry,

William Faulkner, Ernest Hemingway and the like—in the twentieth century. All these writers are noted for their different attitudes and approaches to life and literature which make their contribution to the genre of the short story rich and varied.

The Indian short story in English is a much later development. Rooted in the Indian folktales and fables of the ancient time, it blends indigenous tradition with the western art of story-telling. Leaving aside the sporadically written short stories of late nineteenth and early twentieth century, the real meaningful journey of Indian short story in English started from 1920s, and now it has made a notable effect on the panorama. Modern Indian short story in English has developed side by side with the Indian novel in English, depicting typical Indian characters, Indian milieu, Indian moods and tone. Besides the 'Big Three' in the domain of Indian English fiction—M.R. Anand, Raja Rao and R.K. Narayan—established writers like Khushwant Singh, Bhabani Bhattacharya, Manohar Malgonkar, Manoj Das, to name a few from among the galaxy, have made extraordinary contribution to the repertoire of modern Indian story in English. Anand has a long list of short story collections to his credit—*The Lost Child, and other stories* (1944); *Indian Fairy Tales Retold* (1946); *The Tractor and the Corn Goddess, and other stories* (1947); *Reflections on the Golden Bed, and other stories* (1953); *Power of Darkness, and other stories* (1959). He uses materials from fable, parable, folk-tale, and writes realistic stories and portrays characters affected by a variety of moods. Raja Rao offers a great thematic and formal variety though his output is small. In his *The Cow of the barricades and other stories*, he presents portraits of rustic life, the Gandhian movement and the plight of the Hindu widow, and matters of metaphysical concerns. In contrast to these two masters, R.K. Narayan approaches the Indian scene with no serious angle of study. He provides his readers with a variety of characters, and incidents, sometimes funny and sometimes sad, but never having to propound a philosophy or put forth a theory. His comic vision that sees the little ironies of life, and his genial humour with which he treats his subjects, bring out the poetry and pathos of human existence.

Early in life Narayan developed a habit of watching people around. His career as a reporter and journalist also offered him ample opportunities to watch people keenly, deepening thereby his acquaintance with human characters and the world they lived in. He found 'endless variations' within the broad climate of inherited culture of India with individuals differing from each other: "not only economically but in outlook, habits and day-to-day philosophy" (Author's Introduction, *Under the Banyan Tree*). India offered him a wealth of subjects for his stories, utilizing which he churned out innumerable short stories during his long literary career.

Narayan's early stories were compiled in three volumes *Malgudi Days*, *Dodu and Other Stories* and *Cyclone and Other Stories*. The first two were published in 1943 and the last in 1944. Most of his stories have been republished later in other collections as *An Astrologer's Day and Other Stories* (1947) and *Lawley Road and Other Stories* (1956). A much later collection is *A Horse and two Goats* (1970) containing five tales that have appeared for the first time. Still later collections are *Old and New* (1981), *Malgudi Days* (1982), *Under a Banyan Tree and other Stories* (1985) and *Grandmother's Tale and Other Stories* (1994). Many of the stories in these collections were first published in *The Hindu*, a Madras daily. Narayan also contributed some stories to leading American journals like *The Reporter*, *The New Yorker*, *Vogue* and others. In fact, his early stories were written to be published in journals and newspapers and offered him the scope to earn his living during his period of struggle as a writer. However, his short stories, no less significant than his novels, have created a distinct place for themselves in the literary history in course of time.

The well-known Malgudi, the Indian microcosm, comes alive in his stories with characters that come from all possible corners of the society. Even the ignorant, the illiterate, the hopelessly poor men and women of the lower strata of life are not debarred from an entry into his stories. Insurance clerks, photographers, shopkeepers, doctors, astrologers, postmen, beggars, professional exorcists, prostitutes, dancers, domestic servants crowd the scene of action. They are ordinary men and women living ordinary lives. Still amidst the ordinariness Narayan discovers a moment or an experience that is special and memorable. With his deep insight he also delves into the psychological world of his characters in which dwell their beliefs and superstitions, fancies and imagination, individual aspirations and social obligation. His powerful narrative art brings out the implication of all these aspects within the brief space of the short stories.

The world of Malgudi is a familiar world for the Indian readers and also for the non-Indian ones, because, as Narayan says, 'the characteristics of Malgudi seem to me universal' (Author's Introduction, *Malgudi Days*). During the process of delineating a character or telling a situation of his life, Narayan does not give a 'minutely worked-out detail' as he does it in his novels. But 'through a mere suggestion of detail,' with 'the focus being kept on a central idea or climax,' he brings the story into existence (Author's Introduction, *Malgudi Days*). It begins without any prelude or circumlocution. Curiosity remains intact as he is a master in the use of surprise. Sometimes facts from his own life or real incidents intrude into the realm of his stories. Memorable stories like 'A Breath for Lucifer,' 'Annamalai,' 'A Horse and Two Goats,' 'The Shelter' have their origins in real life experiences. Referring to them Narayan says, "A story may have its origin in personal experience or a bit of observation or a conversation overheard" (Introduction, *Under the Banyan Tree).* 'A Breath of Lucifer' was dictated to him into a cassette when he had to spend ten days in bed with eyes bandaged following a cataract operation, and was attended on by a crazy male nurse. "Annamalai," he says, "is almost a documentary of a strange personality who served as a watchman in my bungalow for fifteen years; ' A Horse and Two Goats' was suggested by an American friend's visit to my house one evening in a station wagon, crammed with an enormous clay horse which he had picked up at a wayside village. 'The Shelter' developed out of a whispered conversation between a couple overheard during a bus journey." (Introduction, *Under the Banyan Tree*)

Sometimes a story is discovered when "a personality passes through a crisis of spirit or circumstances." In some of his stories "almost invariably the central character faces some kind of crisis and either resolves it or lives with it. But some stories may prove to be nothing more than a special or significant moment in someone's life or a pattern of existence brought to view" (Author's introduction, *Malgudi Days*). Stories like 'An Astrologer's Day,' 'The Missing Mail, 'The Doctor's Word,' 'Gateman's Gift,' 'Such Perfection,' Father's Help,' 'Leela's Friend,' 'Mother and Son,' 'Selvi' are examples of such stories.

In the 'Astrologer's Day' the astrologer begins his day not only with his professional equipment but also with his skill and trick to be applied on his customers. The setting is drawn very minutely and vividly, against which he is set to work. It is not by accident that the astrologer is found doing his job in a place that does not have the benefit of municipal lighting. The place is lit up by shop lights. One or two have hissing gaslights, some have naked flares stuck on poles, some are lit up by old cycle lamps and some like him manage without lights of their own. "It was a bewildering criss-cross of light rays and moving shadows" (*Malgudi Days*: 4). The background is developed intentionally to give a reasonable support to the course of events that is to follow. The astrologer works in a semi-dark atmosphere in which he could see something of his customer but his customer cannot see him properly. That the astrologer knows nothing about astrology and lives on bluffing others is clear from the comic rendering. "He was as much a stranger to the stars as were his innocent customers" (4). "Long practice has sharpened his perception. Within five minutes he understood what was wrong. He charged three pies per question and never opened his mouth till the other had spoken for at least ten minutes, which provided him enough stuff for a dozen answers and advices" (4). Narayan's skill lies in exposing the real crisis of life within the brief span of the story: the astrologer's great load of living with the guilt of having the blood of a man on his hands is gone when suddenly he comes to discover that the man he has thought he murdered is actually alive. He recognizes the man standing before him as his customer. He is practical enough to play his trick upon the man who fails to recognize him in darkness, and tries to escape the man's angry resolve to avenge himself. The astrologer uses his ready wit to tell his customer that the man he has been searching is dead, and that he should not come southwards ever again. His dealings with this man as his customer is naturally taken up by the reader as an example of a rare success of his regular bluffing and his advice that he should not come southwards appears just a way to impress the customer with his developed skill. It may also be assumed that he knows the man but does not reveal it lest he misses his earning. The mystery is resolved only through a subtle twist at the end of the story. His involvement in the whole affair comes to light when he confesses to his wife that his fear of years has proved to be a false one. The reader now understands that he has only made his life secure by telling the man not to come southwards. The little irony is that the astrologer does not forget even at that moment of crisis that the stranger does not give him one rupee as he has proposed to do. That earning a living is the chief concern of the poor people like the astrologer is highlighted in a subtle way.

'The Missing Mail,' 'The Doctor's Word' and 'Gateman's Gift' celebrate the value of human relationship and leave the central characters in the midst of a dilemma in which they have to make significant choices according to their priorities, keeping the relationship in mind. At the beginning of 'The Missing Mail' Thannappa, the postman is seen in his duty-bound daily errands. The nature of his work has developed in him a sense of belongingness. He not only carries letters for the people of Malgudi but also knows them all personally and shares a close and intimate bond with them. He knows and understands their joys and sorrows, worries and anxieties. He is a welcome visitor in every house. "Everybody liked him on his beat. He was a part and parcel of their existence, their hopes, aspirations and activities" (*Malgudi Days*: 8). His closest association is with Ramanujam, of number 10, Vinayak Mudali Street, a senior clerk in the Revenue Division Office. The story describes vividly the typical worries and urgencies faced by an Indian family having a daughter of marriageable age and having to search for a groom. Thannappa becomes a part of it and extends his cooperation in the search in his own way. His concern for the marriage of Kamakshi, seventeen year old girl of the family, may seem absurd to the self-centred modern people in urban areas and also in most of the rural areas in modern India. But such relationships were not rare during 1950s and earlier. At that time a postman's duty was not just delivery of letters; he would get involved in their affairs too. Thannappa could not draw the line between showing concern and interfering. To get the family relieved of the burden, he supplies information about prospective bridegrooms. After a long search he finds a suitable groom for Kamakshi and to ensure that her marriage should take place on the appointed day, delays the delivery of a letter and a telegram to her father—the letter informing about the severe illness of his uncle (father's brother) and the telegram announcing his subsequent death. Thannappa ignores his professional ethics and also the fear of losing his job if charged by Kamakshi's father for dereliction of duty. All this he does selflessly, only for the completion of Kamakshi's happy marriage. A touch of subtle irony is felt at the conclusion when Ramanujan announces that he would not report against Thannappa, though he would obviously have attended his dying uncle even at the cost of postponing the marriage. He forgets that earlier he has expressed his anxiety to the postman in regard to the marriage. For, the date of marriage has been the last date of the season and the groom is to be sent away for some training for three years. Yet he says that he "would not have cared to go through the marriage when he was dying" (13). Here is a hint at middle class duplicity vis-à-vis selfless service.

'Gateman's Gift' is an interesting story that throws light on Narayan's hold on common man's psychology. A keen observer of life around him, Narayan finds that human beings play various roles which are culturally assigned to them, and in doing so, they get alienated from their real nature. Division of labour is a product of culture and civilization, and it generates certain roles which become canonized. The gateman in Narayan's story is habituated to the role of a gateman and is unable to get him adjusted to any other role, say, the role of an artist. Narayan portrays the gateman as a comic figure because he behaves like a mad man out of fear that the sealed envelope contains an order of postponing his pension or of some similar misfortune. He is afraid because he feels he has trespassed the role assigned to him by making a model of his office frontage with himself at his post and the chief officer getting down from his car. At last, he is assured that he is offered an award of 100 rupees for his art, but he stops making models henceforward. Certain concepts of Transactional Analysis, a post-Freudian school of psychology, originated by Dr. Eric Berne and developed by Claude M. Steiner, may be remembered in this context. According to these concepts there are six basic maladies of our culture reflecting six forms of cultural deformity such as Gender deformity, Social deformity, Political deformity, Physical deformity, Mental deformity and Spiritual deformity. The network of these deformities forms the cultural labyrinth where people get lost. They hardly perceive the real cause of their problems and get entangled. In the gateman's case social deformity causes mental deformity. The gateman is unable to get adjusted to an artist's role and chooses to remain only a gateman. Division of society based on the nature of work breaks human society into several fragments. In course of socio-cultural evolution, these divisions become hierarchal and result in inequality.[1] The gateman takes the division for granted and suppresses his artistic nature. For him, to do otherwise is sacrilege, and so he would not do it.

'Mother and Son' presents a very natural and touching tale of the relationship between a strong, resolute mother with a terrible temper and cutting tongue, and her young, unemployed son. She is indignant and angry at him as he does not agree to her proposal of marrying her brother's daughter. Trying to be severe upon him in her anger, she says repeatedly, "Even if I see you drowning I will never ask why you are drowning" (*Malgudi Days*: 139). "If he was going to slight her judgment and feelings, she was going to show how indifferent she herself could be." (138). But at a time of test the 'mother's heart' betrays the woman's resolute will. When her son does not come home for a night, the thought of her son having committed suicide in the Kukanahalli Tank crops up in her mind and shatters her to pieces and the true and universal nature of a mother's love for her child comes to the fore. It is always an unconditional and selfless love.

'A Shadow' is another touching story depicting the indestructible bond among the members of a family. The wife comes to term in her own way with the truth that her husband is dead. She could bear seeing him in the photographs but not the film he has acted in. She dreads to see her husband speak, move or sing on screen. "How could people bear to see him on the screen when they knew he was no more?" (*Malgudi Days*: 123)—she wonders. But her son is excited. For him, it is as if his father has come back to life and he could live in his company. He could see it again and again to go through the ecstasy of meeting his father and the pain of parting from him after every show. For his friend in his school it is like any other Tamil picture which he would not at all see. The story with its matter-of-fact narration underlies a deep sense of an irreparable loss.

'Uncle's Letters' is a unique story containing extracts from about ten letters from an uncle to his nephew during different important occasions in the nephew's life starting from his birth to his eightieth birthday. Though these extracts are called letters it is likely that these letters were never sent to the addressee; rather the letters seem to be taken from the uncle's diary in which he wrote something addressing his nephew. A close picture of the interior of an Indian life—the father's joy at the discovery of some meaning in little one's gestures, the child's reluctance to go to school, the mother's concern for the effect of an injury on the child's brain, the child's development into a man and his marriage, the matured man's problem in Indian society—is offered within the brief space of the story. A real picture of Indian society is found in his ironic reference to the bridegroom's party: "With all this, you bitterly reflect that your bridegroom's people created scenes during the grand occasion, criticizing the arrangements, presents, and so forth. Such things are part of our social life and you are not to brood over it any more. What is a bridegroom's party for unless it is to hector the bride's. It is a warfare with its set laws. In any case here is a tip for consolation. You can have your vengeance in your turn when your three sons (or it is going to be four?) are ready for marriage." (*Under the Banyan Tree*: 85)

'Leela's Friend,' 'A Willing Slave,' 'Annamalai' and 'A Snake in the Grass' centre around some important situations arising in the lives of domestic servants or situations that arise due to them in the families they serve. Little Leela shares an inexplicable bond with the servant Sidda in 'Leela's friend.' Ignorant and unaware of the adult ways and of the class distinction prevailing in the society, she innocently asks "Why should not Sidda sit in our chair, Mother?" (*Malgudi Days*: 135). But for her parents things are different. When Leela's gold chain is found missing, Sidda being a servant should be the first suspect. Being a criminal in the past he can never be trusted. That he could be so close and dear a company to Leela is of no account. The adults shower self-congratulation having saved themselves from greater risks by handing him over to the police. But the friendless child laments the loss of her friend's company. The story offers a real picture of the society where the poor and helpless are emotionally exploited. However, the situations are not always the same. If in this situation the employer sacks the servant ruthlessly, in 'Out of Business' the trusted servant swindles the employer and in 'A Snake in the Grass,' the servant deceives the family by saying that he has seen the poisonous Cobra leaving the house, and thus, leaves the children in danger of Cobra bite. In 'A Willing Slave,' the loved maid servant willingly leaves the young child she looks after in order to slave for her husband who had vanished from her life for years together, and suddenly reappears.

Narayan's childhood memories left so vivid an impression on his mind that he could draw the innocent and imaginative world of children with deep understanding, affection and authenticity. 'Father's Help,' 'Crime and Punishment,' 'Dodu,' 'A Hero,' 'Hungry Child' and even 'Leela's Friend' create loveable and very credible child characters like Swami, Dodu, the naughty boy in 'Hungry Child' and Leela. These stories present a charming picture of children's psychology that leaves the readers with a sense of nostalgia. The details of day-to-day life enumerated to create a comprehensive picture of the children's world are fascinatingly authentic.

'Such Perfection' brings in a quaint charm to the realistic world of Malgudi. The story takes the readers to the world of a sculptor where they discover the importance that mystery, miracle, and blind faith receive in the life of an average Indian. Soma, a skillful image maker, makes a perfect image of Nataraj and on the day of consecration, a tempest breaks out with heavy rain, thunderbolt and lightning striking mercilessly. Fear seizes everyone. This strengthens people's belief that 'such perfection is not for mortals.' As the priest says, "This perfection, this God, is not for mortal eyes. He will blind us at the first chant of prayer before him, he will dance. . . . and we shall be wiped out" (*Malgudi Days*: 53). Soma is advised to break a little toe or some other part of the image to make everything safe. But he is not ready to mutilate his creation—something that he has created with great passion and five years' prolonged labour. Instead he offers himself as a sacrifice to propitiate the angry God. However, a sudden gust of wind that makes a tree fall on the house does the work for him. A little toe of the image is severed by a falling splinter. "God himself has done this to save us," people cry (55). The storm abates. The image is installed; Soma is showered with wealth and honour. He lives long but never touches his mallet and chisel again. For some it may be a mere co-incidence strengthening the blind faith of the orthodox and religious-minded people of Malgudi but for the simple, innocent believers it is a supernatural matter—occurring at the behest of an unseen power. Narayan's world takes into account both the attitudes to explain such inexplicable affairs of life.

'Another Community' is a moving story revealing how communal tensions are brewed up out of hatred and how this tension devastates the lives of the innocents. It is one of the rare stories of Narayan with a topical theme. Without being sentimental, without sounding politically motivated, Narayan highlights the agonizing and shameful actuality of communal tension and disharmony afflicting the society. To maintain his detachment while narrating the communal riot, Narayan uses the designation 'one Community' and 'another Community'—the method followed in newspapers—when he refers to the two main communities of India in the backdrop of the riot of 1947. He does not even give his hero a name, lest his community be revealed, and throws a challenge to the readers that they would not be able to find out the name of the community to which the hero belongs: "I am giving the hero of the story no name. I want to find out, if you like, to what community or section he belonged; I am sure you will not be able to guess it any more than you will be able to say what make of vest he wore under his shirt; and it will be just as immaterial to our purpose." (*Under the Banyan Tree*: 67)

The readers however are not in a mood to take up the challenge: they are moved by the projection of stark reality—the mindless murder of the innocent that drowns the voice of reason. A sensitive man, the protagonist in the story, finds nothing in anybody to arouse in him hatred or hostility and is not at all ready to give up his peaceful life for anything. But amidst a mindless enmity and purposeless war he sacrifices not only his life but also the peace in the society that he is so keen and anxious to retain. This single story is enough to dispute V.S. Naipaul's argument that Narayan represents the life of a small South Indian town through characters that were "inviolate" to the "distress of India"[2]. The protagonist in the story is in no way untouched by the violence of Indian society and his response to the outer chaos cannot be called a part of Hindu response. It is the response of a humanist who values human being more than blind rituals.

With a rare skill Narayan detects the causes of eruptions in the form of communal riots and presents an objective picture of the riots in 1947. It is suspicion and hatred that destroys human relationship: "Life seemed to have become intolerable. People were becoming sneaky and secretive. Everyone seemed to him a potential assassin. People looked at each other with suspicion and hatred. It seemed to him a shame that one should be throwing watchful, continuous looks over one's shoulder as one walked down a street. The air was surcharged with fear." (68)

When the protagonist in the story is hit by somebody from another community apparently for no valid reason—for both the men are panicky in the tense atmosphere caused by the news of communal riot hundred miles away—he is ready to hush it up. He knows that there are persons like his uncle who have been preparing for the riot and any such incident of clash would spark off a chain of incidents disturbing the peace in the locality.

> But I will never, never tell my uncle what has happened. I won't be responsible for starting the trouble that will press the button, so to say. That'll finish up everybody, you and me together. What is it all worth? There is no such thing as your community or mine. We are all of this country. I and my wife and children: you and your wife and children. Let us not cut each other's throats. It does not matter who cuts whose: it's all the same to me. I'll tell my uncle that I fell down the office staircase and hurt myself. He'll never know. He must not press the button. (71-72)

But unfortunately for him, the truth comes out and no opportunity is lost for bloodshed and senseless killings of people who are not connected to the incident.

> But the button did get pressed. The incident of that alley became known within a couple of hours all over the city. And his uncle and other uncles did press the button, with results that need not be described here. Had he been able to speak again, our friend would have spoken a lie and saved the city; but unfortunately that saving lie was not uttered. His body was found by the police late next afternoon in a ditch in that wretched alley, and identified through the kerosene ration coupon in his breast pocket. (72)

The story has so topical a theme, but it has not lost its significance even after sixty years of independence; for, the culture of prolonging hatred among different communities is still intact in India and is causing havoc all around. The story is a fine example of Narayan's capacity to analyze the behaviour of the mass.

> Someone or a body of men killed a body of men a thousand miles away and the result that they repeated the evil here and wreaked their vengeance on those around. It was an absurd state of affairs. But there it was: a good action in a far off place did not find an echo, but an evil one did possess that power. Our friend said the tempers of his neighbours rising as they read the newspaper each day. . . . He visualized his office colleague sitting on his right, his postman, the fellow at the betel-leaves shop and his friend at the bank—all these belonged to another community. He had not bothered about their category all these days: they were just friends—people who smiled, obliged and spoke agreeably. But now he saw them in a new light: they were of another community. (67-68)

Narayan shows how suspicion and hatred can change man's attitude and how reason is discarded when a rumor spreads. Yet his faith in the existence of reason and humanity is not marred and that is why the protagonist in the story utters a voice of reason, which, however, remains unheard:

> He tried to smooth out matters by telling his fellowmen: "You see . . . but such things will not happen here." But he knew that was wishful thinking. He knew his men were collecting knives and sticks. He knew how much they were organizing themselves, with a complete code of operations—all of which sounded perfectly ghastly to his sensitive temperament. (68)

Narayan's success lies in delineating the real culprit behind all sorts of riots: suspicion leading to mutual hatred. It is not a particular community or a group of that community which is responsible for the riot. One's lack of faith in the other generates a sense of insecurity and when hatred is added to that insecurity, it bursts any moment.

Some of Narayan's stories reveal other social maladies like corruption, greed, exploitation of the poor and the helpless. These stories are mild social satires. 'Four Rupees' deals humorously with the story of a man who risks his life just to earn a few rupees more. To some it is apparently sheer avarice but to some others it appears as an existential compulsion which Narayan delineates without any intention of censuring. 'Half a Rupee Worth' exposes the unscrupulousness and wiles of a small town businessman Subbiah who exploits the poor when they are going through extreme scarcity of food grains. He seeks to earn more money, more profits. The story ends very significantly: Subbiah, the greedy blackmarketeer goes to the secret godown to get half a seer of rice for sale and upsets the rice bags which come down on him and knock his life out. Narayan exposes the greed that works behind the criminal act of hoarding food grains. In his characteristic style Narayan exposes the crude reality of food shortage, rise of black marketing and existence of mischievous government servants in post-World War India, through the perspective of a self styled black-marketeer. The war seems at first to be the end of civilization, but very soon the protagonist, Subbiah, finds that it is "not unwelcome after all."

> His profits piled up as never before—Saigon and Burma ceased to send rice and that meant the stock he held was worth its weight in gold. People flocked to his shop at all hours, and the door of the iron safe could hardly be pushed in. He bought the big house next door for a godown and then the next one and the next; and then bought a dozen more villages. . . . He loaded more gold on his wife and daughters and increased his own girth. War seemed, on the whole, a very beneficial force—till the introduction of Price and Food control. . . . He felt happy when he heard someone say, "the food department" is a hoax. The government are making a mess of things. (*Under the Banyan Tree*: 176-77)

Subbiah's greed makes him find a way out of Government rules through bribing the officials:

> He retained all the rice he wanted—for sale and personal use—but out of sight and out of paper. He had to give away a lot of money to people who were entitled to examine his stock and accounts, but he never grudged this investment. If he passed a ten-rupee currency note on such an occasion, it meant he had screened from prying

> eyes a thousand rupees worth of grain. When he thought it over, he realized that all controls and restrictions were really a boon. He reflected philosophically: "God arranges everything for the best." He distributed a few annas for charity twice a week, and broke a coconut at the temple on Fridays in appreciation of God's interest. (177)

The revelation of corruption could hardly be done in a better way. But the critics like to focus not so much on the revelation of contemporary reality in the story as on the accidental death of Subbiah under the piles of sacks full of rice hoarded in his godowns. Narayan is described as a 'religious writer' for introducing such examples of poetic justice that are suggestive of his unshaken faith in the benign world order. But it should also be noted that his faith does not distort the reality he projects.

'Forty Five a Month' is the story of Venkat Rao who is sad and angry for not being allowed leisure to spend at home with his wife and daughter. In the urgency of earning livelihood for his family, he neglects them and even deprives his daughter of the simple pleasures of life. He cannot take her out because he does not have time away from his office work. "For forty rupees a month they seemed to have purchased him outright" (*Malgudi Days*: 76). But ironically, just as he makes up his mind to resign and resolves rather to die honorably of starvation but not to work as a slave, he is told of a five-rupee pay hike. All his angry resolve is gone. The humour hides the pathos that underlies common man's helpless struggle for existence. 'Out of Business' and 'A Horse and Two Goats,' show the same helplessness of man. Many of his stories deal with people to whom a few rupees mean the difference between starvation and survival. Using his masterly strokes Narayan brings out the monotony, privation, ennui, boredom, self-denial and frustrations with ease and comfort in such stories. His deep humanism permeates even the most frustrating and unsettling of these real life experiences.

In 'A Horse and Two Goats' the predominant theme is the communication gap caused due to the language difference between Muni, a poor goatherd who wants to sell his two goats and a wealthy American who wants to buy a clay horse standing by the river, which leads to comic complicacies. But the comic absurdity of the story has not blocked the picture of poverty and penury. Poverty is taken for granted by people like Muni.

> His fortunes had declined gradually, unnoticed. From a flock of forty which he drove into a pen at night, his stock had now come down to two goats, which were not worth the rent of a half rupee a month the Big House charged for the use of the pen in their backyard. And so the two goats were tethered to the trunk of a drumstick tree which grow in front of his hut and from which occasionally Muni could shake down drumsticks. This morning he got six. He carried them in with a sense of triumph. Although no one could say precisely who owned the tree, it was his because he lived in its shadow. (*Under the Banyan Tree*: 15)

In 'Nitya' the description of the bus journey exposes the familiar world of Malgudi and at once offers a realistic picture of the transport system in India pointing at the difference between the rural area and the metropolis.

> The bus passed through Ellaman and crossed Nallappa's Grove and climbed the other bank of the river, splashing up water. The driver displayed immense self-assurance and goaded his bus on with reckless gusto. Passengers were tossed sideways and jolted up and down, but no one minded except Nitya. "What sort of journey is this?"
>
> "You must learn to be patient, my boy, ours is a poor country. We cannot afford the luxuries they have in Bombay or Madras." (*Under the Banyan Tree*: 3)

In the same story, as Narayan points at the greed and avarice that motivate some people to act in a particular way, another reality of common man's life peeps up:

> No one protested, but parted with their coins cheerfully. The conductor, hanging on the foot board precariously, pocketed all the cash, which inspired Nitya to note in his diary, "The bus rocks and sways, and sighs with its burden, but won't burst yet. Perhaps the last straw is yet to arrive. But the real question is, who owns this? Definitely not this conductor, though he grows heavier every minute with the coins dropping like manna into his pocket." (3)

Narayan has the capacity to focus on an experience or to probe into human psyche from a particular perspective. A subtle touch or a revelation of the past in a flash, or the turn of events totally unexpected in a situation, or the outburst of a character's emotion amounts to a revelation of what the characters are really up to. Referring to the importance of his characters Narayan says, "If his personality comes alive, the rest is easy for me"[3]. Though in the short story there is limited scope for a writer to portray full grown character, yet in the hands of the master story writers like Narayan the desired effect is easily accomplished. Narayan creates a gallery of colourful portraits in his stories representing the common run of humanity. If there are good-natured people like Thannappa and Gobind Singh, there is no dearth of harmless rogues too. With the black-marketeer Subbiah in 'Half a rupee Worth,' the gambler Kannan in 'Wife's Holiday,' the pickpocket Raju in 'Trail of the Green Blazer,' the Malgudi world comes alive. They all share a common, ordinary existence but they dare to have dreams of the extraordinary, the uncommon. The illiterate knife-grinder, Ranga, in 'The Edge' wants his daughter to be a lady doctor. He lives from hand-to-mouth and sleeps in a dilapidated building to save money for her education, though his very practical and down-to-earth wife wants to take her away from school and get her earn a living in the field. In all their colours the characters are unforgettable. One smiles affectionately at Raju's adventure of putting the purse back in the pocket from which he has stolen. Ironically in the process of doing it with a noble purpose he gets caught and is jailed.

> He served his term of eighteen months and came back into the world—not quite decided what he should do with himself. He told himself, "If I ever pick up something again, I shall make sure I don't have to put it back." For now he believed God had gifted the likes of him with only one-way deftness. Those fingers were not meant to put anything back. (*Malgudi Days*: 110)

In some of Narayan's stories, a character called the Talkative Man is the narrator. Through him Narayan introduces the dramatic mode of narration. The sense of objectivity, dramatic situation, suspense, excitement, entertainment—all this is ensured in the narration of the Talkative Man. He is portrayed as a man of wide travel and experience, who takes immense delight in telling a story successfully to his listeners. But the writer maintains the same ironic attitude towards him as he does towards his other characters and at the same time, exposes the gullibility of common people. The narrative mode is an example of the long established oral tradition of story-telling in India which Narayan adopts deliberately as a narrative technique. In fact, there is masterly combination of tradition and innovation in these stories. 'The Tiger's Claw' and 'The Roman Image' are examples of the Talkative Man's gift for inventiveness, an important quality attributed to him by the writer. 'The Tiger's Claw' exposes the Talkative Man's adventure as a fake one. He boasts to the boys that he once cut three claws of a tiger using a long knife and the same tiger, a man eater, was killed by some hunters who were now worshipped as heroes. After the Talkative man left the boys, they moved on to the square, where the man-eater was displayed,

> We pushed through the crowd and begged to be shown the right forepaw of the tiger. Somebody lowered a gas lamp. Yes, three toes were missing, and a deep black scan marked the spot. The man who cut it off must have driven his knife with the power of a hammer. To a question, the hunters replied, "can't say how it happens. We have met a few instances like this. It's said that some

> forest tribes, if they catch a tiger cub, cut off its claws for some talisman and let it go. They do not usually kill cubs." (44)

Without making any comment on the Talkative Man's white lie and his boasting, the writer exposes his character ironically. He may not be a hero, but his capacity of mesmerizing the audience demands credit. The enchantment of Narayan's world comes from the fact that readers find a kinship, a family likeness with his men and women. He, too, loves his characters and respects their natures. And his portraits never go out of date in a country like India. He says appropriately, "a date-stamp may be necessary for a periodical, but not for a story" (Introduction, *Under the Banyan Tree*).

Malgudi is rendered as a real place not only through the portrayal of characters, but also through the portrayal of birds and animals that are treated as characters of his stories. 'The Blind Dog,' 'Attila,' 'Flavour of Coconut,' 'At the Portal,' 'The Mute Companion,' 'Chippy' are some of the memorable stories on animals. There are evidences of Narayan's sharp observation: he depicts the minute details of their behavioural pattern. "Throughout his work Narayan's skill in depicting animals is noteworthy," says Perry D. Westbrook[4]. 'Chippy' is the story of a faithful dog that is sad and jealous of a new dog that his master has brought home and with whom he has to share his master's care and attention. 'The Blind Dog' brings into ironic contrast the ingratitude of man with the faithfulness and loyalty of animals. It is about a dog that comes across a blind beggar by accident, and feels grateful for being fed by him. Thereafter he serves him as his faithful slave. He helps the blind man, who was earlier confined to one place, go from place to place for begging. He starts earning more by begging. As he becomes free to move, he curbs the dog's freedom of movement by fastening the dog with a ribbon and keeps him to himself and treats him cruelly. Yet the dog's attitude to his master does not change. Once he is freed by a kind man who snips the ribbon fastening him. But after enjoying his freedom for a few days he comes back to his master, this time to be tied with a steel chain, sacrificing his freedom for ever. Narayan points at the aggressive nature of human being, his lack of kindness and gratitude and his obsession with the exercise of power over the weak. At once, he shows ironically the incorrigible servile attitude of animals like the dog. Of all the animal stories 'At the portal' is the most beautiful one. The story presents a delightful picture of a mother squirrel teaching her young one—ten days old probably on his second day's outing—to climb up a wall, while the latter cannot overcome his own fears and anxieties, and learn. The mother, an expert in her art of climbing high, does not actually understand her child's handicap, and continues to give him her instructions, the simple ones—to take a deep breath, not hop up right from zero as she does but to take a dozen paces back and then take it in a run and heave himself up as she demonstrates. The young squirrel follows and imitates all instructions but in vain. She continues to admonish and advise him to make fresh attempts. The author not only could see them talking to each other but can also hear their conversation.

After demonstrating many a times the tricks to climb the potholes, the mother squirrel's patience is gone. She asks her young one, "Are you coming home or not?"

> The young one was in an irresponsible mood and said, "Not unless you carry me as you did that day."
>
> "That day was not this day," said the mother.
>
> "If you were young enough to be rolled up and carried between my jaws, I wouldn't wait for your suggestion."
>
> "Then I can't jump up. I am not coming," said the other one.
>
> "Idiot, you don't know what you are in for. Come along quietly. The whole world has retired, we alone are awake and our enemies are about us. Come up quietly."
>
> "I can't, Mother, don't you see. . . ." The mother did not wait to hear the full sentence. She quietly turned round, jumped down

> on the other side, and vanished, pausing only for a split second to say, "After all, God is above. If you are destined to see the morrow you will see it, that is all. What can I or anyone do for you?" (*Under The Banyan Tree*: 155-56)

Nervous and genuinely frightened, the young squirrel makes several futile attempts to reach the hole, practicing all the tips his mother has given, and finally letting off all efforts, makes a dash for the nearest avenue tree, and gets on to it. The author is so engrossed by the sight that he forgets to think about the proceedings of his proposed meeting. And in his characteristic ironic way he comes to the conclusion that on the next occasion an appeal to the university authorities should be made to reduce the height of pot-holes in their compound walls for the convenience of the likes of the squirrels. Though not a fable, the comic story has something of the importance of ancient fable in it.

Besides men and women, animals and birds, what gives Malgudi its recognizable shape is the recurrent references to the land marks. The place is familiarized by its streets, corners, market places, statues, rivers and trees in his stories and novels and these give the stories a unity of impression. If there are stories that familiarize the important land marks, there are also stories that bestow upon them a sense of history. The stories like 'The Lawley Road,' 'The Martyr's Corner' tell about the making of these land marks. 'The Lawley Road' is a funny and ironic account of the tradition in India of naming or renaming streets and lanes to attain selfish political dividends, in which public funds and public energy are mindlessly wasted. With meaningless enthusiasm to do something great the Municipal Chairman decides to nationalize the names of all the streets and parks in Malgudi, 'in honour of the birth of independence.' The Coronation Park—(named to commemorate whose coronation God alone knew)—becomes Hamara Hindustan Park and soon the town becomes unrecognizable with new names. The Market Road, North Road, Chitra Road, Vinayak Mudali Street and so on, are named after ministers, deputy ministers and the members of the Congress Working Committee. The confusion it creates is a comic reality: "Of course, it created a lot of hardship—letters went where they were not wanted, people were not able to say where they lived or direct others there. The town became a wilderness with all its landmarks gone." (*Under The Banyan Tree*: 100)

Then comes the turn of Lawley Extension named after Sir Frederick Lawley. At the corner of the Lawley Extension and the Market has been standing his statue. With the name of the place being changed to Gandhi Nagar, it becomes necessary to remove Sir Frederick's statue, and for the Municipality it proves to be an uphill task. Ironically, just as the task is accomplished the significant contribution of Sir Frederick to Malgudi comes to everyone's knowledge and the removal of the statue is highly disapproved of by the Government. The Chairman is blamed for the entire exercise and is ordered to reinstate the statue. The statue is reinstated but after a lot of trouble being faced again for it, at a different place and in a different way—and the place, Kabir Lane, is converted to Lawley Road.

Narayan has often been criticized for having made his canvas so small, his setting so restricted in his stories. But he is very much at home in it, because within this restricted setting, he does not find it difficult to touch any sphere of man's activity and any aspect of human psychology. With limitless material and innumerable characters his Malgudi embraces humanity in its entirety. It cannot however be denied that he has shut himself against certain extremely disturbing but yet very real elements in life such as old age, infirmity, death, bloodshed, loss of honour, shameless vices. He is, therefore, blamed for not confronting suffering in his stories. But it is not proper to expect from a writer what he willingly avoids. Narayan avoids display of horror—be it death or hunger—but he reveals a deep, sympathetic understanding of such horrifying reality. Assuming an indifferent and detached approach he lightly puts his fingers on these elements and simply shows his awareness of their existence. C.V. Venugopal describes Narayan's world as a world of 'a comedian's delight,' a world with 'its afflictions and pangs being touched only lightly,' 'enjoyable in the extreme'[5].

As a realist Narayan admires 'honesty' while portraying 'slice of life.' His own experiences in life taught him to take a penetrative look at the world and his readers learn from him to look at life through the lens of sensitiveness and compassion. Realistic rendering of life seen through the eyes of a humourist, filled with Indian sense and sensibility, addressed to mankind as a whole, transcribed in a language smooth and effective—that is how the essence of Narayan's stories can be summed up.

NOTES

1. Claude M. Steiner, *Scripts People Live*, New York: Bantam, 1980.
2. According to Naipaul, Narayan's novels are "social comedies" and at their best "religious books" or religious fables and intensely Hindu. "Some years ago he (Narayan) told me in London that whatever happened, India would go on. He said it casually; it was a conviction so deep it required no stressing. It is a negative alternate, part of that older India which was incapable of self-assessment. It has this result; the India of Narayan's novels is not the India the visitor sees. He tells an Indian truth. Too much that is overwhelming has been left out; too much has been taken for granted." *An Area of Darkness*, 1968: 216.
3. R.E. Wolseley, 'Narayan of India,' *The Nation*, XVI, 4, 3 October, 1953: 273.
4. Perry D. Westbrook, 'The Short Stories of R.K. Narayan,' *The Journal of Commonwealth Literature*, No.5, July, 1968: 47.
5. C.V. Venugopal, 'A Master of Comedy—R.K. Narayan as a Short Story Writer,' *Journal of the Karnatak University—Humanities,* Vol.13, 1969: 178.

Revisiting Narayan's Early Novels

This chapter analyses the first seven novels of R.K. Narayan on the basis of the fundamental aspects of realism revealed in his work, as discussed in the previous chapter. The discussion on realism clarifies that Narayan's novels emerge from an orchestration of two levels of reality—the individual and the social. Thus, at one level, there is the reality of man's elemental nature and at the other, the reality of the set-up in which he is born and brought up. The set-up is important and active as it exerts pressure on individuals to react in a certain way to a certain situation. But the individuals are also driven by their elemental selves and there arise conflict and confusion leading to disorder and disruption. Narayan's comic vision of life helps him to get at reconciliation between the individual self and the society and so matters often take unexpected turns to settle amicably for all. Moreover, the autobiographical element that goes into Narayan's fiction creates an ideal base for the rendering of both psychological and social reality. In fact, a writer's personal experiences, even when not directly rendered in his or her fictional writings, are the actual sources of realism. There may be a little exaggeration in V.S. Naipaul's remark (in his 1994 speech at Talsa), that "a full account of a writer's life might in the end be more a work of literature and more illuminating—of a cultural to historical movement—than the writer's books"[1]. But the essence of the remark is appreciated by all: when the facts from a writer's life are reshaped for portrayal in his fiction, the veracity of the portrayal becomes undisputed. Yet a writer's capacity to detach himself/herself from the experiences he/she gets personally involved is necessary for artistic (objective) presentation of those facts. Narayan was blessed with that capacity and hence the biographical facts enrich and illuminate his fictional writings, lending a touch of authenticity to them. Even his early autobiographical novels, instead of being slavish transcriptions of actual life, transform into great artistic expressions. Personal and intimate experiences wherever they appear in Narayan become universal and timeless.

Swami and Friends

Swami And Friends, the first of Narayan's novels, shows Narayan's acquaintance with himself as a child and boy more than with anyone else. The novel is episodic in nature containing a series of episodes, escapades and adventures of Swami and his companions. But taken together the episodes make a whole and lovable story. P.S. Sundaram aptly says, the novel is "more than a series of episodes. Through it all runs a single thread—the hero as victim—and there is a logical connection from the first line to the last." (1988: 22). Without this logical connection the novel would not have imparted the sense of beauty and sadness that Graham Greene alludes to in his remark about the novel[2].

Being a story about children, *Swami and Friends* immediately brings into mind other such English novels about children—*The Adventures of Tom Sawyer, Huckleberry Finn, The Rainbow, David Copperfield, Oliver Twist* etc. Like these novels, *Swami and Friends* brings to life a children's world in its fullness. The children are found studying, appearing in examinations, enjoying holidays, dreaming, planning, bewildering, quarreling, fighting, making sensible treaties, taking part in hartals, playing cricket, getting involved in dilemmas and dangers, loathing adult interference and at the end, going through some harsh and painful experiences of life. And the readers experience an Indian way of studying, fighting, playing etc—especially in the colonial India. It is as if the whole of one's boyhood is recollected—as if "everyday actuality has taken Narayan's pen and written out the universal epic of all our boyhood yesteryears that are no more" (Iyengar 1983: 365). Swami's reluctance to go to school, his love for the delicious freedom of holidays and, his difficulty to get into the Monday mood of work and discipline, reminds one of Tom Sawyer. The only difference is the purely Indian background against which Swami is pitted. He is a peculiar mixture of timidity and boldness. He is seen through a series of minor or even major events—each working to its own crisis and resolution. He is unable to evaluate experiences but these experiences make him undergo emotional development.

The picture of Swami's family displays the interior of a middle class Indian family. It is a respectable family, mildly religious in a traditional way, neither indigent nor too well-off, profoundly unified in its assumptions about the ends and means of life, and yet it leaves its members comparatively independent. In such an atmosphere Swami develops a coherent and non fractured psyche. He is aware of the intricate and difficult adult ways in which he has to move and function. But he cannot be anything other than his own self. He, with his friends, is perfectly at peace with his world that corresponds to the harmony of nature.

> The river's mild rumble, the rustling of the peepul leaves, the half-light of the late evening, and the three friends eating, and glowing with the new friendship—Swaminathan felt at perfect peace with the world. (18)

He is equally at peace amidst the flurry of activities at home at the time of the birth of his brother. He receives the news of the arrival of a child from his grandmother with enthusiasm. At the time of its birth he could see and hear the "hushed voices, hurry, seriousness, agitation, hot water, and medicine—preparations for ushering a new person into the world," and we have a picture of the Indian homes of the time. He could see his granny in anxiety, making continuous query to someone passing by and no one bothering to answer her. But Swami wants nothing more than the comfort of his Granny's bed and so goes to sleep to wake up in the morning and discover the baby brother. The picture of a new born baby is presented vividly and perfectly when Swami describes him to Pea. He describes him by shutting his eyes, compressing his lips, folding his hands on his chest, protruding his tongue, and tilting his head side to side. Pea laughs uncontrollably. "'But,'" Swaminathan says, "'this thing has a wonderful pair of hands, so small and plump, you know! But I tell you, his face is awful, red, red like chilli'" (49). The apprehension as much as relief caused by the birth of a child in a middle class Indian household—of which Swami is a witness—is minutely and vividly depicted.

The account of Swami's relationship with his family, friends and teachers is presented in a cool, objective and realistic manner. In his relationship with his teachers he is very impulsive and rash. But he is much attached to his friends and in spite of their friendly fights, likes and admires them. Swami and Samuel who share a bond of laugher "see together the same absurdities and incongruities in things. The most trivial and unnoticeable thing to others would tickle them to death" (7). This displays a striking resemblance between Swami and the writer himself. Narayan, like Swami, has shown a natural and strong penchant for seeing the incongruous in the insignificant and the unnoticeable, and for laughing at it and inviting others to laugh with him.

In this novel, facts of Narayan's life correspond to Swami's experiences as a child and this lends a strong element of realism to it. Swami's 'scripture master' (3) who abuses the Hindus and their idol-worship fanatically, reminds one of similar experiences of Narayan in Lutheran Mission School where the Hindus were being lampooned. The devotion of Swami and his Friends to the M.C.C team (Malgudi Cricket Club) corresponds to the addiction of Narayan and his friends to football and their team 'jumping stars' (47). These pictures help the readers develop an understanding of the conflicts in the colonial mindset: the Hindus in

India were sensitive to the derogatory remarks on their religion, but were enthusiastic about cricket, initially a game of England.

Narayan's grandmother played an important role in the formative years of his life. Swami, his counterpart in the novel, finds a friend in his Granny who is ready to give a patient hearing to what he has to say without meddling in his affairs. There is, in fact, hardly any similarity between Narayan's grandmother and Swami's granny. But still they share equal importance as they occupy the same position in the hierarchies of family relationships in Indian society. Narayan's Granny was a strong, efficient, orthodox, but authoritative lady. He was brought up in her care. He grew up in the discipline and routine set by her. She was the deepest influence on his life. He inherited the religious orthodoxy from her. He was introduced to the classical Indian tales, myth, and Vedic poetry very early in life at his grandmother's knee. Swami's grandmother, on the other hand, is a singularly powerless and pathetic figure. She is his companion in loneliness and his saviour in distress. Narayan's attention to such details of family life is noteworthy.

Narayan draws a vivid picture of an Indian summer that speaks immensely of Narayan's realistic art. After harrowing times of examinations come the holidays for the children—the time of great enjoyment and excitement. Nothing in the world could deter the children to make the most of their holidays not even the glaring Sun of the South Indian Summer. During summer Malgudi is one of the most detested towns in South India. Between twelve and three any day in summer dusty blanched roads are deserted. The accuracy of the picture is unmatchable.

Through Swami's interaction with the outer world—an interaction that accelerates a child's growth—Narayan introduces national themes such as India's freedom movement. Swami's involvement in the agitation against the British rule that starts in Malgudi serves two purposes—first, it reveals more about the reactions of children and of the adult separately to socio-political issues of the time, and second, it makes one conscious of the historical importance of the time to which Swami belongs. Though it is a small place apparently unruffled by the upheaval caused by the voice of protest against the colonial rule, Malgudi is not secluded from the National mainstream. The school boys in the town get excited and out of sheer curiosity and playfulness join the strike that begins as a mark of protest against the arrest of a prominent political worker in Bombay involved in the freedom movement.

Narayan has minutely observed the public confusion and the cross-currents in the Indian society during the colonial rule. On the one hand the school boys join the strike against the British throwing the British goods to fire and thereby irritating the headmaster, and on the other hand, they disobey the rules of their institution to form cricket clubs imitating the British practice. The formation of the cricket club, the arrangement of cricket matches, the practice sessions continuing among all odds, Swami's confrontation with the Board School headmaster in the process of his attempt to find ways and means to make himself available at the practice session, and in the end his failure to take part in the match—all this gives Narayan a scope for minute reading of the minds of children. He could very well perceive that cricket matches were the colonial legacy. Narayan's observation of the social trends as demonstrated through his presentation of the cricket fans justifies the theory that the relationship between the colonizer and the colonized is one of reciprocal antagonism and desire, and that post colonialism suggests both continuity and change.[3]

The colonized revolted against the political and the economic oppression and sought emancipation from all sorts of subjugation. But they also developed, willingly, an intimacy with the colonial culture. The Indian boys getting fanatic about cricket match is a proof of their adopting British culture. An intimate picture of colonial India is projected from the perspective of a boy soon going to be an adolescent.

The Bachelor of Arts

Critics aptly maintain, in their own different ways, that if, *Swami and Friends* is the story of a character as a school boy then *The Bachelor of Arts* is the story of the same character as a graduate[4]. Both Swami and Chandran, the protagonists of the two novels, belong to Malgudi, the place that responds positively to the changes of time. It is also maintained by critics that Chandran is drawn on the writer as a boy[5]. If Chandran is a student of Albert Mission College of Malgudi, Narayan was a student of Maharaja's College of Mysore. Rama, his inseparable friend, is drawn perhaps on Ramachandra Rao of *My Days*. Kailash in Madras is modelled after his younger alcoholic uncle. Chandran ends up as a newspaper agent, just as Narayan came into journalism. The writer's experiences as a young man and a graduate go into the making of the story and the characters.

Irrespective of the autobiographical elements, Narayan's capacity to project mundane reality is proved once again in this novel as he describes Chandran, his family and their lives. Chandran belongs to a middle-class family in which people are usually religious-minded. Their faith, religious practices and superstitions find their way into their lives naturally. Religion is an unquestioned and unpremeditated affair in their lives. But at the same time, they are modern and progressive in the serious pursuits of life as well as in their search for pleasures and pastime. Rooted to their soil, they are not averse to English Education System or to English culture and values. Rather, there is a harmonious union between the two. Moreover, these people of the middle class are psychologically more active and their consciousness is more vivid and harrowing. Chandran, a typical middle class young man in colonial India, is modest, unself-confident, tender, terse, sharp, self-protective and unformed.

Like all Narayan's heroes Chandran's immediate preoccupation is with his family—his father, mother, and brother. His next concern is with his friends and teachers in the Albert Mission College. Chandran's proper regard for his father, a natural gesture in an Indian family, his intimate and cosy relationship with his mother and above all, his sense of responsibility towards his younger brother Seenu—all together present an authentic picture of family life in India. The picture of his mother at prayer and at work etches out a typical Indian mother.

Chandran's is a close-knit family. The members are emotionally dependent on each other. Each feels responsible for the other one's welfare. Opinions and ideas are shared before taking any decision for any of the members of the family or for the family as a whole. Chandran cannot ignore his father's strong views on any matter concerning him. He dares not dissatisfy him but at the same time, he tries to overcome the fear of his father, which he thinks is not befitting a young man of his age and achievement. He knows late coming upsets his father. In order not to upset him he takes all possible care to enter the house stealthily until assailed by a surge of self-respect.

Chandran's encounter with his friends and teachers at Albert Mission College, his debates and discourses with them, the importance he attaches to his lessons and other academic activities like participation in debates, forming a Historical Association on his professor's request, are rendered minutely and very authentically. The characters of his acquaintances—Mohan, Ramu, Gajapati, Mr. Brown—are drawn from his perspective. As a student of Albert Mission College he is average but well-known among his friends and teachers. He maintains a good rapport with them. As a learner he hovers between Indian nationalism and a healthy respect for his British teachers.

Young Chandran's one-sided love-affair is rendered brilliantly with irony and humour. He gets infatuated with Malathi, a girl he comes across by chance on one of his 'river ramblings.'

On his usual walk down to Nallappa's Grove, crossing the river and going to the opposite bank, and away into the fields, even at home and around he could do nothing but think of her only. His plan of going to England for further studies, his regular enjoyment of reading novels (even a gripping one like Wells Tono Bungay)—all take a back seat. Now marriage is in mind. He is ready to set example by marrying this girl if she belongs to another cast or sect. He even goes to the extent of thinking indignantly of India's caste system as it appears to be the greatest obstacle on his path, at that moment. "If India was to attain salvation these watertight divisions must go—community, caste, sects, sub-sects and still further divisions" (56), he thinks. Narayan's peculiarity lies in the ironic way he introduces the much discussed topic of reforming Hindu customs: Chandran is so eager to marry Malathi that he is ready to fight against the Hindu fundamentalism under the banner of rationalism and it is ludicrous that he thinks of taking up such a project only to serve his personal desire. The comic effect produced by such reflections also lays bare the mindset of an average Hindu who is blind to the existing social evils unless and until his own interest is affected.

Chandran belongs to a time when girls in middle class Indian families were not allowed to meet boys. So Chandran has to go the river side, avoiding company of his friends, only to have 'an optical communion' with the girl. After a few days of this blissful state, Chandran makes a progress by collecting information about the girl and then by announcing his intentions of marrying the girl. After many heated arguments with his mother relating to the girl's age, caste and horoscope, his parents contact the girl's parents but the marriage fails to materialize in the end mainly because of unpropitious horoscopes. Though ludicrous, it was a fashion of the time that frustration in love would induce young men to leave home. Chandran also insists to be sent to Madras for a change, after the girl marries somebody else. Surprisingly then he takes up the role of a wandering holy man. The new role is like a mild and painless suicide, befitting his anguished and timid spirit. But very soon he realizes the meaninglessness of all that he has been doing. He suddenly falls out of love for Malathi and calls it his infatuation, and there comes a surge of emotion for his father, mother and brother. He decides to come back to the warmth of the family and the comforting huddle of Malgudi life.

This realization is followed by his happy homecoming. He gets a job as a newspaper agent with the help of his father. The prospect of a European education offered by his father is ignored lest his father faces financial strain. Chandran now agrees to marry Susila, another girl, appropriately fair, well-connected and possessing a propitious horoscope, suitable to his parents in all respect, and eventually, finds ecstasy in marriage. After the marriage he is "a new man, his mind full of Susila, the fragrance of jasmine and sandal paste, the smokiness of the Sacred Fire, of brilliant lights, music, gaiety, and laughter" (164).

The novel is packed with irony and humour of a gentle and sympathetic kind. Narayan's irony is directed towards some real religious, social and psychological aspects of life. It is ironic that Chandran's realization, though not spiritual, comes under a banyan tree in a remote village at the foot of a range of mountains in keeping with the Indian way. As a realist Narayan likes to expose the fake nature of so called 'Sanyasis' who could easily befool the God-fearing Indian and remain safe in disguise. Though blind faith in the power of the mendicant is almost absent today, particularly in the urban areas of India, the picture was quite different during 1940s or 1950s. With a sharp and ironic observation Narayan exposes how the profession of mendicant ascetic was adopted for various reasons other than spiritual suffering. For Chandran it is an escape from frustrated love, an easy alternative of suicide.

> He was different from the usual *Sanyasi*. Others may renounce with a spiritual motive or purpose. Renunciation may be to them a means to attain peace or may be peace itself. They are perhaps dead in time, but they do live in eternity. But Chandran's renunciation was not of that kind. It was an alternative to suicide. Suicide he would have committed but for its social stigma. Perhaps he lacked the barest physical courage that was necessary for it. He was a *Sanyasi* because it pleased him to mortify his flesh. His renunciation was a revenge on society, circumstances, and perhaps, too, on destiny. (108)

Later Chandran's self-analysis reveals not only his psychological state but also his critical view of the hypocrisy and falsehood involved in the making of the ascetics.

> After wandering in a world of illusion and as a fake Sanyasi, he comes to terms with the reality of life. Reconciliation with the family, friends, society and its customs and traditions is inevitable for an average man like Chandran. But before this reconciliation, it is a journey from innocence to experience. Change and growth are unavoidable realities. But there are certain basics of life which do not undergo change, and to be at peace and understanding with them is wisdom. As in *Swami and Friends* here too, the Narayan hero finds happiness in submission to those unchangeable basic principles of life.

The Bachelor of Arts, being a pre-Independence novel, has a lot to reflect about the social and psychological relationship prevailing at the time between the colonizer and the colonized. Chandran's casual remarks on Prof. Brown and his friends point at the grudge brewing up in the Indian mind against the British rulers.

> He kept gazing at Prof. Brown's pink face. Here he is, Chandran thought, pretending to press the bell and listen to the speeches, but really his thoughts, are at the tennis-court and the card-table in the English Club. He is here not out of love for us, but merely to keep up appearances. All Europeans are like this. They will take their thousand or more a month, but won't do the slightest service to In-

> dians with a sincere heart. They must be paid this heavy amount for spending their time in the English Club. (5)

An average educated Indian's suppressed desire to enjoy the European way of life is also revealed through Chandran's observations:

> Why should not these fellows admit Indians to their clubs? Sheer colour arrogance. If ever I get into power I shall see that Englishmen attend clubs along with Indians and are not so exclusive. Why not give the poor devils—so far away from their home—a chance to club together at least for a few hours at the end of a day's work? Anyway who invited them here? (5)

Again, he points to another funny reality,

> The white fellows are born to enjoy life. Our people really don't know how to live. If a person is seen with a girl by his side, a hundred eyes stare at him and a hundred tongues comment, whereas no European ever goes out without taking a girl with him. (15)

Chandran's fear of being rusticated from the college and his secret desire to be appreciated by a white man get the better of his grudge against the colonial rulers.

The article read by Veeraswami in the meeting arranged by the historical association of the college is another instance of the conflict between the colonized and the colonizers. His article "pilloried Great Britain before the association, and ended by hoping that the British would be ousted from India by force" (45). He wants to read another paper reflecting ironically more of his mind regarding a blatant social reality.

The English Teacher

After *Swami and Friends* and *The Bachelor of Arts,* in 1945 came *The English Teacher,* the three of which make a set. If Swami grows to be Chandran, then Chandran grows to be Krishna in *The English Teacher*. Like Swami and Chandran, this characteristic Narayan hero is seen engaged in the characteristic Narayan struggle. Like Chandran, Krishna is young, ardent and self-deprecating, hesitant and unsure about himself. But he is less brittle and more complex a personality than Chandran. He is the first person narrator and life is seen from his perspective in the novel.

Krishna is a lecturer at the Albert Mission College, a local college in Malgudi, and his wife and daughter are staying at a different place, with his parents-in-law. He is good at his work and knows the demands of his job and makes adjustments accordingly. But there is a sense of vacuum in life that often torments him. However, the gloom and monotony that he suffers from is broken when he comes to know from his father that his wife and daughter would be coming to stay with him and that he would have to start a home with them. Though hesitant and unsure at first, he gets prepared to have everything ready—everything that they would need to run their home smoothly. He starts his small family with his wife, Susila, and their seven month old daughter, Leela. Now there is a sense of purpose in life, a sense of growth. The household chores of day-to-day life, prudent housekeeping of his wife, her religious-mindedness and his very amused reaction to it, their small fights and small pleasures—amidst all these Krishna discovers himself and realizes his love and devotion for his wife and daughter. Their love and belongingness deepen and intensify. From a world of formal relationship and abstract preoccupations he moves to a world of genuine response and human reality "Life now becomes present, actual, surrounding and supporting" (Walsh 1992: 53).

The depth and strength of Susila's character, her simple traditional upbringing, and respect for her husband, her exquisite manners, and serenity of mind, self-confidence and self-respect—all contribute to the growing and maturing relationship. They keep their romance alive and discover the wonder of marital bliss. Their love is based on shared interests and is rooted in the child for whom both care immensely. The quality attributed to Susila tally with the qualities of an ideal Indian wife, adored by men since ages. Susila is the phantom of delight and fills Krishna's life with sheer elation and ecstasy. There is magic in her presence and an unearthly loveliness in her tall form, dusky complexion, in the small diamond ear-rings and in the 'Jasmine' in her hair.

But the period of grace and joy is brought to a sudden and brutal conclusion. Tragedy befalls when they are planning to leave the rented house and buy a house of their own and according to their choice. Susila catches typhoid. Her illness, first wrongly diagnosed as malaria, leads to delirium, then collapse followed by nursing, coma and death, and finally a grim and unsparing process of Indian funeral. The music and the poetry in the account of life in the first part is replaced by a clinical coolness of description of death and its after-effects. But at no point the cool, matter-of-fact description fails to convey the deep concern and anxiety, the unnerving fear and apprehension, the excruciating agony of Krishna which he suffers during the period of Susila's suffering, and the numbness, the stupefaction he experiences during the preparation for Susila's last journey to the cremation ground. To quote from Krishna's diary:

> We are on our homeward march, a silent and benumbed gag. As we cross Nallappa's Grave once again, I cannot resist the impulse to turn and look back. Flames appear over the wall. . . . It leaves a curiously dull pain at heart. There are no more surprises and shocks in life, so that I watch the flame without agitation. For me the greatest reality is this and nothing else. . . . Nothing else will worry and interest me in life hereafter. (96)

From his cheerful visit with his wife to the prospective new house to his solitary visit carrying his dead wife to the funeral ground to perform funeral rites, it is a short but eventful journey that makes an intensely moving and entirely flawless story. "Not a word is wasted, not a word rings false," says Iyengar (369). The next part of the novel is about Krishna's numbed misery and anxiety during the process of playing the roles of both father and mother to Leela—now his three-year old daughter. Besides, this part depicts significantly the extraordinary mystic experience of Krishna communicating with his dead wife. The part of Krishna's experiment in psychic communion with Susila with the help of a medium introduces a whimsical or fantastical element into the story that has so far been so transparently true to life. Still critics don't discard it as something strange and impossible. Iyengar, who finds it difficult to feel the first and second halves of the novel blend naturally and make an artistic whole, believes that "Automatic writing and attempts at psychic contact with the dead are not altogether uncommon: and the soil of India doubtless breeds every type of idealist and eccentric waif and vagabond." (1983: 369)

P.S. Sundaram has a similar view in the matter. According to him, the theme of love, hope and frustration in family life is by no means uncommon, but it has been treated in the novel as an experience, unique and extraordinary: "On the other hand, the psychic experiments and messages from the spirit world appear strange, but by no means incredible." (47)

Krishna's effort to recover his connection with his dead wife, the whole and detailed process of psychic communion that he establishes could be nothing but hallucination. But it is there in a very subtle way and one has to take cognizance of its existence in a different realm of the mind. The narration of the psychic phenomenon carries conviction.

Every time Susila's spirit appears the atmosphere becomes surcharged with strange spiritual forces. Their 'delicate aroma fills every particle of the air' and he lets his mind float in the ecstasy, with perceptions and senses deepening. "Oblivion crept over me like a cloud. The past, present and the future welded into one" (183). In a state of 'superb and noble intoxication' he recites the name of his wife like a 'hypnotic melody,' and after a few minutes of trance, finds her sitting on his bed with an extraordinary smile in her eyes. At the end standing together at the window, gazing on 'a slender, red streak over the eastern rim of the earth,' they experience the boundaries of their personalities suddenly dissolving. "It was a moment for which one feels grateful to life and death" (184). The whole experience becomes a process of learning for Krishna as he passes from one phase to another.

In his search for a harmonious existence Krishna decides to exclude rigorously everything which disturbs that harmony, even if it means his college work. He decides to resign from his job, in spite of his deep love for English literature. But he is no longer ready to "stuff Shakespeare and Elizabethan meter and Romantic poetry for the hundredth time into young minds and feed them on the dead mutton of literary analysis and theories and histories," while what they need is "lessons in the fullest use of the mind" (178). So he decides to "write poetry and live and work with children and watch their minds unfold" (180). He bids farewell to his friends, Gajapathy, Sastri and others, amidst goodwill and adulation, in a grand send-off arranged for him.

Of all his novels *The English Teacher* assumes an importance and uniqueness, mainly because, it is heavily autobiographical, "very little part of it being fiction" (*My Days*: *134*). Krishna is a fictional character living in Narayan's fictional Malgudi. Nevertheless, his experiences of life are those of Narayan himself. Krishna is drawn on Narayan and Susila on Rajam, Narayan's wife, who in real life met with a similar fate as Susila. Leela is Hema, Narayan's only child. Narayan has not been able to give any direct expression to his deep personal grief even in *My Days* which he wrote many years after her death. It is through his art of writing novel that he has given shape and meaning to his grief and found his own way to come to terms with his irreparable loss and inconsolable sorrow[6]. It is remarkable to note that even the psychic experiences of having contact with his dead wife are not borrowed from the writings on life after death[7]; rather they have grown out of intense moments of encounters with what Narayan has perceived as 'reality.' Narayan's artistic skill lies in the alchemic act that turns the personal into the universal and the finished work of art becomes purged of the taint of the merely subjective.

Narayan introduces real and concrete characters like Krishna's mother and mother-in-law and adds to the objectivity of the narration. Krishna's mother comes to help him set up the family and stays with him for a few weeks as desired by his father. After Susila's death she has to take charge of the situation again. She takes care of Leela though Krishna keeps to himself the sole charge of bringing up Leela. His mother is truly unhappy for that, but Krishna lets her have her cry quietly. His thoughts in the situation are akin to those of a man who in real life has come across death from close quarters, and has grown callous to distress and disappointment. He observes,

> I was used to such situations and treated them with business-like indifference. Condolences, words of courage, lamentations, or assurances were all the same. I had become a sort of professional receptacle of condolence and sympathy, and I have received them in such quantity these months that they had ceased to move me or mean anything. Death and its associates, after the initial shock, produce callousness. (98)

His mother's housekeeping, her attitude to her son, daughter-in-law and grand-daughter, the silent suffering of his parents-in-law at the time of Susila's gradual collapse, even Susila's recollections of her childhood with her brother before marriage offer the novel a wide dimension for realism. The novel brings its readers very close to Indian domestic life and in this respect Narayan is compared to Katherine Manesfield[8]. However, the setting of Malgudi, another aspect of Narayan's realistic art, is not much focused in this novel.

Narayan's concern with the colonial humiliation is evident in the very first chapter of the novel in which the British Principal's emphasis on English spelling is humorously rendered.

> We were summoned to his room at the end of the day. Under normal conditions, he would welcome us with a smile, crack a joke or two, talk of nothing in particular for a couple of minutes and then state the actual business. But to-day we found him dry and sullen. He motioned us to own seats and said, "Could you imagine a worse shock for me? I came across a student of the English Honours, who did not know till this day 'honours' had to be spelt with a 'u'?" He finished his sentence with a sharp, grim laugh. . . . He began a lecture on the importance of the English language, and the need for preserving its purity. Brown's thirty years in India had not been ill-spent if they had opened the eyes of Indians to the need for speaking and writing correct English. The responsibility of English Department was indeed very great. (5-6).

A subordinate staff in the college, Krishna cannot oppose his principal on his face, but his grudges are expressed in front of the Reader of his department, Mr. Gajapathy, who openly supports the principal. Krishna says,

> "Mr. Gajapathy, there are blacker sins in this world than a dropped vowel. . . . Let us be fair. Ask Mr. Brown if he can say in any of the two hundred Indian languages: 'The cat chases the rat.' He has spent thirty years in India."
>
> "It is all irrelevant," said Gajapathy.
>
> "Why should he think the responsibility for learning is all on our side and none on his? Why does he magnify his own importance?" (6)

The tension experienced by the colonized on the colonial world is vividly expressed in the above paragraph.

The novel also offers a realistic picture of health service in India during the time. Though Krishna never complains against the doctor who is consulted for Susila's treatment, the doctor's callousness is evident in his diagnosis and treatment. The condition has hardly changed particularly in small towns and villages after so many years of independence. The doctor prescribes medicine without visiting the patient and when there is no improvement after several days of swallowing pills the doctor comes to visit the patient reluctantly. He has no doubt about his diagnosis and even when it is proved wrong after blood examination, the doctor takes it very lightly.

> 'Malaria'! the doctor said. 'I was only dreading lest it should be malaria—the most erratic and temperamental thing on earth. I wouldn't trust it. But typhoid is the king among fevers—it is an aristocrat who observes the rules of the game. I would rather trust a cobra than a green snake; you can depend upon the cobra to go its way if you understand its habits and moods.' (77-78)

The novel is full of such significant details. These details from ordinary everyday world maintain the balance between the two completely different aspects of the novel—the common and the unbelievable, and keep the sense of reality intact. Notwithstanding the arguments over the artistic credibility and coherence of the various parts of the novel[9], the novel deeply appeals for its compelling veracity and authenticity.

The Dark Room

The Dark Room, published in 1938, between *The Bachelor of Arts* and *The English Teacher*, does not belong to the category of autobiographical novels. With its poignant story of a married couple—Ramani and Savitri—the novel takes us again into the familiar world of Malgudi. This time the story throws light on the plight of the Indian women in general with details of the life of the couple. The picture is remarkably realistic. Walsh quotes Narayan telling about the genesis of the novel:

> I was somehow obsessed with a philosophy of woman as opposed to man, her constant oppressor. This must have been an early testament of the 'Women's Liberation' movement. Man assigned her a secondary place and kept her there with such subtlety and cun-

> ning that she herself began to lose all notions of her independence, individuality, stature and strength. A wife in an orthodox milieu of Indian society was an ideal victim of such circumstances. My novel dealt with this philosophy broadly in the background. (1992: 22)

The novel reflects the manner in which the patriarchal power structure determines gender stereotyping, leading to legal inequalities between the male and the female. The multiple aspects of the feminine discourse are introduced in the novel.

Ramani's wife Savitri, the mother of three children, belongs to a well-to-do middle class family in Malgudi. She is a typical Indian mother in the way she looks after her three children, Babu, Sumati and Kamala. Her concerns about their well-being are vividly portrayed. A typical man in the male dominated society, Ramani is assertive and exigent and demands to be treated as the Lord of his wife. He is cruel to the children and insensitive to their requirements. Savitri is given no right to interfere in the way he deals with the children. "How impotent she was, she thought; she had not the slightest power to do anything at home, and that after fifteen years of married life" (5). She feels that her husband has been exploiting her goodness. If she had tried at the beginning of her married life to be assertive, things would have been different. She regrets for not having done so. She is yet, not deeply dissatisfied with her allotted part of a docile wife. Utterly dependant for livelihood on her husband, she is ready to tolerate her husband's ill-temper and whims without protest.

Savitri and her children have to read Ramani's mood first in order to know how to behave themselves in his presence. Ramani gives the signal which they receive and understand. If he is in a happy mood they too can be happy in their own little ways. They feel relieved when the signal caught is a positive one. As the children think, "Ah, Father was going to be pleasant. It meant they could just hang about the dining hall and listen to their elders' talk; otherwise they would have had to keep to their books for some time and then crawl away to their pillows" (11). It is torture even when Ramani is happy. The wife and children would have to talk, to laugh, to pay attention corresponding to his demands. Or else they would have to bear the brunt of his sudden temper and subsequent tantrums.

Ramani is happy that he possesses a beautiful woman as his wife. She is for him an object that fans well the flames of his ridiculous male ego. Hence at the cinema,

> Ramani sat in the first-class seat with his wife by his side, very erect. He was very proud of his wife. She had a fair complexion and well-proportioned features, and her sky-blue saree gave her a distinguished appearance. He surveyed her slyly with a sense of satisfaction at possessing her. When people in the theatre threw looks at her, it increased his satisfaction all the more. (22)

Ramani treats his wife as a possession, and not as an individual having a mind of her own. He stands in contrast to men like Chandran, Krishna and even other Narayan heroes, who value family relationship above all and are loyal and committed to their wives and children. Ramani, on the contrary, is too self-assured, too sure about his worth. He, unlike them, is sadistic and unscrupulous, arrogant and sexist.

In the first part of the novel the experience of the disintegration of family is realized. The second part reveals this disintegration with greater intensity. Ramani employs in his office the rather elegant and fiercely independent Shanta Bai, a woman recently separated from her husband. He begins to have an affair with her. Narayan gives the details of how Ramani gets attached to Shanta Bai. Ramani assembles a house for Shanta Bai in the office. In the process of furnishing it he even borrows Savitri's favourite piece of furniture, a bench made of tick wood. Ramani, at first pushing himself forward as her brother, ends up in being her 'soothing lover.'

At the beginning Savitri in her own timid ways tries to set things right. But when her husband's infidelity becomes a talk of people around, she is ready to fight, but to no avail. In spite of her loud and strong protest and her threat to leave home, Ramani gives no assurance to end this relationship. She is rather allowed to walk out of the house and is forced to leave the children behind. "What possession can a woman call her own except her body? Everything else that she has is her father's, her husband's or her son's" (88), she says, clearly hinting at the actuality involved in the life of an Indian woman from birth to death. She leaves home all alone. Earlier as a reaction to her husband's misdemeanour she used to take recourse to the dark room of her house or rather to the dark corner of the dark room. Now she attempts to commit suicide in the river Sarayu and this act of suicide can be viewed as recourse to the dark room, a figurative one. However, she is saved by the lock-repairer and umbrella mender, Mari. He is also a part time burglar, always sheltered by the angry but kindly wife Ponny. For a short time after being rescued, Savitri tries hard to be self-sufficient, but ends up realizing how completely dependent she is on her husband and how impossible it is for her to live without her children.

> And she grew homesick. A nostalgia for children, home, and accustomed comforts seized her. Lying here on the rock floor beside the hot flickering lamp, her soul racked with fears, she could not help contrasting the comfort, security, unholiness of her home. . . .
>
> The futility, the frustration, and her own inescapable weakness made her cry and sob. . . . This is defeat. I accept it. I am no good for this fight. I am a bamboo pole. (146)

She is weak and defenceless and needs support for survival, and that is why she has to put up forever with her husband's wilfulness and the ignominy of his infidelity. She reconciles to her fate, though with some reservations, and comes back home.

Savitri finds that nothing has changed, except that only a part of her is dead and she would rather live with it happily than fight for what she would never obtain. As for Ramani, at first he is shaken by his wife's sudden fiery and rebelling spirit. But a thorough egoist, he is back to his self, after the initial shock at the turn of events. He can never allow anybody to dictate to him. He could think of rectifying himself with 'a little persistent persuasion' by her but not by her sullenness or dictation. He expects to be coaxed and requested so as to condescend. He has his own concept of India women that suits his purpose.

> He held that India owed its spiritual eminence to the fact that the people here realized that a woman's primary duty (also a divine privilege) was being a wife and a mother and what woman retained the right of being called a wife who disobeyed her husband? Didn't all the ancient epics and scriptures enjoin upon woman the strictest identification with her husband. He remembered all the heroines of the epics whose one dominant quality was a blind stubborn following of their husbands, like the shadow following the substance. (109)

Ironically his interpretation of Indian epics and scriptures shows the misconception about the position of women in the ancient time. It is the misconception of men as self-conceited and ill-informed as Ramani. Therefore, he decides in his own indignant and pompous way to be firm with a woman who he thinks has behaved like a servant, not a wife by threatening to leave, and so wait for her to come back on her own unconditionally.

Ridiculously enough he has different standards for Shanta Bai. For him, she is "a splendid creature with her understanding heart and cultured outlook" (110). He takes an unconventional step not only by appointing her in his office but also by giving her a place to sit in his room—"It was all nonsense to keep men and women in water-tight compartments; women were as good as men and must be treated accordingly" (57), he says. Though he is often snubbed by her, he is ready to oblige her in all possible ways. Yet the only redeeming factor about him is that he looks after the children well in his wife's absence. Moreover, when his wife is back, he cannot but grant her a little bit of space and freedom.

Narayan the realist knows that there is hardly any scope for mutual change and that women like Savitri come back not out of love for their husbands, but for dragging a disgraceful life. Only after she knows that she is unable to support herself, she has no other way but to come back to her husband. All her finer sensibilities are now dead as a result of her husband's cruel behaviour. He still does not recognize her as an individual, but treats her as a possession. Narayan's story is based on his assessment of the women in pre-Independent India when child marriage was in vogue. A domestic battle in a time when girls were married off at an early age and were not educated to support themselves, physically or psychologically, was usually a battle between two dissimilar powers.

Shanta Bai, though not good-looking like Savitri, is young and can make herself attractive by her little make-up and stylish manners, something similar to "Garbo manner: the temperamental heroine and the impending doom" (68). With her candour, smartness and snobbish replies, she can undo the airs Ramani puts on. When they are together the role almost reverses; she is the person in charge of the situation and he the subservient. In spite of her power over Ramani, the employer, Shanta Bai's position as a woman is as vulnerable as that of Savitri. She was married at the age of twelve to a cousin of her own who was a gambler and drunkard. At the age of eighteen she left him realizing that he would not change. Her parents did not approve of this and so she had to leave home. She did her matriculation, and then came to Madras with the help of an aunt, and joined the women's college and completed her B.A. She did some odd teaching jobs and also became companion to a few rich children. "On the whole it has been a great struggle," she says (51). A comparison with Ibsen's *A Doll's House* clarifies Narayan's vision. Nora, the central character in *A Doll's House*, frees herself from the plight she has been put to for being dutiful and unselfish. She leaves home to get her education and Ibsen wanted to raise an awareness in men that 'in killing women's souls they had killed their own' (G.B. Shaw on Ibsen). Her advice goes on as long as Savitri does not feel guilty for having raised her voice against her husband. Amidst all this, Ponni stands as a contrast. Belonging to a lower caste she is likely to be uneducated. But with the strength of her character and her basic goodness, she stands apart. She is clear in her views of men and firm in her dealings with them. So she advises Savitri, "Sister, remember this. Keep the men under the rod, and they will be all right. Show them that you care for them and they will tie you up and treat you like a dog." (105)

The novel ends with a tragic realization of Savitri that she is not entitled to the basic right to live as she likes. When she recognizes her rescuer passing the dusty street with his tool-bag slung over his shoulder and a couple of dilapidated umbrellas under his arm; his dark face was shining with sweat under the hot sun (161), she wants to give him a good treat—"food, water and a magnificent gift and inquire about her great friend Ponni" (161). She remembers Ponni saying that she would ask him to visit her house. But soon she remembers her limitation; how can she help him when she herself has nothing of her own. She lets him go on his way. The dark room of Savitri reminds one of Virginia Woolf's *Room of One's Own*. Savitri's dark room is however different from the room suggested by Woolf. Woolf's room signifies strength, but Savitri's room being dark signifies the awareness of her helplessness. Savitri's attempt to assert her individuality is suggested through her eagerness to give Mari a good treat. But her awareness of her own status in the house prohibits her from showing sympathy to Mari. She could however offer him a treat in secret without the knowledge of Ramani. But her sense of honour forbids her to do so. She acknowledges her status in Ramani's house and that is why abstains from inviting Mari to her house. These denials add to her suffering; but this time this poignant suffering attached to her self-respect suggests a tragic awareness. She has also developed a knowledge of others' sufferings. Mari's hard life is suggested through Savitri's reflection: "the poor fellows face shone with sweat; perhaps he had been tramping the street in the hot sun, foodless; perhaps he had not earned a pie yet in the town" (162). Narayan beautifully understates his concern for the subaltern in his novel. The slight reference to untouchability also makes the setting of the novel socially relevant.

The Dark Room occupies a special position among Narayan's novels for displaying the status of women in an orthodox milieu of Indian society. Narayan's unbiased attitude as a realist is once again displayed in his portrayal of women characters taken from different parts of the social setup—the protagonist Savitri, her friend Gangu and Shanta Bai, The portrait of Ponni as a lower cast woman, displays Narayan's understanding of certain other forces at work. For instance, Ponni, unlike Savitri, need not bother about the shallow social prestige; she is free to behave as she likes and shows generosity to helpless Savitri; but Savitri has to remain a puppet, suppressing all her human feelings. At a time when the women's liberation movement was gaining force in the West, Narayan expressed his sympathies to women's issues, embodying them in his fiction. P.S. Sundaram says appropriately, "It is neither tragedy nor melodrama: still less is it a didactic or cynical tract. Nothing is extenuated in this faithful picture of what happens in many homes in India, nor aught set down in malice. It is, to adopt a line from Wordsworth, 'a simple tale for thinking hearts'"[10] (1988: 38).

Mr. Sampath: The Printer of Malgudi

Mr. Sampath, *The Financial Expert* and *Waiting for the Mahatma*—the three as a set signal a new phase in Narayan's development as a writer. They mark his journey from an enclosed, contemplative and personal art to a more strenuously imagined and external fiction. *Mr. Sampath*, the first of these post-independence novels of Narayan is a fictional rendering of Narayan's experience as the editor of *Indian Thought*. At the outbreak of the Second World War Narayan found it difficult to have anything printed in England and at home, due to shortage of newsprint and printing ink. He could not have his writings published as much as he wanted in *The Hindu*. So he started a journal of his own, a quarterly called *Indian Thought* and kept himself busy. The character of Srinivas, the editor of 'The Banner' in *Mr. Sampath* is the outcome of Narayan's experience as an editor, though Narayan never became as successful as his counterpart in the novel. Mr. Sampath, the printer of 'The Banner' is drawn on a real Sampath of his acquaintance. In *My Days* Narayan mentions that the multifaceted Sampath of real life also became a busy film personality without, however, neglecting his press work (2006: 180).

Thus, personal experience and persons of his acquaintance from real life find a place in this novel, too. But the autobiographical elements in this novel are reshaped and reconstructed according to the colour of the novel's theme, making these fit for the particular context, in contrast to the earlier novels where there has been an immediate transmission of such elements. The new method is used in this novel and the novels that follow it. New facets of life and more complexities of human relationship are explored. The stories are populated by myriad characters with their varied problems, creating a gallery of God's plenty. Life is made more general, more comprehensive and of course, more diversified.

Thus, in *Mr. Sampath* we have Srinivas, Sampath, Ravi, the landlord, Somu, Sohanlal, De Mello, Shanti, Mrs. Srinivas, Mrs. Sampath, Ravi's mother and the like, each different from the other in interests, attitudes and preoccupations. In the novel place, work, social obligations and personalities—in everything there is found a striking duality. Srinivas, the typical young, ardent, idealistic Narayan hero, is afflicted at first with an uncertainty of purpose and mild hopelessness about the future and indecision. A question of career has seemed to him as 'embarrassing as a physiological detail'; and 'agriculture, apprenticeship in a bank, teaching, law,' he has given everything a trial once. But with every passing month he has felt the excruciating pain of losing time. He is sensitive, modest and wry about himself, but has a hidden resolute will that helps him settle in journalism, with a temporary break into film making. It is his work as an editor that finally gives meaning to his own existence as well as that of his family. As a journalist he does not exactly represent the author. Life, however, is seen through his eyes. He is an ardent idealist as the founder-editor of 'The Banner.' His mind is always preoccupied with the thoughts of the article he is to write for his readers that would cater to their interest and requirements. Thus his articles on the problems of growing towns reveal the socio-economic conditions of the time. In a regular feature entitled "Open window" he writes about the need for the abolition of slums and congestion. "It described the tenements, the pigsties constructed for human dwellings in the four corners of the town by rapacious landlords." (6) Narayan's awareness and observation of the evils in the society are evident in such remarks.

However, Srinivas's existence as a man is rooted in his commitment to family life. He comes to Malgudi, leaving his joint family at Talapura, in search of livelihood and then is followed by his wife and son. Though inexperienced and inept to manage domestic affairs satisfactorily and to fulfil the round of domestic demands, he calls himself a family man and tries to satisfy his wife and son, and keeps the connection with his brother and other members alive. The minuteness and exactness with which Narayan portrays family life manifests his immense capacity for sharp observation and clear understanding of the realities of life. The character of Srinivas who sees a vast scheme of God in the mundane affairs of day to day life is portrayed as a typical God fearing Indian.

Sampath, in contrast, has more control over outside matters than over family matters. The husband of a rough, uneducated woman and the father of five children, coarsely but lovingly brought up, he reflects a typical Indian attitude towards a male child when he wants his son's picture to be drawn by the artist. Unlike Sampath, Srinivas has no reservation about the sanctity of marital relationships. Through Sampath's comic self justification Narayan offers a realistic picture of the mindset of a section of society for which polygamy is a norm.

> Some people say that every sane man needs two wives—a perfect one for the house and a perfect one outside for social life. . . . I have the one, why not the other. I have the confidence that I will keep both of them happy and if necessary in separate houses. Is a man's heart so narrow that it cannot accommodate more than one? I have married according to Vedic rites; let me have one according to civil marriage law. (179)

Srinivas meets Sampath in a dramatic way just when he is looking desperately for a printer to assist him in his work. Sampath accepts his offer and agrees to do the job for him whereas a number of printers have already declined for fear of running into trouble with the administration. Srinivas's unpleasant and discouraging experiences as an editor bring to light the cumbersome process of official procedure in India that frightens people to take up any responsibility.

It is only Sampath who undertakes the task with great interest and enthusiasm. He is not just the printer who carries out the orders of the editor—he is clever to handle the complicacies involved in the administrative process, to deal with the strike in the press, to get the journal out on time even if he has to work all night, to take the bundles in the early hours of the morning to the railway station, and cajole and bully the station master into handing them over to the guards of trains going in either direction. In all this he is helped by Srinivas, though he is not actually in need of anyone's help. And later he takes the decision all by himself to stop the journal without even consulting his boss and circulates a printed slip to that effect for the information of the reading public—"Owing to some machine breakdown and general overhauling, 'The Banner' will not be issued for some time" (77).

It is Srinivas's interaction with a contrasting character like Sampath that gives rise to various social and economic complicacies that constitute the theme of the story. Unlike Srinivas, Sampath is vociferous and flamboyant. Though he has the mastery of printing and great managerial authority his heart is not into the trade of printing. His interest lies in theatre, make-up, costumes, stage and films. He leads Srinivas into the venture of film-making in the most opportune time and persuades Somu Sundaram, the District board President, to film production. Soon comes into existence 'Sunrise Pictures' in place of the press office 'Truth Printing Works.' 'Sunrise' grows with financial help from some people interested in film making. Somu becomes the film-producer, Sohanlal the film-financer, Dc Mello the brain behind the 'studio organization,' Sampath the chief executive, Srinivas the script-writer, Ravi, the accountant; Shanti, the ravishingly beautiful woman, is assigned the role of Parvati in the mythological story of 'The Burning of Kama' (God of Love) chosen to be filmed. Ravi, the gifted but unrealized artist, is engrossed in a vision of beauty once seen in the Iswaran Temple, and lost. Later in Shanti he finds his long-lost vision. But Sampath's romantic involvement with her leads to his madness and creates unwarranted complicacies.

The novel is packed with dramatic and funny events, each of which however exposes human oddities and eccentricities. Narayan's natural ability to see the comic in each and every realistic and authentic character or event brings different aspects of life sharply into focus. Characters like the landlord who arrives to collect rents, and his heir reflect their matter-of-fact approach to life. Situations like the opening ceremony reveal the sheer foolishness of people holding position of importance. These are the source materials for Narayan's ironic perception. Narayan portrays the much practised inauguration ceremony that reminds one of such occasions in real life during which the invited V.I.P. guests are not found properly briefed and without being ashamed deliver speeches that have little relation to the occasions. One is reminded of Nissim Ezekiel's famous poem 'Farewell to Miss Pushpa T.S.' The situation in the novel shows how the President arrives when the ceremony is practically over. He is taken to the seat of honour, garlanded, given a bouquet, and requested to speak to the audience. He says modestly that he knows nothing about films and yet goes on speaking for an hour denouncing mythological pictures and stressing on the need to use the cinema to educate people in cleanliness, domestic economy and the problems of agriculture. They must boycott films dealing with demons and gods. Next moment after being reminded that the film the Sunrise Pictures are going to shoot is mythological, he takes a contradictory stance without wasting time and begins to say the opposite of what he has been saying just before:

> Our epics undoubtedly are a veritable store house of wisdom and spirituality. They contain messages which are of eternal value and applicable to all times and climes, irrespective of age, race or sex and so on. . . . India has a lesson to teach to the rest of the world. (134)

The funny details of the film industry arouse irresistible laughter. The frantic and unproductive energy employed in the film studios leading to the mangling of ancient stories beyond recognition, the crazy temperamental tantrums of the actors—all this reveals the hollowness and hypocrisy prevailing in the film world. The sketch of the shooting of the film presents a vivid and credible picture of the technical details and the details about the actors and other people involved in it. The actors are temperamental. The actor playing the role of Shiva in a fit of unreasonable rage demands more importance, more money, and then walks out of the project. He is immediately replaced by Sampath, who considers himself fit for any task that comes his way. Srinivas is surprised—"Sampath's versatility took his breath away" (185). The heroine is given undue importance. The rule of the set is decided according to her moods and whims. She receives all attention and her demands are immediately fulfilled. But the most ridiculous is the composition of music and the shooting of dance act.

> A song blared forth from the loud-speaker—a song with a sentimental lilt, and drums producing a kind of hot-air rhythm. The music department fully realizing the need of the hour had produced a brand-new tune by adapting a couple of tunes born in Hollywood from a South American theme. Srinivas despaired on hearing it. It produced anything but the holy-of-holies feeling that he had hoped would be the essence of the scene. As he saw Somu and Lal tapping their feet instinctively to the music he was filled with a desperation which he could not easily place or classify. Other feet picked up the rhythm, and presently he saw Sampath slowly stirring in his meditation. He rose to his feet. He twisted and wriggled his body and assumed the pose of a dance—carving one saw on the temple walls. He moved step by step and approached the chair, which marked Parvati's place. (185-86)

It is ludicrous that this peculiar mixture of western and Indian dance and music is passed by the film personalities in the name of the 'revival of our classical art.' The glamorous film world is shown as full of hypocrisies and self-deception.

The novel ends with Ravi succumbing to his mad passion and landing up in police lock-up; the shooting of the film ending in a fiasco and the film unit breaking up; and Srinivas having his last meeting with Sampath before separating ways forever. Srinivas, who turns out to be Ravi's saviour at a critical moment of his life, refrains from showing any interest in Sampath's affairs. This shows his growth as a worldly-wise man. *Mr. Sam-*

path displays a more than usual variety of tones—stretching from "the intensely serious to the deliriously comic, and from something approaching farce and romp in the film studio section to the coolly realized actuality of the details of family life." (Walsh 1992: 67). The novel has many attractive elements which on the surface appear dispersed but they do not fail to reflect the maturity in the author's perception of life with its various facets.

The Financial Expert

Narayan's excellence and maturity as a novelist is most recognized in *The Financial Expert*. The newly emerging world of Malgudi—the world that Iyengar calls the exotic world of half-headed or half-hearted dreamers, artists, financiers, speculators, twisters, adventurers, eccentrics, cranks, cinema stars, sanyasis—is found more perceptibly in this novel. The former sheltered existence and the placidity of Malgudi of Swami's time get broken. Not only men from outside but also plenty of money, a plethora of ideas and many cultural varieties force their way through Malgudi causing a pressure on human existence. Change is visible on every front—change for the better or for the worse. Traditions and customs are followed without denying space to the newly acquired modernity; the new ways of life are followed which gradually form new sets of beliefs and values. The centre stage is now occupied not by the typical Malgudians but by its new members like Margayya.

Margayya is the most notable character in *The Financial Expert*. It is his rise and fall that constitutes the story of the novel. His actual name is Krishna, but he is called Margayya, meaning the path-finder—one who shows the way. He shows the way out to those in financial trouble. In the five parts of the novel, he is seen going through five phases of success and failure, each coming in turn. Through the story of his life, Narayan draws, with deft strokes, a very realistic picture of the social and economic trends of post war and post independent India. In the first part of his life as a businessman, Margayya plays the role of a financial adviser to the poor peasants. His emergence is "an unexpected and incalculable offshoot of a corporator's zeal" (1). He is a modest money lender who transacts his business under a banyan tree in front of the Malgudi Central Co-operative Land Mortgage Bank. He advises his customer to borrow money at a low rate of interest from the Co-operative Bank and lend to those in sheer need of money at a higher rate. To one who has already received a loan, he advances a little loan (for interest) so that the little loan might wedge out another loan from the Co-operative Bank. Margayya keeps himself as the centre of all that complex transactions, and makes all the parties concerned pay him for his services, the bank opposite him being involved in it willy-nilly. He, thus, unhesitatingly defeats the very purpose of co-operative movement for promotion of thrift, and elimination of middlemen. His crooked banking reveals the age-old social malady of the exploitation of the poor, ignorant and illiterate rural Indians by the clever and greedy people crowding the newly developing urban India. Margayya is however portrayed in Narayan's characteristic way. He exposes the rampant materialism of modern society that has become the basic principle of life and that has replaced the values of the old Indians. Margayya has a great passion for money and a remarkable faculty of generating and multiplying it. He values money as God and values it more than human qualities. He believes that money can obtain all good things and shudders to think of a life without it. He believes that all the dishonour and humiliation he has faced early in life is due to the lack of money. His recurrent reflections on the fascinating power of money, sets the tone of the story perfectly. He thinks of the people who make money even on a dead body. He feels a kind of disgust at the thought of it but still wonders to see what people can do for money.

His money-lending business is carried on with his 'tin box, a grey discoloured, knobby affair,' which is small enough to be carried under his arm, containing practically his entire equipment—"a bottle of ink, a pen and blotter, a small register where pages carried an assortment of names and figures, and above all—the most important item—loan application forms of the Co-operative Bank" (2). The last are his greatest asset in life, and half his time is occupied in acquiring them cleverly by using his own agency at work—his customers. But this cannot go on forever. The Secretary of the Bank, accompanied by Arul Doss, the peon, stops his business for a day and threatens at the same time of further action against him. But this cannot stop him forever. Only when his son, Balu throws his private account book into the gutter that this chapter of his life is practically brought to a close. After it he takes guard elsewhere.

The materialistic attitude is described in the high terms of philosophy. It makes the business of printing a book on sexology appear to him as an alien one. He gives thousand excuses to persuade himself to believe that he is in the wrong business doing a wrong thing and thus harming young minds like that of Balu and old minds as well. "I would do anything to avoid it," he says, and swells with his goodness, nobility and importance and the clean plans he is able to make for his son (95). Margayya represents that section of the society which does as it satisfies its need and says as it suits its ego and vanity. Adopting means of pretence, he manages to sell the rest of his interest in the book to Madan Lal for an outright cash payment.

Hence in the next phase, he is found in a position to lend money to his former clients at high rate of interest. He becomes again the financial adviser and money lender to the peasants, with his own offices in the Market Road. He finds his offices to be the best place in the world, in spite of the mild rumble of the Malgudi gutter and the not so mild smell of it. He revels in the crowds, noise and bustle which seem to him like background music to his own thoughts because he realizes that a prospect for him depends on the people who are part of this world. They are going to be his future clients. In his new role as a financial advisor he is assisted again by Dr. Pal. With his own shrewd calculations he uses Dr Pal's resources to his advantage and allows Dr Pal to benefit from it. For his tremendous success, Margayya is referred to as a financial small savings he takes to give fantastic wizard who receives deposits and pays fabulous rates of interest to the depositors. His complex methods are beyond anyone's comprehension. He becomes a celebrity and is looked upon with greater admiration and awe than a film star and is courted by the high and mighty, blessed by the poor whose interest in return. For him it is dream come true.

But the final phase of his career sees him as an 'insolvent Margayya.' His insolvency comes after he falls out with Dr Pal. In his mad yearning for money Margayya fails to notice the corrupting influence of both money and Dr. Pal on his son Balu. Both have led Balu astray. Acting on impulse he drags Dr. Pal by the scruff of his coat and hits him with one of his sandals, and in the process sows the seeds of his own ruin. He could have dealt with his son with a bit circumspection and diplomacy, could have shared his property with him as he had demanded and saved himself. But he does not do so. Outraged by his impulsive act, Dr Pal destroys him. He spreads rumours about Margayyas's dwindling financial position and spreads panic among the depositors. They in turn take back the deposits bringing Margayya's rising business down to collapse. After being hounded for three or four months by clients and customers, lawyers and the like his life comes back to normalcy. He is ready again with his old knobby trunk, his only property now, to start afresh at the banyan tree in front of the Co-operative Bank and advises Balu to accompany him. His career completes full circle in life. He is now Balu's pathfinder. The turn of events in his life comes naturally as he hovers between two guiding factors of his life—his family, the constant and money, the variable. Narayan delineates convincingly the reality of his mad passion for material success and his extreme fondness for Balu, and the subsequent rise and fall in his life.

It is Margayya's attitude to life that saves him from the ignominy likely to be caused by ruins. Though he is a worshipper of money, he is ready to give up the money when the happiness of his son or daughter-in-law is in question. The novel ends with Margayya being shown as happy and content, playing with his grandson. He comments—"Life has been too dull without him." Margayya accepts the vicissitudes in his life with perfect equanimity. Money is still a passion. Yet, his fall from affluence to insolvency does not affect him, not even psychologically. He is ready to start it all over again. Therefore, this turn of fate does not make the novel a tragedy. Rather, as Graham Greene says,—Balu's "progress from charming childhood to spoilt frustrated manhood is perhaps the saddest episode Mr. Narayan has written" (Introduction, *The Financial Expert,* vii).

Waiting for the Mahatma

Narayan's *Waiting for The Mahatma* is different from his other novels. It is the dual structure of the novel—a combination of comedy and tragedy in the plot bringing two different kinds of action into relationship with each other—that makes the difference. The relationship between two young lovers, Sriram and Bharati, forms the comedy part and the assassination of Mahatma Gandhi, the great political leader and saint, forms the 'tragedy' part. Following the definitions of comedy and tragedy offered by Northrop Frye, Shiva M. Pandya finds in the novel a blending of incompatible emotions and justifies the incompatibility[11]. According to Iyengar two factors make *Waiting for the Mahatma* different from the preceding novel—*The Financial Expert*, and the following one—*The Guide*. First is that action stays out of Malgudi and goes as far as to Delhi; second, the two central characters are engaged in politics. These two, being quite uncommon in Narayan, deserve special attention.

In fact, the introduction of the Mahatma as an important character in the novel makes it impossible to confine its scope to the small and simple South Indian town of Malgudi. It is for the first time that Narayan's Malgudi representing India to a great extent, comes in direct touch with a national figure and a national movement. Therefore critics often discuss the novel as a political novel and find fault with Narayan's understanding and his presentation of political matter.[12] They seek to fit the novel forcefully into some preconceived notions, and having categorized it as 'a political novel' they criticize it for not fulfilling the terms of political novel. It may be rewarding to remember M. Bakhtin's observation on Dostoevsky in this context. He says that Dostoevsky's work does not fit into "any of the preconceived frameworks in histrio, literary schemes that we usually apply to various species of the European novel."[13] What Bakhtin says of Dostoevsky can be applied to Narayan. In fact, Narayan, has not intended to write a political novel. He only portrays a slice of Indian life that was bubbling with various political activities, during the period of freedom struggle.

Critics find fault even with Narayan's portrait of Gandhiji. They, in fact, fail to understand that Narayan does not attempt a character sketch of Gandhiji in his novel.[14] Narayan's purpose is not at all to portray him as a historical figure with all minute details of his personality and life. It is not a 'Gandhi novel' meant to enlarge our awareness of Gandhi or his era. Narayan brings Gandhi to the fold of his fictional characters only to show the influence he exerted on the different sections of the Indian society with his simplicity, saintliness and charisma. P.S. Sundaram rightly observes that the trouble with the critics who find fault with Narayan's portrayal of Gandhiji lies in the fact that those critics are touchy, because they look upon Gandhiji as Jesus and Muhammad and such a critic has his "own idea of the proportion and propriety to be observed in a political novel dealing with the struggle of independence (1988: 67). Critics like Shiva M. Pandya, too, find no fault with Narayan's portrait of the Mahatma in his novel. To quote Pandya, "The action in which Gandhi is involved is the epic struggle between the forces of good and evil . . . The evil he wanted to vanquish stirs at many levels: individual, social and political. At individual level unrestrained indulgence in greed, anger and lust without any regard or consideration for humanity . . . at social level untouchability, degraded position of women, intercommunal discord . . . at the political level foreign rule were the gigantic forces of evil."[15] Pandya's observation is revealing because it helps one understand how Narayan analyses Gandhiji's influence on these different levels in his novel.

More than 70 years after India's Independence and the martyrdom of the Mahatma, it is now possible to interpret the novel in a new light. Scholars all over the world are now interested not so much in Gandhiji's life but in the way Gandhiji has influenced different types of people including an illiterate Indian peasant and a personality like Martin Luther King. The famous author, Doughlas Allen, the editor of 'Philosophy of Gandhi for the 21st century,' recently said in an interview, "Gandhiji is a catalyst, someone who gets you to think and challenges status quo."[16] Doughlas further says, "Gandhi's philosophy has to be integrated to suit today's needs. His was not a static way of looking at the world. . . . Gandhi tries to understand the root causes of terror and hatred-domination, exploitation, humiliation. Gandhiji still touches people."

At the beginning of the novel *Waiting for the Mahatma*, the Malgudians are seen to be waiting for the Mahatma with great interest and curiosity. They generally have a 'simple and relaxed way of living' but with the Mahatma's arrival, they are caught in the political current of the time. Unlike Bharati, they are lacking in any kind of political passion, but the knowledge they have already acquired about Gandhiji's greatness, make them enthusiastic. His actual arrival at Malgudi, and delivering fervent words are enough to create a stir in the otherwise dormant and idle world of Malgudi. When he is gone, everything returns to its normal state. The minute details with which Narayan describes the huge gathering awaiting the arrival of Mahatma Gandhi braving the scorching heat of the sun, sitting uncomplainingly for hours, create real and vivid impressions of the way Gandhi made his path into the hearts of the masses.

Gandhiji's views and philosophy of life have not been shown as being important in themselves. Rather Narayan has tried to make a study of the impact of his views and his philosophy particularly on young men like Sriram. Thus the story of Sriram and his involvement in politics becomes central to the theme of the novel. And here again Narayan's good-humoured irony becomes the key to his apprehension of reality. At the beginning, Gandhiji's words are having a ludicrous effect on Sriram who is already fascinated by Bharati. When Gandhi is urging people to give up all bitterness and grow love for the people they are fighting against, Sriram relates his words to his love for the girl. He thinks: "Oh, revered Mahatmaji, have no doubt that my heart is pure and without bitterness. How can I have any bitterness in my heart for a creature who looks so divine?" (32)

Sriram, obviously, joins politics as a means to pursue his love interest, Bharati. But soon the impact of Gandhiji's indomitable personality as well as the great magnetic power of his words on Sriram becomes clear and visible. Initially, he has no understanding of Gandhian philosophy or his politics. But as he listens to him, he begins to think, and then realizes that he has started seeing life from a different perspective:

> Sometimes Sriram found it impossible to follow his words: He could not grasp what he was saying, but he looked rapt, he tried to concentrate and understand. This was the first time he felt the need to try and follow something, the first time that he found himself at a disadvantage. Until now he had had a conviction, especially after he began to operate his own bank account, that he understood eve-

> rything in life. This was the first time he was assailed by doubts of his own prowess and understanding. (30)

From the beginning of Mahatma's entry into Malgudi to the end of the freedom struggle and his assassination, the impact of the Mahatma on Sriram can be felt very well. But the irony is that Sriram looks up to Bharati for encouragement and moral support for every decision and every action of his life. That is why, in her absence, he is led to be involved in terrorist politics. As a realist Narayan knows that the common people lack in firm faith and so are easily distracted.

The success of Gandhi's freedom struggle was also a result of the sacrifice of his non-violent army of soldiers. Narayan touches upon the reality of the life they led under Gandhiji's motivation and guidance. Bharati, one of them, stands apart among all Narayan's characters. She makes a man and patriot of Sriram. She is a follower and close associate of Gandhi and it becomes possible because she has been brought up in Gandhiji's ashram after the death of her father during the 1920 movement. A true disciple of Gandhiji, Bharati represents the new generation of Indian women. She is self-confident with a positive ideology. In spite of her self-controlled and self-assured ways, she adds a tone of romance and warmth to the novel.

Bharati is more like the heroines of the Shakespearean comedies—strong-willed, independent, sprightly and powerful. She has chosen her path with proper understanding and total conviction. She has set her goal before her eyes and nothing can divert her attention or interest. She has her own understanding of life. She would not marry Sriram until she gets the consent of the Mahatma, the only guiding force of her life. She represents all those women who braved the anger and disapproval of their male counterparts during the struggle and jumped into the struggle sacrificing the pleasures of their lives or even sacrificed their lives. Bharati is not even aware of the kind of male ego Sriram is suffering from, when he thinks he could imagine her only as his wife, not as a social worker. But, Sriram does not have the courage to do anything or say anything that "might scare her and take her away from him, nothing that might make fruitless all the thousands of miles he had come" (243). So he remains on his guard. The impact of rising feminism seems to have influenced Narayan's views of the world and its people.

Narayan refers to Gandhiji's deep concern for the position of women in India. As Bharati mentions, "the thing that pains Mahatmaji now is the suffering of women." She further says,

> On the 15th of August when the whole country was jubilant, and gathered here to take part in the Independence Day festivities, do you know where Bapu was? In Calcutta where fresh riots had started. Bapu said his place was where people were suffering and not where they were celebrating. He said that if a country cannot give security to women and children, it's not worth living in. He said it would be worth dying if that would make his philosophy better understood. (243)

The fact that women were learning how to protect their honour even at the cost of their life shows the growing consciousness among women regarding the dignity of their position in a men's world: "Mahatmaji had advised women as a last resort to take their lives with their own hands rather than surrender their honour" (244) and Bharati is always prepared to end her life to save her honour.

Besides this issue of Indian women, Narayan has thrown light on other socially relevant themes like poverty, untouchability, prostitution and communalism. The shameful caste system that used to prevail in the society those days is portrayed through the description of the sweeper who has a long broom and short broom attached to his body. As the Mahatma explains, "It meant that he is both a municipal sweeper and that he has scavenging work to do in private houses also. The long broom ought to be the municipal emblem." (49)

The prevalence of caste system in India and Gandhiji's passionate and relentless struggle against it is a matter of immense significance. According to Sriram's grandmother, the illiterate old woman, "The Mahatma was one who preached dangerously, who tried to bring untouchables into the temples, and who involved people in difficulties with the police." (62)

When Sriram hears Gandhi's views on the caste system and untouchability, he begins to think about it for the first time. He realizes that there exists such a malady which he has taken for granted and which actually requires to be attended to. He remembers how his orthodox grandmother bullies the ragged scavenger who comes to their house everyday to sweep the backyard and how she would not let him approach nearer than ten yards, and habitually adopt a bullying tone while addressing him, and how he himself would join her.

Narayan creates a vivid impression of the places in towns where the poor and the downtrodden live and are left to suffer. The Mahatma, in the process of his attempt at their uplift, decides to stay in one of the dozen huts belonging to the city sweepers

> who lived on the banks of the river. It was probably the worst area of the town, and an exaggeration even to call them huts; they are just hovels, put together with rags, tin sheets, and shreds of coconut matting, all crowded in anyhow, with scratchy fowls cackling about and children growing in the street dust. The municipal services were neither extended here nor missed, although the people living in the hovels were employed by the municipality for scavenging work in the town. . . . these men spent less than a tenth of their income on food or clothing always depending upon mendicancy in their off hours for survival. Deep into the night their voices could be heard clamouring for alms, in all the semi-dark streets of Malgudi. . . . Reformers looked on with wrath and horror, but did little else, since as an untouchable class they lived outside the town limits. . . . (37)

Critics have always found fault in Narayan's rendering of the caste system in all his novels. D.A. Shankar in his 'Caste in the Fiction of R.K. Narayan' says, "In *Waiting for The Mahatma* Narayan offers a fairly realistic picture of the location where the outcaste live, indicating at least some familiarities with such places on the superficial level, the level of the transient or tourist." (McLeod 1994: 140) He adds, "Narayan is obviously aware of the role of class and caste in Indian life and the situations that they create in human relationship, but when we attempt to discover in his work some exploration of the relationship that they bear to characters and their actions, we are in for a disappointment. Caste, in fact, has little or no bearing on the psyche of Narayan's characters: there is no structural or organic relationship between characters and caste." (142)

Such observation can be contradicted as Narayan is not bothered about the details of these issues. His renderings carry a sense of actuality and at the same time, they convey his mild criticism of the society. There is irony and humour in his tone. He is all admiration for a man like the Mahatma who dedicates his life for the welfare of the untouchables and raises his voice against the injustice meted out to them. He also shows how the new generation gradually has learnt to accept the idea that caste system in India is ugly, inhuman and also unscientific.

Corruption, another social reality in the world of Malgudi, is manifested by the presence of people like the timber contractor who can mindlessly and illegally fell trees and sell huge logs and at the same time justify themselves in the name of business. These people who destroy their own greenland for nefarious purposes are no better than Vasu of *The Man-Eater of Malgudi*, the modern day Rakshasa who destroys wild life with the same thoughtlessness. Even Gandhiji's message of non-violence and his call for National Service mean nothing to them. They contribute a part of their illegally acquired wealth to Gandhiji's Harijan fund and are satisfied that they have done their duty for the country. Corruption in Malgudi is further exposed through the delineation of the character of Natesh, the Municipal Chairman, who has been for weeks preparing his palatial house, Neel Bagh in the aristocratic Lawley Extension to receive Gandhi (38). He describes how he has spent two lakhs in the building, twenty five thousand rupees for garden and lawn only to receive a great soul like Mahatmaji. Otherwise a simple man like himself who can comfortably live in a hut has nothing to do with such a big place, he says. For the Mahatma's satisfaction, he replaces his gaudy chintz of the doorways and the windows by Khaddar, pictures of hunting gentry of George V's wedding by pictures of Moulana Azad, Nehru, Sarojini Naidu, C. Rajagopalachari and the like. Narayan's ironic rendering of the hypocrisy and pomp of the Indian leaders reveals the art of exhibiting reality in his novel.

Besides Natesh, there are the District Collector, the District Superintendent of police and many others who are enthusiastic about Gandhiji's arrival but have never realized his ideas. They rather pervert them to suit their own coarser personalities. The Collector is there to receive the Mahatma but ironically he is the "Custodian of British Prestige." He takes the trouble to go through the address of the Chairman before it is sent for printing. In order to make sure that it in no way betrays military secrets, he has to censor it at several places. He makes sure that "Anyone who reads the address would conclude that politics were the last thing that Mahatmaji was interested in." (42)

However, simple but shrewd, Gandhi foils all the plans and arrangements of these petty politicians by acting on his own. Even the people of Malgudi can see the difference between the Mahatma and these people. From Narayan's point of view, the Mahatma represents an ideal for the masses, an ideal that may be aspired for but cannot be attained. He is an ideal portrayed in the backdrop of reality. In *Waiting for the Mahatma* Narayan describes not the India Gandhi dreamt of but the one in which he was born and brought up.

The masterly stroke of realism comes in his portrayal of the grim situations prevailing in the Indian jails and of the communal feelings running high in the post-independent India. The novel ends with a note of uncertainty in the life of Bharati and Sriram which again points to the greater uncertainty and confusion that arose after Gandhiji's death. The post-independence change in Malgudi is indicated when Sriram notices that Karni's shop is gone and with it is gone the portrait of Maria Theresa. This marks the end of colonial presence. The blending of levity and seriousness, which is mostly a modern trend, finds its way into Narayan's novels. *Waiting for the Mahatma* is no exception. But what sets it apart from other novel is that in it the serious outweighs the comic. Even the comic interlude involving Sriram and the assumed death of his grandmother has a serious statement to make. Sriram's unhappiness and regret at the death of his granny, the elaborate rituals of funeral and finally the discovery that she actually is not dead is depicted to present Narayan's ironic view on a socially relevant situation. Instead of rejoicing at the discovery that Sriram's grandmother is not actually dead the superstitious Malgudians are swayed by the priest's words. As she has risen from the pile of wood she is not allowed to come back to her ancestral home in Malgudi because it is against the ancient custom. She is forced to go on a pilgrimage for it is dangerous to violate an ancient custom. According to the priest, "The whole town will be wiped out by fire or plague. It is very inauspicious. Do anything you like, but she can't come into the town." (124)

It is important to note that whatever external changes Malgudi might have undergone in its journey from innocence to experience, in its basics it remains the same as ever. Narayan's sharp observation and cool analysis take both change and continuity into consideration in his realistic narrative and depicts them with the naturalness of life.

NOTES

1. Naipaul on Narayan, *The Hindu, Literary Review*, May 4, 2008.
2. Graham Greene says, "Swami is the story of a child written with complete objectivity, with a humour strange to our fiction, close to Chekhov than to any English writer, with the same underlying sense of beauty and sadness." Introduction, *The Bachelor of Arts*, London: Pocket Book Edition, 1951: vii.
3. Ashish Nandy speaks of two forms of colonization. One is the physical conquest of territories. The other is the colonization of the minds, selves and culture. The first mode is violent, transparent in its self-interest and greed. The second mode is that of the rationalists, modernists and the liberals who claim to have the responsibility of civilizing the uncivilized world. *The Intimate Enemy: Loss and Recovery of self Under Colonization*, New Delhi: O.U.P., 1980: xl.
4. R.M. Varma says "If *Swami and Friends* is a story of childhood, *The Bachelor of Arts* is a story of adolescence and maturity, the latter being only an extension of the former. The scene of action shifts from Albert Mission School to Albert Mission College, the Cambridge of Malgudi, where the hero, Chandran is preparing for his B.A. Final Examination" (1993: 19). P.S. Sundaram says "In an upper and middle class Indian family, college follows school both logically and chronologically: and *The Bachelor of Arts* seems almost inevitable continuation of the school days of *Swami and Friends*" (1988: 25).
5. R.M. Varma says "Love in marriage or marital harmony, the theme of *The English Teacher*, is taken directly from Narayan's life. As a matter of fact, *Swami and Friends*, *The Bachelor of Arts*, and *The English Teacher* form an autobiographical trilogy; for they largely describe the three consecutive phases of Narayan's own life. Swami, the school boy in the first novel, is Chandran in the second; and Chandran, the college student in the second is Krishnan, the English Teacher, in the third. But all the three names are only fictional substitutes for Narayan himself' (1993: 29). P.S. Sundaram says "There is more of Narayan's own life in the second novel than in any other except the fourth, *The English Teacher*. Chandran's

experience in Albert College seem obviously based on Narayan's in Maharaja's College, Mysore" (1988: 26).

6. Walsh aptly remarks, "*The English Teacher* dramatizes Narayan's personal life at a most devastating point. This is a fact which offers even more evidence for the maturity of detachment and control shown in the novel. No doubt the act of writing itself proved a potent instrument of personal therapy, an activity which helped to control the chaos of life by submitting it to the discipline of art. Writing itself becomes a part of life and an influence propelling the author towards a more complex and balanced reality." (1992: 56).
7. There is no scarcity of books on the existence of souls and the possibility of communion between living persons and those who are dead. For example, *Death, Its Causes and Phenomena*, by Carrington and Meader, *The Unknown* by C. Hamerian, *Life Beyond Death* by Swami Avedananda.
8. Comparing Narayan to Katherine Mansfield, Walsh says, "She (Katherine Mansfield) is a poet of a family with young children, and the material of which her poetry is made, is New Zealand life. The personal past, the known place, the home, the physical context and chores of the household, family relationships, and in particular the diction and harmony of young and old, these are the points through which the line of her art goes. And much the same might be said of Narayan. Like Katherine Mansfield, Narayan uses three generations to give solidity to the family presence" (1992: 51). According to Uma Parameswaran, "Seen from the autobiographical side, Susila's contraction of typhoid virus in a dirty latrine is extremely pathetic; but viewed from the artistic point of view as a device whereby the heroine feels the touch of Death on her lips, I think it fails." *A Study of Representative Indo-English Novelists*, New Delhi: Vikas, 1976: 54. P.S. Sundaram, on the other hand, observes, "Whether Narayan is actually putting down his personal experiences under a thin disguise, or all this is mere invention there is an artistic coherence in all that is written and a sense of actuality, which is all that should matter from the point of view of the novel." *R.K. Narayan*, New Delhi: Arnold-Heinemann India, 1972: 55.
9. P.S. Sundaram also observes, "Krishna has made his peace with life, is entirely at ease with death, and is duly grateful to them both.

We may not be capable of such adjustment. But should that make us doubt the veracity of the story, or refuse to give it as a story the tribute we gladly pay to *Gulliver's Travels* or *Robinson Crusoe*?." *R.K. Narayan As a Novelist*, 1988: 47.

10. P.S. Sundaram: *R.K. Narayan As a Novelist*, 1988: 38.
11. Shiv M. Pandya, *Studies in Modern Fiction*, New Delhi: Vikas, 1983: 182-83.
12. Narayan's American friend Metro finds *Waiting for the Mahatma* "weak in motivation." *The Writerly Life*, 2001:189-90. Narasimhaiah feels that Narayan has made a muddle of Gandhian principle in the novel. He is disappointed with the novel because it does not enlarge our awareness of Gandhi or his era one bit (*The Swan and the Eagle: Essays on Indian English Literature*, Simla: Indian Institute, 1968). Agreeing with Narasimhaiah, A.N. Kaul says that it happens to be the weakest of Narayan's novels, neither a successful political novel (if it meant to be that) nor good comedy, and that Raja Rao's *Kanthapura* and Mulk Raj Anand's *Untouchable* are comparably superior 'Gandhi novels' when compared to *Waiting for the Mahatma*. 'R.K. Narayan and the East-West Theme,' *Considerations*, ed. Meenakshi Mukherjee. New Delhi: Allied, 1977: 47.
13. Y.P. Morris, ed., *The Bakhtin Reader*, London: Edward Arnold, 1994: 89.
14. Narayan was also aware of the demands of the foreigners from the novel that portrays Gandhi. His American friend Metro complained that he did not learn anything about Mahatma Gandhi and that the "narrative lacks punch." *The Writerly Life*, 2001: 190. Another noted critic K. Radha cites Uma Parameswaran views that the portrait of Gandhi in *Waiting for the Mahatma* is weak and uninspiring and is lacking in "characterization and language." Narayan, Parameswaran says, is "uninteresting when moulding good men, and positively out of his depth with supermen"; thus the novel fails because "Mahatma Gandhi was a superman. Sriram, the hero, is a good man" (66). Sriram is moronic, she adds, and Gandhi is in the same mould as a moron. Narayan takes certain familiar characteristics and incidents associated with Gandhi and he sticks them in haphazardly at the first opening he gets, adds Parameswaran,

who also gives examples of Gandhi's speeches that are not well planned by the novelist. Narayan "merely drops Gandhi's statements like bricks." Cited from Parameswaran's *A Study of Representative Indo-Anglian Novelists*, 65-67. K. Radha places Chaman Nahal's *The Crown and the Loincloth* above Narayan's *Waiting for the Mahatma* while comparing the two Gandhi novels. She says, "Gandhi, in Narayan's novel, does not impress the reader in spite of his direct appearances." According to her, "Nahal's portrait of Gandhi is more realistic and life-like than Narayan's: there is no idealization or emulsification of Gandhi." She concludes by saying, "The Mahatma, whom Churchill described as a half-naked fakir, appears to have more flesh and blood in *The Crown and the Loincloth* than in *Waiting for the Mahatma."* 'Mahatma Gandhi in R.K. Narayan and Chaman Nahal,' *R.K. Narayan Critical Perspectives*, ed. A.L. McLeod, New Delhi: Sterling, 1994: 112.

15. Shiv M. Pandya, *Studies in Modern Fiction*, New Delhi: Vikas Publishing House, 1983: 194.
16. Doughlas Allen on Mahatma Gandhi in an interview, *The Hindu, Sunday Magazine*, Jan 29, 2006: 2.

Revisiting Narayan's Later Novels

This chapter is a continuation of the third in the sense that eight other novels stretching between 1958 and 1992 are analyzed in it to throw more light on the essentials of the realistic art of R.K. Narayan. These novels are *The Guide, The Man-Eater of Malgudi, The Vendor of Sweets, The Painter of Signs, A Tiger for Malgudi, Talkative Man, The World of Nagaraj* and *Grandmother's Tale*. These novels portray the everyday activities, the mundane realities in the life of modern men in a social set-up that is undergoing fast and visible changes mostly by coming in contact with the Western culture. All the important aspects that have galvanized his creative art in the previous novels—his keen observation of life and manners, his deep insight into human mind, his attention to the minute details while portraying a particular aspect of life, his gentle irony and fusion of humour and pathos, his sympathy for and understanding of human conditions in a society driven by different forces, and finally his detached and dispassionate outlook,—all find their way into these novels too. However the only difference between these and the previous ones is that he has mellowed with time and his creative power is found at its best in these novels.

Like his contemporary Indian novelists in English, Narayan addresses a heterogeneous audience by choosing themes and situations which have more or less the same importance all over the country and that evokes a universal appeal. That is why the regional variations in social structure, values and customs or in human problems do not generally appear in his work. But the themes of social change like the disintegration of the old hierarchical and agrarian society, the breakdown of large joint family, the years of struggle and sacrifice in the colonial period shaping and colouring Indian experience, the encounter between the East and the West with its impact not only on people but also at the level of ideas and outlook, man-woman relationship, and above all, the unchangeable values of small Indian towns or villages are introduced in his novels. Romantic love, supremacy of social hierarchy and emergence of the individual, the place of faith in the socio-cultural life of India, adherence to rituals, the cult of Guru, renunciation as an ideal are also the themes that Narayan dwells upon in them. In the rendering of these themes he exhibits a charm, an intimacy unmistakably discernible. He is full of warmth and shows an unprejudiced understanding of existence. His social awareness and vivid imagination are enough to capture readers' attention. His novels never provide discourses on sizzling social issues. For example, in *The Dark Room* or in *The Painter of Signs* he reflects on the problems of women at different phases of social development but does not allow the social issues like feminism overshadow the stories in these novels. He only speaks of an experience that is immediate in his surroundings and stirs in his readers a deep response, without, however, losing its timeless value. In the novels written towards the very end of his career, he just appears wiser, brighter and more sophisticated, drawing themes from a still broader spectrum of life.

The Guide

The Guide which won the Sahitya Academy Award in 1960 received enormous attention and great enthusiastic response from critics. The novel gave Narayan a wider recognition as a matured creative artist. William Walsh attributes its success to a 'sensibility preserved from ambivalence, or fracture,' 'an unusual unity in the point of view' and 'a social tradition in which the comic and the sad are not marked off one from the other' (1992: 114). But the most distinguishing feature of the novel is its unique structural conception—the zigzag technique used to tell the story of Raju, the protagonist. Narayan uses in this novel both first-person and third-person narratives, a braided time-scheme and an open-ended conclusion. At the beginning, Raju is seen from the perspective of the omniscient narrator. He has just got out of jail and has ended up in an abandoned place where he finds Velan, a simple, innocent man from the neighbouring village, Mangala, situated on the outskirts of Malgudi. The narrator narrates Raju's experiences with Velan and other villagers who first take him for a saint and then for a spiritual guide to lead the village out of a drought by undertaking a fast. In between the narration comes Raju's own (first person) account of his passage from the world of innocence to the world of experience. He relates to Velan his progress from a wide-eyed child to the owner of a railway stall to the tourist guide to the lover and impresario of the classical dancer Rosie to a jailbird. Raju reveals his shady past to Velan under compulsion—to demystify the latter about his spiritual powers and to escape the task thrust upon him. But Velan is unmoved by this revelation and continues to see him as a Guru and thus, compels Raju, in a way, to go ahead with the fast. At the end of twelve days' fast, Raju is found collapsing by the river, as he feebly murmurs to Velan, "it's raining in the hills. I can feel it coming up under my feet, up my legs" (221). Nobody knows if rain has actually set in or Raju is in delusion. But as K. Venkatachari appropriately says, "Whether or not it is Raju's self-delusion that rains have set in is not so important a consideration as his coming to terms with an ethos that makes it possible for one to believe that fasting could intimidate even the Rain God."[1]

Narayan writes in his memoir the real circumstances from which he derived the plot of this novel. He speaks of the severe drought during which all the sources of water including the big reservoir of Kishanganj Bazaar in Mysore became dry and both the people and the authorities felt helpless. The destructive impact of the drought began to be felt on every sphere.

> As a desperate measure, the municipal council organized a prayer for rains. A group of Brahmins stood knee-deep in water (procured at great cost) on the dry bed of Kaveri, fasted, prayed and chanted certain mantras continuously for eleven days. On the twelfth day it rained and brought relief to the countryside. This was really the starting point of *The Guide. (My Days* 2006: 166-67)

The novel begins with the circumstances that lead Raju to undergo enforced sainthood. It shows Narayan's preoccupation with the middle class—a class in which religious ethos and practices play an important role in shaping the minds. In fact, conformity to religious ideas and values, beliefs and superstitions is universal. But India with its deep and complex religious background and age-old customs and traditions more rigidly conform to them. Hence, Malgudi, the microcosm India, witnesses similar adherence to tradition, religion, and superstition. The people in Malgudi and in nearby Mangala are illiterate and poor. They are, at the same time, indolent, listless and unenterprising. They believe in chance, in destiny or in the efficacy of prayer to solve their problems, but not in their own abilities. They would rather suffer perpetual misery than to think of a practical solution of a problem. The incident behind the story of *The Guide* brings to the fore this attitude which lies uppermost in the lives of the Indian people. It is irrelevant to trace in the novel Narayan's faith in rituals as a way out of mundane problems. The novel only exposes Indian people's penchant for being guided by this faith.

The novel is set in the solidly constructed environment of Malgudi which offers Narayan a canvas to draw a veiled social, cultural and political history of India. Raju's childhood is spent watching haunts of idyllic Malgudi,—the shade of a tamarind tree across the road, an ancient, spreading tree, dense with leaves, amidst which monkeys and birds live, breed and chatter incessantly, feeding on the tender leaves and fruits. Pigs and piglets come from somewhere and their nose about the ground thick with fallen leaves (12). Through Raju's boyhood experiences

> we get, too, a vivid picture of the bullock-cart with its wooden wheels grating and grinding the dust off the road; and the bells jingling round the necks of the bullocks; the smell of the straw; men, vehicles, hogs and boys: a whole panorama of life enchanting to a boy.[2]

In the portrayal of Raju's childhood and boyhood experiences with his parents Narayan reveals the remarkable tenderness and warmth that prevails in the lower-middle class domestic life in India. Raju and his mother sit side by side on the floor to have their dinner together. His mother keeps the rice-pot within reach, and serves him and her simultaneously and they finish their dinner, by the sooty tin lamp stuck on a nail on the wall. She, then, unrolls a mat for him in the front room, and he lies to sleep. Sitting by his side, his mother waits for his father's return. Her presence gives Raju a feeling of inexplicable coziness. To take advantage of her proximity, he complains of something bothering his hair and immediately she runs her fingers through his hair and scratches the nape of his neck. As she starts telling a story, he goes to sleep.

With minute visual images Narayan raises a real and concrete sketch of Raju's intimate relationship with his father. There is also a fine portrait of his father's social life and the atmosphere in which he grows up to be a Railway Guide. They live in a small house opposite the Malgudi Station—a house built by his father with his own hands long before trains are thought of. It is a mud house roofed with coconut thatch. Prudent and economical in his approach in all matters, he chooses the spot that is cheap for being outside the town. He has a shop built of real planks and gunny sack where he sits all day to sell peppermint, tobacco, betel-leaf, parched gram (measured out of tiny bamboo cylinders), fruits yielded from the papaya trees he plants around and cut in slices with dexterity and also whatever else the wayfarers on the Trunk Road demand. Sometimes little Raju takes his place though he does not understand anything of his business rules. At home, his father milks the buffalo and every morning he is in-charge of teaching Raju his alphabets and numbers. Sometimes he takes Raju to market in some passing bullock cart as he goes there to buy things for his shop. His father keeps his shop open till midnight keeping his mother waiting at home, worried about his food and sleep. The shop, the centre of his livelihood, is also the centre of his social life. A crowd of peasants and drivers of bullock wagons and the other customers of the village always gather in front of his shop to buy things or to chat with him. The topic of their discussions are varied—prices of grain, rainfall, harvest, and the state of irrigation channels, old litigations with Magistrates, affidavits, witnesses in the case and appeals, and such others being repeatedly referred to. Their roaring laughter—possibly caused by the memory of some absurd legality or loophole, reveal their capacity to enjoy life against all sorts of odds. Narayan also presents, as says C.D. Narasimhaiah, "A true homogeneous community where corporate living is possible around the village peepal tree: the spacious brick platform round it; the stone figures anointed with oil and worshipped by women; and on the other side of this spacious platform the village elders sitting and conferring on local problems; children chasing each other and dogs slumbering."[3]

The picture, artistically rendered in the novel, displays the author's capacity to seize and store some minute but significant moments from actual experiences of a common man's life[4].

Raju's account of the whole process of his learning renders an authentic and familiar picture of the traditional Indian method of teaching. The familiarity strikes a chord with most of the people of the last generations who had been part of it. Raju undergoes unwillingly the rigours of compulsory education, first right under the care of a zealous father 'flourishing a twig menacingly' as he teaches him the Tamil alphabets and numbers, and as Raju's mind is distracted by birds 'chirping and flying in the cool air.' "The modern notions of child psychology were unknown then; the stick was an educator's indispensable equipment,' says Raju. In contrast to the modern concept of education without corporal punishment, the philosophy that the unbeaten brat will remain unlearned had been the belief (11). This traditional Indian way of learning is rendered with a touch of the comic and irony, as when he describes how the boy has to go over the contours of the letters endlessly with a slate pencil until they become 'bloated and distorted beyond recognition.' (11)

But more delightful is the portrayal of the Pyol school—the typical village school held on the broad verandah of the village headman's house where all classes are held at the same time. The schoolmaster addresses his pupils as donkey and traces their genealogy 'on either side with thoroughness.' The unruly, indiscipline young pupils get on his nerves. Sometime the school master feels bored and enters his house for a nap or a dozen domestic calls, leaving the urchins on the verandah to roll on each other, fight and scratch, bleat and yell. The pupils also invade the master's secrecy and peep in to find him sitting before the oven, baking something and inviting from him the fierce reaction for their unpardonable behaviour. But his anger is short-lived as he depends on the patronage of his pupils and their parents to be supplied with things he requires. When he wants something he adopts 'a kindly, canvassing tone.' The pupils feel honoured to serve him and pester their parents to give what he wants. Their parents are ready to oblige too, as a mark of their gratefulness for keeping the mischief mongers in charge for the major part of the day. And such is the relationship that grows between the teacher and the student that the former escorts the latter to his new school after his lessons with him are over. The method of teaching in the Pyol-school is typical of the time. The reluctant Raju walks alone to the school in a halting and slow pace—as if walking endlessly to reach his school—talking to himself on the way, pausing to observe the passers-by or a country cart limbering along or a grasshopper going under a culvert. But turning into the market street he could hear his classmates shouting their lessons in unison. It is a traditional method of teaching, different from that of the fashionable Albert Mission School situated close by.

The existence of the Convent School side by side the Pyol School reveals a clear picture of the Indian education system that has hardly changed in the twenty-first century. The two quite different types of School also expose the economic and cultural differences prevailing in the Indian society. Raju's father has set notions against the Convent School; he thinks that such a school intends to convert the Hindu boys to Christians and is insulting in its attitude towards Hindu Gods. He believes that the traditional school is 'best under the sun,' and the ancient master is the best as students passing through his hands have become very successful in life. Young Raju, however, knows the reality: "It was purely his imagination or the invention of the old man who taught me. No one could dream that this was in any sense a school, let alone an outstanding school" (23). In spite of all the "apparent violence and purposelessness," the students in pyol school do well under the ancient master and become good enough to join the Board High school to read heavier books.

Narayan evokes the real atmosphere not as a social commentator but as an artist creating a real backdrop in which characters of flesh and blood are presented. In the process he mentions the construction of railway tracks and the station in Malgudi—one such real event that introduces change in the Indian society, and particularly in the urban areas. Raju's father gets the privilege of running a shop at the railway station. Unlike the 'Hut shop,' this one is spacious, paved with cement and fitted with shelves. It is hard to fill the shelves in spite of all the bunches of bananas, the troughs of fried stuff, the bread, buns and cigarettes. The two shops stand in contrast to each other emphasizing the change in time—the physical changes as well as the change in the mindset of the younger generation. A school drop-out, Raju gradually takes charge of the railway shop. He is thrilled by the modernity and bustle he notices in the newly acquired business of his father. The old customers are left in peace with his father. Soon enough a certain bridge is found ready near Malgudi facilitating regular services on the rail. After his father's death Raju equips his shop according to the changing demands of the day. His father has not used wrapping paper. But Raju adopts the new policy of using wrapping papers. In his search for them far and wide, he gathers a big dump of, "old books, stolen books and all kinds of printed stuff" (43). The school and college going students, even the station master himself, enjoy the privilege of drawing reading materials from the stack and reading while waiting for the trains to come. And while sorting them, Raju also starts reading things that interests him, bores him, and baffles him. He says,

> I read stuff that picked up a noble thought, a philosophy that appealed, I gazed at pictures of old temples and ruins and new buildings and battleships and soldiers and pretty girls around whom my thoughts lingered. I learnt much from scrap. (44)

Interestingly, it is this learning he widely makes use of cleverly with surprising acumen as he plays different roles in his passage from a railway guide to a spiritual guide.

With an all-round growth brought about by the railways, Malgudi suddenly comes to be recognized far and wide as a place of tourist interest drawing attention to its rivers, hills and forests. Tourism as an industry gets a strong foothold. Anand Bhawan Hotel, Malgudi Photo Bureau and the like come to existence opening opportunity for ancillary business. Narayan's keen observation of the all-round changes in the post-colonial Indian society that struggles through the shackles of agrarian society to reach the world of industrialization and material comfort, offers a realistic picture of the time. The old ways of living give way to the new. Family, love and marriage start acquiring new meanings. Money, not values, is considered to be the corner-stone of life. Next to money is valued fame and power.

Raju adapts to the changes well, and using his business instincts and tricks grows from an amateur guide to a professional and full-time railway guide. To assist him he has Gaffur, always ready with a taxi, to take the tourists to their destinations. They are paid for their services, both in cash and kind. Raju motivates the tourists to visit again or to visit with their families. As a guide he reads their minds, their moods, and reaches to a conclusion about their habits, tastes and disposition and then uses it to his advantage to serve and succeed as a guide. He says,

> If he was of the academic type I was careful to avoid all mention of facts and figures and to confine myself to general descriptions, letting the man himself do the talking. You may be sure he enjoyed the opportunity. On the other hand, if an innocent man happened to be at hand, I let myself go freely. . . . But it was years before I could arrive at that stage of confidence and nonchalance. (51-52)

Practice makes him perfect. He then becomes the most sought after guide of Malgudi. His life takes dramatic turns when he meets Rosie and Marco, tourists from Madras. "My troubles would not have started (Raju said at a later stage in the course of narrating his life story to this man who was called Velan) but for Rosie" (8-9). Rosie is married to Marco whose interests are directly antagonistic to hers. She is an aspiring classical dancer and Marco is a devoted student of ancient art and is interested in the figures of dancers in the temple frieze far more than his wife, the actual dancer. On the other hand, Raju is fascinated by the grace and rhythm of the movement of her body. He falls in love with her at first sight and takes advantage of all opportunities that come his way to foster his relationship with her. Forsaken by her husband for her illicit relationship with Raju, Rosie falls back on Raju. In the next phase of his life Raju witnesses fluctuating fortunes at home and in professional life. The hard realities come to replace the early pleasures of romance. He forfeits his claim of the railway-shop due to neglect and mismanagement. He ceases to be a railway-guide. His expenses soar, debt accumulates frighteningly with the Sait, a wholesale merchant, and in a reckless mood of levity he antagonizes him, and as a consequence, faces court action. Both his friend and mother desert him.

The next change that happens is Raju's role as the impresario to Rosie, who after allowing her name to be changed as Nalini, becomes a dancing sensation. He takes great pains to build her career as a dancer. With her natural talents her career soars high. Moving among the elite and the sophisticated members of the society, Raju feels 'vastly superior to everyone.' Money begins to come in plenty. Rosie's name becomes public property. But Raju develops a jealous monopolistic attitude, displaying a typical male attitude 'I had a monopoly of her and nobody had anything to do with her. . . . She was my property. This idea was beginning to take root in my mind" (168). Raju is afraid that with her ambition fulfilled, she may now want to be back with her husband. That makes him hide the copy of Marco's gorgeous book on 'The Cultural History of South India" and later forge Rosie's signature to acquire the jewel box. Raju's relationship with Rosie comes to an end, and Raju is sent to prison for two years on charges of forgery. Though Raju has blundered all along, he finds prison life to his liking and makes the most of it. This sudden change of fate does not affect him adversely. He rather uses his inherent qualities—his old habit of affording guidance and solving problems—to the advantage of the prisoners and the staff. Raju's prison life offers Narayan an opportunity to take his readers to the interior of an Indian prison.

Released from the prison, Raju reaches the temple on the bank of Sarayu. Velan, mistaking him for a sage, seeks his advice to solve his personal problem. His nature to 'get involved in other people's interests and activities' asserts itself again. The edifying experiences of his turbulent life have not completely curbed his instinct to star-gaze and make-belief. At first he plays the role of a sage as he finds it to be an easy and safe way of earning food for him. But then the illusion grows, his inanities and platitudes are considered to be pearls of wisdom—not only by the villagers but by him too. He is surprised at 'the amount of wisdom welling from the depth of his being' (41). The role that frightens him first turns out to be fascinating due to his customary nonchalance and tact.

The turning point comes when the drought affects the village. Raju is forced to undertake the fast in the mistaken belief of the villagers that this is what he wants to induce rain and save the village from the drought. Raju is thus trapped in the delusion he creates. In a desperate bid to free himself from the trap he tells Velan the whole truth of his life. Velan is unmoved. Raju "now saw the enormity of his own creation. "He had created a giant with his puny self, a throne of authority with that slab of stone" (96). Now he has to stand up to their expectation, to make himself fit for the throne. Feeling enraged at the persistent thought of food during the fast, he takes a sort of 'vindictive resolution' to chase away all thoughts of food. The resolution gives him a peculiar strength to go on successfully with the fast. There is wisdom in acceptance of the inevitable. And when faith shakes wisdom holds out.

There are several factors responsible for Raju's predicament. He is no doubt a victim of circumstances. But more important is Raju's own nature—his impulse to get involved in the affairs of others, to accept the role thrust upon him and to play that role with an eagerness to reach perfection. Raju's character justifies his action and all that happens in his life. Narayan creates his characters with great fidelity and penetration and brings them to life using minute details of their social milieu and psychological state. Narayan's concern, however, is not mere creation of characters. They enliven the whole atmosphere in which they are placed and give out all the time a sense of vividness and authenticity. Through them he explores the state of socio-economic affairs of the country at that time.

Rosie's account of her birth brings to light socio-religious customs prevalent in India at the time. She is born to the family traditionally dedicated to the temples as dancers who are treated by the society as the 'despised caste of dancers,' as public women, "we are not considered respectable; we are not considered civilized" (75), she says. In order to remove the stigma and to earn respectability for her, her mother plans different things for her—good education and marriage to a respectable family. In the process, Rosie takes her Master's Degree in Economics and marries Marco, a man well beyond her caste and clan, a man of high social standing. He is wealthy and an intellectual. As a precondition, she sacrifices her career as a dancer. Narayan's concern for the plight of the traditional temple dancers (Devadasis) and his suggestion of getting them educated and then arranging civil marriage for them are revealed through the portrayal of Rosie's affairs. But he is also aware of the limits of his suggestion. He knows that the conservative Indian society does not allow the housewives to practice classical dance in public, and hence the dancers are denied the opportunity to excel in their art and enjoy marital status at the same time. Narayan could also see some signs of change in the society. Marco takes recourse to matrimonial advertisement to find a suitable bride, and Rosie reaches him through it. They do not consult horoscopes or invite their elders' intervention. The prospective groom meets the prospective bride to examine her, her certificate and the like, and marriage is settled. This is followed by a marriage in a court, before a registrar. Their marriage acquires legal sanction making social sanction redundant.

Rosie, like Bharati and Daisy, is a new and modern woman. But, unlike them, she is not at peace in her role as the new woman. She is tossed between her two worlds—the conventional world to which she actually belongs and the world acquired through her ambitions for independence and achievements. On the one hand, she acknowledges her indebtedness to Raju and on the other asks him to leave her alone to her own fate. On the one hand, she deserts her husband to live forever with her art; on the other, she thinks of going back to him, sacrificing everything and begging forgiveness. She is happy to flourish as a dancer, but is guilt-conscious, conscience-stricken—"Is this right what I am doing?" (106). Though she blames Raju for bringing disgrace to her life by committing forgery, she does everything possible on her part to free him on bail and later to fight his case till conviction. It is for her relationship with Raju that his mother and friend—the two most important persons of his life—desert him forever. Even at that time Rosie sticks to her place in the house, though sad, yet unperturbed in the face of all abuses and reprimands. She mutely watches Raju's mother leaving home along with his uncle as a mark of protest. Ironically, Rosie herself deserts Raju leaving him to his fate at a later period of time. She still flourishes and soars to greater height in her art and career, alone and independent. She has her own 'sustaining vitality' that lets her go and Raju's concerns for her—his jealousy or over-possessiveness or self-congratulating thoughts for having made her what she is—appear ill-founded.

A new facet of family relationship unfolds the description of the bond between Raju's mother and his maternal uncle—the two elderly persons are drawn with amazing accuracy and deep affection. In the short space given to them in the novel, they come out life-size, alive and active. The characters of Raju's mother and Rosie set in contrast the opposite trends operating in the society. The former advises the latter to go to her husband and fall at his feet; she also tells her how to bring one's husband—unreasonable, savage or moody—round by doggedness, perseverance and patience. She wonders at knowing that Rosie has come all along the way alone, whereas in her time she used to be accompanied by her husband whenever or wherever she was to go. Other peripheral characters like Gaffur, Raju's well-meaning friend, the Saint with his ledger clutched under his arm and his "multi-coloured turban" are portrayed with fidelity and sympathy. Velan, the simple, credulous man from the village, is drawn with equal conviction. He is "very much the stuff that disciples are made of," who takes Raju's confession simply as a piece of singular condescension on Raju's part," "a mere proof of Raju's goodness and humility" (Walsh 1992:129). Velan's attitude of submissive respect towards Raju is prompted in part by the temple itself and in part by his own traditional expectation, and in part by Raju's bearing and appearance. And for a man of Raju's character, it is enough to tempt him to assume a manner appropriate to the context—the guise of a holy man. Raju smoothly, though to some extent helplessly, glides into the part, sometimes feeling guilty at his own duplicity and at others debunking himself a little. When Velan's sense of Raju's holiness is shared by other villagers it leads to mounting pressure on Raju.

Narayan's rendering of the Indian legal system is found to be refreshingly real and delightfully satiric. Raju describes the star-value of his lawyer. He is one who saves many a neck from the noose, absolves many a public swindler in the public eye and in the eye of the law. He presents Raju's case as a comedy of three acts—in the first Marco is the villain trying to drive his wife mad, in the second his wife being rescued from privation and death by a humble humanitarian called Raju, who sacrifices his time and profession for the protection of the lady and for enabling her to rise so high in the world of arts and making her the prestige of the nation and the cultural tradition, and in the third, the villain returns with the sinister purpose of blowing up her rising career through a fabricated case of forgery. The last part is presented with all the elements of suspense, thrill, art of scheming etc. being incorporated into it. But the prosecution case, though unspectacular, is strong. Extracting the truth from Mani,

Raju's guilt is proved. When Raju is sentenced with imprisonment of two years the lawyer claims to have reduced the punishment of five years to two, by his fluency and competency. The picture speaks volumes about the loopholes in the legal system of post-independent India, and about the vain, pompous and lying lawyers.

The picture describing the Indian attitude of turning every situation to an occasion of religious festivities or of business opportunities glares on the face of reality. As Raju goes through the ordeal of fasting, the hum of humanity increases around him. The news spreads far and wide through a particular journalist passing there by chance. People from all corners rush to Malgudi and for them special trains are scheduled for Malgudi. Taxis, buses carry people to Mangala. There is an unimaginable crowd squeezed in the small village to view the whole incident. Shops spring up overnight—makeshift shops selling coloured soda bottles, bunches of bananas and coconut toffees. The Tea Propaganda Board opens a big tea-stall with posting pasted on the temple wall for advertisement. The tea-bar installed to serve free tea in porcelain cups sees the public swarming around it like flies, and the flies swarm on all the cups and sugar bowls. The ridiculous way in which the Health Department in India functions does not escape Narayan's eyes. It arrives to take precaution fearing an outbreak of some epidemic in the crowded place without water and vaccinate against 'cholera, malaria and what not.' Film shows—all about mosquitoes, malaria, plague, tuberculosis, dengue, river-valleys, projects and ministers delivering speeches—are shown in public interest. A few young stars just for fun bare their biceps with a big crowd watching them. An area is cleaned up to make people sit and watch a film-show. Popular film songs are played on a gramophone to attract an audience. Even a man opens a gambling booth with a dart-board on a pole and erects a merry-go-round and there are men selling balloons, reed-whistles and sweets. A portion of the crowd is busy worshipping the saint, with Velan, the master of the ceremonies, being in full charge of him. The school master is in charge of the telegrams and letters pouring in from all over the country wishing the Swami success. A few, sitting near the Swami, sing devotional songs to the accompaniment of a harmonium and *tabla*.

A change in the scene comes with the arrival of an American with an interpreter from Madras whose business is production of films and TV shows. He sets the stage before shooting the film on Swami. All attention is now drawn towards this man. He asks all sorts of silly questions answering which the Swami feels fatigued. There are the doctors who are reluctant to speak to the journalist about Swami's health on matters of principle. “Sorry, we are government servants—we cannot do it without permission. Our reports are released only from headquarters” (219), they say. Only when the Swami’s condition becomes grave towards the end of the twelve days’ fasting that the doctors and the government show great concern and decide to persuade him to end his fasting. The pictures make a mockery of such slow and cautious government policy. The whole scene depicts, as Walsh aptly says, two of Narayan’s deepest convictions about human life: one is the sense of individual alienation—the way the isolated individual faces the enormous, fundamentally indifferent crowd—and the other is the way human character is constituted by the expectations of others. The second one operates stronger than ever in this novel. “It is this double insight which the career of Raju embodies and justifies” (1992: 69). The suggestion at the end of the novel that rain may be on the way and Raju might be dying adds a genuine artistic stroke to a story based on reality[5].

The Man-Eater of Malgudi

Apparently, the plot of *The Man-Eater of Malgudi* depends on a simple movement from harmony to disharmony and back to harmony and this simple movement runs parallel with the myth of Bhasmasura. The myth of Bhasmasura is introduced by Sastri, the orthodox semi-scholar who describes Vasu, the taxidermist by profession, as the Rakshasa of the Indian myth. He believes that evil carries the seeds of its own destruction. Harmony or order in Malgudi means the regular and habitual pace of life. The protagonist Nataraj's uneventful life with his wife and son, the house he inherits from his father, the people who like and dislike him, his press on the Market Road, with a view to the fountain, the well-furnished parlour welcoming the people to come and rest, the poet and Sen as his constant companions, Sastri, the old man, who does all the works of his press, even the river where they all go at different times either to finish their daily chores or for other purposes—all belong to that familiar order. Anything that comes from outside and tries to bring about change is not welcomed or accepted by the Malgudians. Shiv K. Girla rightly describes them as "a happy set of lotus eating Malgudians' ' (1984: 162) into whose world Vasu, unscrupulous and power hungry by nature, intrudes. His diabolic plans to depopulate the Mempi forests of wild animals immediately project him as the demonic figure that disturbs the 'order' in Malgudi.

It is Vasu's intelligence along with his arrogance that sets him apart from others. He sets himself as a rival to nature and carries on his relentless fight against nature. He considers nature as man's worst enemy which requires to be conquered with the help of science and human intelligence. Moreover, he challenges every man who contradicts him. He shows an attitude of sheer intolerance and disregard for life, human or animal. He defies all institutions, traditions, emotions and values that man holds precious. In fact, Vasu represents the autocrats who have no faith in the values of life (Vasu even argues against the institutions of marriage), and who can, therefore, go to the extreme for satisfying his ego. Vasu's 'hubris' was at the root of his fall; not only the demons in myths but also the arrogant autocrats of real life have carried the seeds of their own destruction. That is why the autocrats fall sooner or later and may very well be replaced with other autocrats. Vasu's mysterious death is rendered as a bizarre and fantastic happening after Sastri describes how Vasu kills himself while slapping the mosquitoes sitting on his forehead. Sastri's reiterated references to the mythological stories of Bhasmasura, in order to explain his ultimate act of self-destruction, focus on the allegorical framework of the novel. The composite design of Narayan's art provides credibility to the bizarre story of killing: the strength of Vasu's iron-fist has been already proved in his breaking the iron cot and his intolerance at the buzzing mosquitoes has been insisted upon from the beginning.

In the myth, peace is restored and order brought back after the demon is ousted. Similarly, in *The Man Eater of Malgudi*, all the confusion and disorder should have ended and normalcy should have been back after Vasu's death. But a close study of the novel makes it clear that here Narayan has given a twist to the plot by showing that Vasu's death has brought about further disorder because crimes like murder are supposed to be profane in the world of Malgudi and Vasu is still supposed to have been murdered. Hence 'order' comes back to Malgudi only after Sastri explains that Vasu has not been murdered but killed by himself. Narayan makes conscious attempts to make the fantastic event of Vasu's death look convincing. He makes the setting of the novel realistic and not mythical. But his concern with the real life in *The Man-Eater of Malgudi* is ignored even by established critics. K.R.S. Iyengar, for example, describes the novel as "a modern version of one of Deva-Asura conflicts of very ancient times" (1983: 382). Meenakshi Mukherjee, though does not attribute any symbolic meaning to names like Vasu and Nataraj, observes: "It is evident, however, that the story of *The Man-Eater of Malgudi* follows the familiar pattern of a tale from the *Puranas* where a demon gets too powerful, threatens the heavens with his elemental forces of disorder, but finally goes up in air like a bubble, leaving the universe as calm as (ever) before. At the end of the novel, the blue curtain of the printer's room is peacefully drawn again, and Sastri disappears behind it to print the labels for K.J.'s Soft Drinks." (2001: 143-44)

Jayanta Kumar Biswal says almost in the same vein, "Neither Nataraj nor the other Malgudians have any role in Vasu's death except that they are participants in a religious festival. The irony embedded in Vasu's death once again, vindicates the sacred traditions. When humanity is threatened, the grace of God, which comes in mysterious ways, destroys the wicked and saves others." (1987: 106)

Biswal further argues that what saves the Malgudi community from Vasu is not an accident, but, as William Walsh suggests, 'the blessings of the Gods or just the stubbornness of life itself' (1992: 145). Biswal says, "The hypothesis of the blessings of the gods' cannot be easily rejected in an Indian context. With Vasu's death peace and order are once again restored to the society. Nataraj is roused from his complacency and this brief disorder if not to anyone else at least to Nataraj and Sastri alone, brings renewed faith in God's subtle ways of saving humanity." (1987: 106)

K. Chellappan says, "But this is part of Narayan's technique of bringing the myth down to the dusty earth. The universal war between god and evil is brought out in this story of two familiar human beings; and in this modern fable, too, the sublime evil is brought out as sheer absurdity." (McLeod 1994: 28)

Though Walsh finds that the characters in *The Man-Eater of Malgudi (*he refers to Nataraj) are solidly established in a social world (134) his ultimate interpretation is that *The Man-Eater of Malgudi* "can be taken as a dramatization of the theory of the necessary flaw, the mysterious balance tremblingly sustained in being by fallibility" (1992: 145). L. Narayan Murty finds "an impeccable affinity" with the ancient mythological episode of Bhasmasura. He compares Nataraj with Lord Shiva (Nataraj being another name of Shiva). Bhasmasura is given the boon of indestructibility by Lord Shiva who in turn tries to experiment the effect of it on Lord Shiva only. Similarly Nataraj gives shelter to Vasu and is harassed and tantalized by him only. Murty points to the irony of character and the irony of situation[6]. But he forgets to note that the affinity he draws is too superficial because Vasu's death is considered as a murder and so as a crime. And, in spite of all its ailments, the small town of Malgudi is not ready to accede to any kind of killing—man or animal, killing committed either by Vasu or by Nataraj. The myth blended with irony—an aspect which Murty has failed to notice—reveals realism as an important and inevitable facet of Narayan's novels. Narayan's world is a world of real beings, good and bad, but not of gods and demons. P.S. Sundaram talks about this—the coexistence of good and evil, simplicity and corruption. But still he interprets Narayan's world as a mythical world[7].

A thorough study of the novel shows that characters in Malgudi are ordinary men and women with their little joys and sorrows, ordinary aims and ambitions, simple ideas and beliefs, hopes and frustrations, virtues and vices, failures and achievements. It is this life, flowing through generations, that sets the order. Life in Malgudi is seen and shown through their eyes and from their points of view. Therefore, everything is found projected from different perspectives—sometimes from Nataraj's, sometimes from Sastri's, some other times from Vasu's. The writer's own authorial comment remains hidden and suppressed, though not absent. By treating both his people and plot with delicate irony he subtly communicates his stance on Indian life—rather his criticism of it. Without making a direct attack Narayan exposes poverty, exploitation, corruption and the deceitful ways of Indian life.

It is ironic to note that the Malgudian order we are talking of is not a perfect or unblemished order. Malgudi has its share of sordid and calculating men and women. There is corruption in Malgudi and so it suits Vasu who exploits the corrupt system and finally manages to escape through the loopholes of law. He tries to get a license to shoot animals in the Mempi Forest. Though he fails to get such a license, he manages to get a permit to kill birds and small animals. With that he kills heedlessly whatever he likes, and the law stands helpless to stop him. Even the judiciary falls prey to the loopholes in its system when Vasu makes the Court send a letter to Nataraj making false allegations against him.

Corruption in Malgudi is also hinted at through the comic portrayal of the characters of the bus conductor and the adjournment lawyer who survive or rather prosper well in the small town of Malgudi. The bus conductor makes money illegally by pocketing a lot of cash collected from passengers. He packs the bus with passengers more than is permitted by law, allows the driver to drive recklessly and "fills his pockets with the wayside fare, never issues tickets" (45). Even the circle inspector, for his own vested interest, shuts his eyes to everything and lets the unlawful go free. The lawyer makes money by adopting clever means and taking advantage of his clients' helplessness. The police contribute to the corrupt systems prevailing in Malgudi. It shows its inability to take actions against Vasu who is so relentlessly killing animals for his own selfish purpose and is planning so defiantly to kill the temple elephant. "We cannot take action unless there is concrete evidence or a consequence," says the D.S.P. on being informed (147). As elsewhere in India, the poor and ignorant people of Malgudi suffer as the clever ones take advantage and spread lawlessness.

Men in Malgudi are mostly idle, inactive, indecisive and god-fearing. Their religion is confined to rituals and blind faiths. They hardly do anything meaningful. The temple festival is non-utilitarian. Nataraj, Sastri and the poet do not stop the religious procession even when they know that Vasu is waiting for the procession to fulfil his evil intentions. Through the irrational attitude of Nataraj and his friends Narayan points at their lack of courage, their inaction and circumscribed outlook. Vasu criticizes and at the same time takes advantage of these shortcomings and carries the situation far beyond the control of the Malgudians. Therefore, Vasu's death order is restored—but it is an order with all its evil aspects intact in it. Sudesh Mishra rightly says, "After the nature of Vasu's death is conveyed to Nataraj by the glib Sastri, we revert to a pre-Vasuan and not a modified post-Vasuan, world of dharma. The Rakshasa was purely an aberration, neither adding to nor subtracting from the theatre of Malgudi." (McLeod 1994: 94)

Vasu is supposed to show things from another perspective[8]. In contrast to the Malgudians, Vasu is a rationalist. He believes in man's muscle power and intelligence rather than God's will and-might. He is ironic and sarcastic in his views of the people around him and their problems. He says, "More people are to die on the roads, if our nation is to develop any road sense at all!" (33) and

> Anyway, do you know why we have so many melas in our country? So that the population may be kept within manageable limits. Have you not observed it? At Kumbh Mela, thousands and thousands gather; less than the original number go back home with cholera or smallpox, or they just get trampled. How many temple chariots have run over the onlookers at every festival gathering? Have you ever paused to think why it's arranged thus?" (149)

Vasu is modern and scientific in his outlook as opposed to the sentimentality of Nataraj, but without humanity and compassion the working on his mind turns perverted and sinister.

Malgudi suffers from other maladies too. The exploitation of Devadasis in the name of God and religion, prostitution, poverty, and untouchability are present there. Narayan presents a world in which social stability and economic security are in a vulnerable state and therefore, may be attacked by adverse external forces at any time, and may face temporary, if not permanent, dislocation. Thus, Narayan's world is real and concrete, not noble and sublime. It allows the eccentric to exist. The ways of this world, though rendered in a ludicrous way, are realistic too. The use of myth helps him focus on the god-fearing and lethargic middle-class Indian people who sincerely believe that the evil is meant to be destroyed by itself, and that there is no individual responsibility assigned to anyone to do away with that evil.

The Vendor of Sweets

The Vendor of Sweets belongs to a period when Narayan's creative genius was at its peak. But the novel does not share the ambitious design of plot or the broad spectrum of interest of other novels of the period—especially of *The Financial Expert, The Guide* and *The Man-Eater of Malgudi*. In spite of the vivid and authentic portrayal of the world of Malgudi and its people, the novel is comparatively less rich and varied because it confines itself to the theme of family relationship especially to the relation between father and son. Of course, family is the immediate context in which Narayan's sensibility operates well, and his dozens of novels and short stories treat family relationships with remarkable ease and conviction. Even the relationship between father and son is touched upon in many of his novels such as *Swami and Friends*, *The Bachelor of Arts, The Financial Expert.* But in all these novels father-son relationship is of secondary concern, whereas in *The Vendor of Sweets* it is the chief concern and the novel treats the complexity of this relationship more comprehensively and with greater concentration and detail. This helps the novel surpass its narrow boundary.

The Vendor of Sweets portrays the relationship between a doting father and his estranged son—between Jagan and Mali. As Ved Mehta informs us, the novel has taken its origin in a lawsuit in actual life brought by a wasteful son against his indulgent father, a sweetmeat vendor, to get more money from him[9]. In Narayan's novel, the conflict between the two does not lead to a lawsuit but to the father's retreat to the forest leaving everything behind for his son. The introduction of the new and rare aspect of the Hindu ethos of renunciation becomes another redeeming factor of the story.

Jagan is the owner of a flourishing sweetmeat business. He has spent his childhood, his boyhood and his youth in a traditional lower middle-class Indian family. Through his reminiscences of the past, fifty years back, a close picture of it is graphically drawn. He remembers the time when his father's family was living in a hut in the backyard of the place he is living at present. His childhood had been happy and carefree. He had spent his time with his brother hunting for grasshoppers amidst weeds—a common childhood pastime of children mostly in rural India. In the blazing summer afternoons Jagan and his elder brother would be active, perusing the grasshopper resting in the paltry shade of the weed plant. Carrying a small-tin, his brother would cup his palm over the grasshopper and trap it to his tin as befitting an elder brother: "if it was a little one, it was passed on to Jagan; but on no account could Jagan be permitted to catch one himself. He could only stand behind his brother and wait for his luck, with his own tin in hand." (141)

Sometimes their sister would track them down there and threaten them to talk to their father about it and frighten them with the fear of punishment in hell. Jagan would be afraid but his brother, defiant, would threaten her back. Jagan's childhood reminiscences—his chasing the grasshopper in summer noons along with his brother—directly come from Narayan's memory of his childhood. Narayan's elder brother in real life taught him how to catch grasshoppers (*My Days* 2006: 35). Of course, there is no mention of the sister's interference, in the autobiography.

The charm of Indian joint family is felt in the description of the warm and close relationship Jagan and his brother shared with their father. Between them there had been a mutuality of interest. They helped their father build the house, laying the bricks with their own hands. They helped also by fetching water from a well across the road and storing it in old Kerosene tins and drums. They were with their father when the hut was being pulled down and the new house was being built. As long as Jagan's father was alive he used to be in charge of all matters of the family. When he asked Jagan and his wife to accompany him to Sanatan Krishna temple at Badri hill to treat their barrenness they simply obeyed. "When father said anything so specific there could be no discussion on the subject" (167). He felt tongue-tied to say anything in defence of his wife. There were things which they were not supposed to discuss with their father nor even with their mother. According to P.S. Sundaram, "In the kind of home which Narayan describes in his novels, fathers and sons, however deeply attached to each other, are seldom other than embarrassed in each other's presence. Conversation between them is monosyllabic; the father gives an order and the son obeys. Plans and ambitions are communicated through mother. Jagan's relationship with his own father was on these lines." (1988: 93)

This was the norm of a common Indian family of the time. The change that has ushered in with the passage of time is felt when Jagan's relationship with Mali becomes strained and complicated. An invisible barrier stands between them that grows bigger with every passing day. It comes into being the day Mali's mother dies of a malignant tumour. Deeply attached to his mother Mali is left puzzled and dismayed at her death. He ceases to speak to his father normally after this. The 'course, raw pain' Jagan feels that fateful day at the sight of Mali remains 'petrified in some vital centre of being' (37). He finds his reticent son inaccessible to him. However, with the extended family system fading from existence, Jagan is left alone to look after his son. Playing both father and mother to the young boy he develops a deep but absurdly embarrassed affection for him. In his excessive fondness and concern for his son, Jagan overdoes his paternal duties and his son is keen to avoid or rather escape his nagging nature. His son grows harsher and brusquer in his behaviour to his father as days pass by. Left to himself and to his business ethics, Jagan is strict and is in complete control of himself and of the situation. In matters relating to Mali he is uncertain, timid and apprehensive. He yields to the pressure of Mali's haughty manners and arbitrary decisions. He indulges in the thought that being a Gandhian he cannot use force. But in reality his diffidence prevents him from disciplining Mali. Hence the relationship he shares with his son exists on a plane completely different from that of his relationship with his father long time back.

Living through a period of transition Jagan becomes a juxtaposition of paradoxes. He claims to be a Gandhian by principle. So he does not allow adulteration in his shop. He uses pure cow ghee for making sweets even if it is costlier than buffalo ghee because Gandhi has said that the latter is not good for health. In his youth he had his head cracked trying to pull down the Union Jack from a Government building, had spent a few years in jail, promised Gandhi to spin everyday and for twenty years has been keeping the promise. He plies the Chakra religiously just as he worships Goddess Laxmi every morning. He wears a loose jibba over his dhoti, both materials spun with his own hand. He uses the leather that comes from naturally dead animals to make his footwear. As a follower of Gandhi he shudders at the idea of cow and buffalo being slaughtered for human use. He believes that money is the source of all evil. But despite all his Gandhian ideology, as a businessman, his chief objective is to make money. Following a common practice of businessmen in India he divides his earning of the day into two parts—one as 'free cash' not taxable and the other meant for everyone's inspection and so taxable. For it he maintains two accounts—one for himself and the other for tax collectors. What he calls 'free cash' is converted to 'crisp currency,' tied into a bundle, and put away in the loft at home. The duplicity of his character is revealed ironically. Though he claims to be a Gandhian he abhors charity work openly, and is reluctant to entertain beggars or poor people at his shop. His mind is filled with disgust at the sight of the vagrant, collecting dining leaves cast out of the homes of Kabir Lane, scouring them with his hand, and filling his belly with any vegetables and rice that might be left on them. He even thinks of changing the habit of using leaves and of introducing plates that could be washed and kept, and not thrown out after dinner for vagrants to pick.

Jagan's inability to follow the spirit of the teachings of the Bhagavad Gita is also explicit. He is an avid reader of Bhagavad Gita. He preaches its ideology with great earnestness. But in practising the ideology he shows any common man's lack of proper understanding of the ideas advocated in the scripture. Even his decision to renounce everything and retire does not reveal his attainment of the wisdom that the Gita professes—the wisdom of attaining complete non-attachment or equanimity. As he fails to decide whom to give the key to the backdoor of his house, he takes it along with him. More ironically, he takes the cheque book with him as religiously as he takes the Chakra. When Mali is put in the lock-up on charges of violation of prohibition laws he helps the cousin arrange for his release. He leaves the keys of the shop in the safe hands of his cousin with instructions to take care of it along with Shivaraman and others, until Mali is ready to take over. Moreover he instructs the cousin to come over to the retreat if there is anything urgent or to render an account.

Mali is the product of the modern times and therefore denounces all ideals and values that the previous generation holds precious. He completely disapproves of his father's stubbornness in following Gandhian ideals of simple life choosing not to mend the dilapidated bathroom, not to have a telephone connection, not to use a toothbrush, not to engage a cook and not to view oneself daily in a mirror. Yet at the same time the integrity of his own character is questionable. He leaves college and gives up study on no solid ground. He takes to novel-writing but fails in his ambitious endeavour. He goes to America to get lessons in creative writing. He proves his father's fear that America could "corrupt his body with wine, women and meat, and his soul with other things." In America Mali takes to eating beef and pork. Jagan is afraid of the public outrage his beef-eating might invite in case it comes to public knowledge, and therefore, tries rigorously to protect him from it.[10] Moreover his fatherly feelings are thrown again into a greater confusion when he is confronted by Mali's world that so cruelly dismisses his cherished notion of marriage and morals. The discovery that his son and his American Korean companion are not really married but live together makes him feel that his house unsullied for generations has become tainted, contaminated, has become a moral plague spot with this sin of Mali. His sister and orthodox elder brother have already distanced themselves from him for his liberal outlook. Now they would distance themselves further to be spared the indignity of his son's unsavoury activities. Jagan too cannot allow these to go on. He takes every possible step to insulate himself from the evil radiations of an unmarried couple living together. Still his confusion does not come to an end.

Jagan is troubled by Mali's absurd business plans of manufacturing machines for novel-writing. Mali has already arranged for American collaboration in both technical and financial matters and banks on his father to finance the project by investing about fifty one thousand dollars—almost about two and half lakhs in rupees. The prototype of his machine has knobs for characters' emotions, complexities, climax etc, which by being pressed would provide innumerable shades, kinds and combinations of story patterns. Here is a satire on the modern trend of writing books on public demand without having to wait for the inner urge essential for creation. However, Jagan is not ready to squander his money on the novel-writing machine, and Mali is contemptuous about the sweetmeat business.

Narayan, in fact, exposes the modern rebels as much as the conservative conformists through the characters of Mali and Jagan. They are divided by disparate priorities and values, by their preferred lifestyles, one's modern and the other's traditional. Mali as the modern rebel does not earn the readers' sympathy. He is insensitive, disrespectful, an ungrateful parasite, a vain and pompous man. He is the unethical and remorseless product of modern consumerism who helps himself to his father's money hoarded in the loft, without his permission. He even lacks modern man's rationality and practical approach to life. He is no less absurd than his father in handling his business or personal affairs. Jagan's life in the past set against the backdrop of Mali's relationship with Grace provides a contrast between the East and the West, the values cherished in an orthodox Hindu home and the lures of life of a modern Westernized young man. The tragicomic clash of the two generations ends with Jagan's decision to retire and to 'shake things off'—"unmistakably, completely, without leaving any loophole or a path back" (175).

The Vendor of Sweets may not be reckoned among the best of Narayan's creations but it is filled with his ironic observations of life and of the eccentricities of his characters and his subtle sense of humour that enrich his realistic human comedy.

The Painter of Signs

The Painter of Signs, written after a silence almost ten years since the publication of *The Vendor of Sweets*, makes a welcome appearance. A touch of specific period sense is imparted in this novel in a clever manner, when Raman, the hero, mentions the time noticing around him the visible changes that have taken place in Malgudi—"Malgudi was changing in 1972. It was the base for a hydro-electric project somewhere on the Mempi Hills, and jeeps and lorries passed through the Market Road all day. The city had a new superintendent of police who was trying out new ideas. Policemen were posted every few yards" (12). From the days of *Swami and Friends* to 1972, it has been a long journey for Malgudi. From the colonial to the post-colonial days and again to the seventies, Malgudi, like any Indian town of the post-independence days, has witnessed an all-round change—change on physical as well as cultural, economic, political, social and psychological planes. The new generation of Malgudi finds itself in a new milieu with new ideas, new ideals, new problems and newer solutions. But amidst all the manifestations of newness, the old, eternal spirit of Malgudi creeps into life. The old and the new exist in an incongruous relationship. The old is questioned as much as the new—the former not yet fully banished and the latter yet to have full social sanction. Thus, with the age-old faith, tradition, convention and superstition, are blended the scientific temperament, reason, growing freedom of women, rising sexual permissiveness, modernity and contemporaneity. Man is torn between the two and therefore, grows protean, self-contradictory and complex. He is aware that the inner forces drive him to act in certain ways and that his inner self is a reality at a different level. This has necessitated the writer to focus his attention both on the external reality and the internal reality. Raman in *The Painter of Signs* is a characteristic representative of his time. His character is vividly portrayed through his various actions, interactions, introspections, streams of thought and interior monologues. The other characters and their actions are seen largely from his perspective.

Raman, the young bachelor of about thirty, is a painter of signs by profession. After the death of his parents in a train accident long ago, he has been brought up under the maternal care of his aunt. Life has been smooth and congenial for him. He is a solitary person and is at ease with his solitude. He is skilled and adept in his work. He has set his own standards of quality and excellence. He sees sign-painting as an expression of calligraphy and hates to see his delicate art defiled by ignorant and unskilled artists. He is also a college-educated man who has a cupboard overflowing with books he has collected since his college days—from Plato to *Pickwick Papers*. Raman's choice of work makes it evident that the modern time has opened up new opportunities to choose a career corresponding to one's natural ability. A professional approach to work is a sign of time as well.

As a bachelor Raman enjoys his independence, and his work takes him all over Malgudi. Malgudi, the large business town at present, provides him enough opportunity for business. He is polite and businesslike in his dealings with his client. But his inward speech is sharper and plainer than these; he is free to be acidic inwardly and that gives him a kind of satisfaction. His encounters with the lawyer, the bangle-seller, the Town Hall Professor, illustrate different aspects of his character and of the society.

Through Raman, Narayan apprehends modern man's penchant for rationality. Raman is determined to establish the Age of Reason. "I want a rational explanation for everything" (5), he says to the prospective lawyer. But his rationalism is challenged by the blind believers like the lawyer and his own aunt. The lawyer believes in astrology and follows his astrologer's advice undeterred, at every step of his life. Raman's aunt too advocates the importance of stars in life. Raman questions its validity. He, in fact, represents the questioning mind of the youth in an age of science. A bigger challenge is posed by the centenarian temple priest who he comes across in the temple during his visit to a nearby village. The priest claims to have inexplicable, extraordinary mysterious power at his command, and nobody dares contradict him. In India the clash between religion and rationality is perennial. As Raman's friend Gupta, another rationalist, says—"Superstition, faith, the working of real incalculable forces, all three operate in our country; but we can never be certain where one begins and the other ends . . . we are in a mixed up state. Social workers have to take this into account" (113).

The novel claims another distinction for its treatment of sex. Sex, the most predominant theme in fiction, has always been treated by Narayan in a restrained, reticent and almost cold manner. For him it is too private a matter to deserve an open fictional treatment. His later novels, however, show a growing uninhibited interest and candour in the topic. The references to extra-marital illicit relationship of Rosie with Raju in *The Guide,* Vasu's unabashed sexual adventure with women in *The Man-Eater of Malgudi* and in the lengthy flashback of marital sex in *The Vendor of Sweets* are obvious evidences of the growing freedom from the self-imposed reticence on the part of the writer as well as the freedom of the society from sex-related taboos, prevailing before. In *The Painter of Signs* this freedom is shown to have gone a step farther. Raman is obsessed with sex although his middleclass morality restrains him. His indulgence in pre-marital sex would have been unthinkable, a few years ago, for an average middleclass Indian.

The sight of a woman's thigh lures Raman. Daisy the social worker comes to his dreams without her clothes on. The very word 'population' brings to his mind the word 'copulation.' Even the triangle symbolizing birth control titillates him. When alone with Daisy he is overpowered by his strong desire to possess her, make love to her, "to dash up, seize her, and behave like Rudolph Valentino in *The Sheik*" (92). Daisy takes timely precautions, but later on, they pronounce themselves as lovers and enter into a physical relationship. Raman's comical attempt at self-suppression thus ends with sex gratification. He throws light on the all-pervasive impact of sex on man's life. As Raman reflects Money and sex: "obsessive thoughts, too much everywhere—literature, magazines drama or cinema deal with nothing but sex all the time." (14)

Comical complications ensue from Raman's romantic involvement with Daisy, around which evolves the main plot of the novel. Their love story deals with a variety of aspects of love—romantic ardour, frustration, agony, loneliness, reconciliation, delusion and disillusionment. It renders the meaning of love and marriage in the modern context.

Raman and Daisy decide upon a marriage according to Gandharva style in which once the two souls meet in harmony, the marriage is consummated perfectly, and no further rite or ceremony is called for. Daisy is happy as it seems a sensible type of marriage, without ancient customs. For Raman this is the best because in case of a failure in marriage, the Gandharva-style marriage is as easily snapped as made. Daisy lays down her conditions as a prerequisite for marriage:

> One, that they should have no children and two, if by mischance one was born she would give the child away and keep herself free to pursue her social work. ". . . if you want to marry me you must leave me to my own plans even when I am a wife. On any day you question why or how, I'll leave you." (159)

Raman is reminded of the ancient king Santhanu of the Mahabharata who ties himself to such preconditions of Ganga to marry her. Like him, Raman is so intoxicated in love that he readily agrees to fulfil the conditions. Raman's divided self makes him analyze, from different angles, every aspect of marriage—beginning from Daisy's attitude to housekeeping to her role as a wife and mother. Daisy leaves everything to Raman to decide because she considers domestic affairs only a worthless occupation.

The novel ends with a big irony that the relationship between these two lovers never culminates in marriage and Daisy never comes to Raman's house which he prepares for her with a lot of care and attention. Now that his aunt has left the house, making way for their marriage, he is left alone. Daisy declines to marry Raman as a sudden realization comes upon her—"Married life is not for me, I have thought it over. It frightens me. I am not cut out for the life you imagine. I can't live except alone. It won't work" (178-79), she says. She goes out on a long tour—on a bigger mission towards birth control. Raman's attempt fails to melt her resolve. They part ways, and there is pathos in their parting. Raman definitely comes back to his bachelor existence withdrawing himself sadly but gallantly from Daisy's life. As there has been no tragic collapse for heroes like Chandran, Krishna, Margayya, Jagan, Sampath and Raju, so there is none for Raman, in this comedy of sadness.

Daisy, the family-planning zealot, spreads awareness of birth control with a missionary zeal. The response of the poor and illiterate villagers of the adjoining villages of Malgudi is quite favourable too. The topicality of the theme is a proof of the essential realism of the story. Raman is commissioned to the work of writing signboards for the family planning centre of Daisy. As he sets down to work he thinks ironically of the task Daisy has taken up and in the process inadvertently throws light on the enormity of the task, its relevance in modern India afflicted by population explosion and subsequent poverty. In portraying Daisy's character Narayan announces the emergence of the much liberated, self-assertive modern woman. Daisy is the product of the time. She is different not only from her traditional female counterparts like Susila and Savitri, but also from her modern counterparts like Bharati and Rosie. Susila is traditional but strong; her role is confined to her home. Bharati is a pure idealist, an ardent follower of Gandhi. Savitri is the oppressed one who is forced to suppress her rebelling spirit and reconcile, because she does not have the education or the economic independence to stand on her own. For her survival she needs a man to support her. But Daisy is quite different from all these women. She is highly individualistic, self-confident, self-reliant and liberated. She is different even from Rosie because, unlike the latter, she does not seek a man's support to fulfil her ambition, nor does she blame herself at any time for her actions or decisions.

Daisy is modern in the true sense. Through her portrait Narayan shows how modernity has infected Malgudi. No one has any knowledge of her identity or her parentage. She is a sudden descent from Malgudi—an outsider. She works in her own office. She admits Raman into her office fearlessly even when she is alone. She also calls on him at his house all alone. She plans to be accompanied by Raman on her tour to the adjoining villages to write signs advocating family planning. All this has been, in fact, new for the Malgudi world. Her zeal and intensity at work, her adaptability to difficult situations are new things to be seen. She travels tirelessly by taxi, bus, train or even lorry and takes whatever food is available, without having taboos of any kind. She sits wherever she finds a place for it, bathes in the public well, and accepts any hospitality, even in the lowliest of hut. She does not care for comfort or convenience. She is extremely undemanding by nature. In all this she presents just a picture opposite to that of Savitri of *The Dark Room*. She explains to Raman, "Let us live at least for a while as millions of our population live; otherwise we will never understand our own people. Living in a city is not real life. Urban life is standardized, and meant to keep people apart" (57). Narayan's concern for the underprivileged is also expressed through Daisy's attitude to them. Though he is not vocal, his anxiety over the growing population in India and the pangs of poverty is expressed well. Strictly adhering to rules set by herself, and following her own methods Daisy explains to the poor uneducated, ignorant men and women the power of family planning. Her manner shows firmness and conviction. In her uninhibited, unabashed but rather bold ways of dealing with her work she anticipates a time much ahead of hers. Even today, in the twenty-first century, the questions of sex-education face a lot of controversies and debates. She knows the disadvantages of big families. She has left her own big joint family which she describes as a vast, meaningless organization, where one can do nothing beyond the monotonous routine of life. Letting her personal safety and womanhood endangered, surviving all ordeals, she has come to Madras, completed her education with the help of a missionary organization, adopted a new name, trained herself in social work and finally, devoted her life for the poor and the unprivileged.

Daisy's beauty as well as gentleness enthralls Raman while her strength of character, her hard-edged zeal for work and mysterious independence perplex and appall him. She makes a deliberate show of strength even when she is swept by her tremendous capacity for love. She shows 'a firmness, a calculated coldness in her look' which comes through her 'elegance and femininity' and discourages one from taking chances with her (37). She is a perfect combination of femininity and masculinity. "She carries a furnace of conviction within which burns up all ambiguities, doubts and qualifications" (Walsh 1992: 157), which others of Raman's generation suffer. Narayan explains her character in his own words to S. Krishnan: "In *The Dark Room*, I was concerned with showing the utter dependence of women on men in our society. I suppose I have moved along with times. The girl in my new novel is quite different, not only is she not dependent on man, she actually has no use for them as an integral part of her life. To show her complete independence and ability to stand by herself, I took care not to give her a name with any kind of emotional connotation. I am calling her simply Daisy. She is a very strong character. All the same, when you read the novel, you will find she is very feminine also. There is conflict. That is the whole point."[1]

Raman's aunt, on the other hand, is a typical traditional Indian woman, a motherly figure who is devoted to the well being and comfort of her nephew notwithstanding the blow she receives from him. She is a storehouse of strength, too. In protest to Raman's decision to marry a girl whose caste, religion and parentage is not known, she leaves on a permanent pilgrimage to Benares and Badrinath hoping to die on the banks of the sacred river. Raman, who has taken her for granted all these years, suddenly realizes her worth and her importance in his life. A detailed picture of his aunt's enormous industry at home to keep him properly nourished and her own simple living with minimal wants reflects the way an Indian household runs. However, to a modern mind like Daisy's it is but a life of domestic slavery from which his aunt has freed herself. "Why do you grudge her for the few years left for her?" (179), she asks Raman who is pleading with his aunt to stay back.

The various incidents and the characters, even the fantastic and grotesque ones, have a proper placing in the scheme of Narayan's plot that centres on the reality of life. Everything about life portrayed in his tale gives a sense of inevitability, and authenticity and therefore, holds dear to the readers.

A Tiger for Malgudi

Of the last four novels, written during the last ten years of Narayan's prolific career as a novelist, *A Tiger for Malgudi* is the only full length and full-fledged novel. There is no manifestation of creative diminution of any sort in the novel but it certainly shows a major shift in his attitude to certain facts of life, especially to Hindu philosophy. He has chosen a theme very largely different from that of his earlier novels—the theme of true renunciation and true asceticism. In the process of delineating the theme he creates a real and not a fake 'sanyasi'—an ascetic. In the 'Introduction' to the novel, Narayan explains what has led to the writing of the novel and also, gives an account of his concept of a 'sanyasi' in Indian context. As Narayan says, he comes across a newspaper report that amidst the ocean of humanity at the Kumbh Mela Festival which recurs every twelve years at the confluence of rivers Ganga, Yamuna and Saraswati in Allahabad arrives a hermit with a tiger as his companion. He does not hold the animal in a leash since he claims they have been brothers in their previous lives. The tiger is reported to be moving about freely without hurting or scaring anyone. Narayan also comes across a few other instances of enduring friendship between tigers and human beings. Next he comes upon a bookmark, a four-inch-long strip of cardboard with the picture of a young tiger pleading, "I'd love to get into a good book." This is what turns into a creative inspiration for him—inspiration to translate into action his desire, already taken root in his mind, to let the tiger actually get into one of his novels, though in his characteristic humorous way he says, "the goodness of the book itself I can't guarantee" (7). As he explains further, human beings monopolize the attention of fiction writers. Man is too smug to realize the importance of other creatures. He is ignorant of the fact that they, too, possess their ego, values, outlook and the ability to communicate, though they are incapable of audible speech. Man assumes that all else in God's creation exists only for his sport, amusement, comfort or nourishment. It is a sin and Narayan makes an attempt to compensate for this sin by making an animal the protagonist of his novel. Moreover, for his purpose he chooses a tiger, not a mouse, so that "the chief character may not be trampled upon or lost sight of in a hole" (8). A tiger can be a befitting substitute for man.

So far as the ascetic, the other important character of the novel, is concerned, Narayan's explanation is that an ascetic (or a 'sanyasi,' or 'sadhu,' or 'yogi' or 'swami') is one who renounces everything and undergoes a complete change of personality with a complete obliteration of his past. The cause for it is not known. It could be an external factor or an inner compulsion—a "personal tragedy or frustration, a deeply compelling philosophy of life, or a flash of illumination driving one to seek a change." "A sanyasi is a wanderer living on alms, never rooted to any place except when he seeks seclusion of a cave or forest at some stage for prolonged meditation" (9). And in the course of it he acquires supernatural powers of different kinds—he could become "invisible, levitate, transmute metals, travel in space, control animals and men, live on air, and so on and so forth" (9). And this power is used not for "profit or self-promotion" but to "mitigate pain or suffering in others" (9). Beginning from *Swami and Friends* to *The Bachelor of Arts*, *The Dark Room, The English Teacher, The Financial Expert, The Guide* to *The Vendor of Sweets* and *The Painter of Signs*, ascetics of various types appear under various circumstances. Some of them are counterfeit as they adopt this life for its sheer vagrancy, or to exploit the public in the garb of holy men, some have it thrust upon them and some others receive mixed reactions of distrust and deference. But all of them undergo Narayan's ironic treatment. But here there is a genuine type treated solemnly and portrayed with inner conviction—one who according to Narayan, has acquired extraordinary powers after attaining spiritual experience. So, he says, "Now in my story the 'Tiger Hermit' employs his powers to save the tiger and transform it inwardly—working on the basis that, deep within, the core of personality is the same in spite of differing appearances and categories, and with the right approach you could expect the same response from a tiger as from any normal human being." (Introduction: 9-10)

It comes from the same writer who, years back, while replying to the strange questions of his readers in a western country regarding mysticism in India, has tried to explain, "Perhaps you think that all Indians are spiritually preoccupied. We aren't, we have a large background of religion and plenty of inner resources, but normally we also have to be performing ordinary tasks, such as working, earning, living and breeding. . . . we have traffic, crowds, shops, pimps, pickpockets, policemen, and whatnot as in any other country. . . . You have to realize that unemployment among educated classes is a grim reality in our country; and a young person has to overcome this deficiency before aspiring for the luxuries of a mystic state." (*The Writerly Life* 2001: 454)

Narayan, the hardcore realist, seems to have matured with time, and in this novel, seems to have reached a stage to believe mysticism as a real, though not common, experience like any other experience of man, that can be attained once aspired. Thus, we have a tiger and a hermit for characters in this novel.

The novel with a tiger as its hero brings to mind the Indian classic *The Panchatantra* by Vishnuraman, a learned Brahman who undertakes to teach three dull and ignorant princes the polity and worldly wisdom by means of stories acted out by animals. Animals like lion, bull, monkeys, jackals are portrayed as his dramatis personae in his entertaining and edifying fables. The animals talk and act like the human types they represent. Narayan's novel can be called a fable in this sense. But it is different from Vishnuraman's beast fable in that it has no moral lesson to teach. It rather resembles George Orwell's beast fable *Animal Farm* expanded into a sustained satire on the political and social conditions of a country under an autocratic regime. In telling his story of the tiger, Narayan brings the animal world in contact with the human world—the world of modern Malgudi, the representative India. He has already given proof of his keen observation of human action and behaviour and his deep insight into human mind in his earlier works. Here, just as he has shown his power in observing and describing the behavioural pattern of the animals with an eye for detail, so he shows an uncanny power in interpreting convincingly their 'codes, signals and idioms' (50). The accuracy of observation makes the interpretation sound true and credible.

Narayan's story begins with the aged tiger lying in his cage ruminating on his past, beginning with his cubhood and wild days in the jungle, and later life in captivity as a circus star. He attains freedom when he breaks loose from a film-shooting camp and wanders into the town. The terror-stricken public attempts to get him shot, but the ascetic appears on the scene, protects him and adopts him as a companion. The tiger is subsequently blessed with spirituality and wisdom by the ascetic. Therefore, as he recalls the past, he makes a wise analysis of the behaviour and action of both men and animals and explores the motives behind these. He is also aided by the ascetic in his attempt to understand and evaluate men and animals. In the process of narrating his experiences, he compares and contrasts the world of animals with that of men and realizes certain truths of life. And Narayan's realistic art finds full expression in the process.

In his early days, the tiger, named by the owner of the circus as Raja, has been a cave-dweller, a jungle beast, dwelling in a cave at the far end of Mempi Range, which trails off into the plain. The cave has been on the edge of a little rivulet. The days have been full of frolicking on the sandy bank and in the cool stream. He has been growing up in the safe keeping of his mother, ignorant and unmindful of the dangers that life might be having in store for him. The first truth of life—the impermanence of everything in this world—dawns upon him, when his mother dies leaving him to fend for himself. He experiences the hardships of life, the attacks of the enemies but ultimately survives all odds to become the Supreme Lord of the Jungle, afraid of no one, striking terror in others. It is a period in which he experiences the frenzied enjoyment of power. But yet animals like the big lion, the secretive and agile leopard, the small ones like the porcupine with its stab of quills, monkeys who live at a height and birds like crows, kites, vultures, eagles, with their ability to fly to still greater height, the owl with its cynical cackle and hoot have been the ones to challenge his prowess and expose his weaknesses. As Raja grows young, he finds his mate, an attractive tigress, and soon has his family with four little cubs. His happiness is gone when one day the tigress inadvertently strays into human habitation of a nearby village in search of prey. She is shot dead along with her four cubs that instinctively have followed their mother.

Coming in search of his wife and children, Raja has his first encounter with human beings—callous and devilish in the frenzy of power. He is amused at their ignorance and self-assurance (25). Then he comes face to face with men and discovers another side of their nature—their cruelty and immense capacity to torture: "A human being may look small, without prominent teeth or claws, but he is endowed with some strange power, which can maneuver a tiger or an elephant as if they were toys." (28)

Raja is captured by Captain, the owner and proprietor of the Grand Malgudi Circus, who saves him from being shot dead by the shikaris and brings him to Malgudi to perform in the circus. Later the captain lends the tiger to a film-maker to perform for a film. These are important phases during which he learns more about life. As a circus tiger he experiences loneliness, immobility and hunger. While performing for the filmmaker he suffers intolerable humiliation and torture. In an attempt to get himself free he kills Captain and discovers that man is but a flimsy creature in comparison to a tiger's size and strength. He is surprised to know that he has been cowed down by so miserable a creature not even half his height.

Raja realizes that man assumes power over animals only by his intelligence, his mental power. As long as Captain acts as the trainer, and shows kindness, sympathy and understanding, his whip is enough to tame even tigers and lions. He would not touch the gadget. He would rather say, "I'd be ashamed to employ this on any animal. No trainer worth his name can be proud of it if his animal is coerced and beaten down with such a contraption. It's no training. It's stampeding an animal into obedience with electric shock" (104). But overcome by 'a certain degree of greed,' though indifferent generally in money matters, and by a gradual corruption through contact with the film world, and 'drunk with authority,' he sacrifices the real power, his intelligence. Narayan offers a befitting assessment of man's behaviour in the animal world through Raja. Walking freely out of the circus, Raja throws the entire town of Malgudi into a state of confusion, excitement and fright. His next encounter is with the gunman Alphonse who makes some funny and vain attempts to kill him. He is however rescued by the ascetic who then exercises some strange power over him.

Raja begins to understand human speech. All his animal strength is sapped. He is made to understand that though violence and aggressiveness are natural conditions of existence for every creature in this world, they cannot be 'everlasting.' The ascetic tells him

> Sooner or later it (the potential store of violence) has to go, if not through wisdom, definitely through decrepitude, which comes on with years, whether one wants it or not. The demon, the tormentor, or the tyrant in history, if ever he survives to experience senility, becomes helpless and dependent, lacking the strength even to swat a fly. You are now an adult, full-grown tiger, and assuming you are fifteen years old, in human terms you would be over seventy years old, and at seventy and onwards one's temper gets toned down through normal decay, and let us be grateful for it. You cannot continue your ferocity forever. You have to change. (145)

And the tiger changes under the spiritual training of the ascetic.

From this stage there starts a new phase of learning in Raja's life. In spite of his initial unwillingness to have anything to do with human beings, he comes to realize that under the ascetic's influence, he is no different from human beings. The ascetic becomes his master and he, his disciple. Together they leave Malgudi and seek shelter in the green foliage of Mempi Hills, where he gets illumined. Raja is advised not to crave for the unattainable and not to brood on his shortcomings but to think of improvement. He learns a great deal from his Master, knows himself, and understands the world he lives in, feels and expresses his thoughts. He learns that a 'sense of time' is not necessary for those who try to attain spirituality. It is important only for those who are engaged in worldly activities. He learns more about his master who has been once a man of the world, busy and active, living by the clock, scrutinizing his bank book, greeting and smiling at all and sundry because he has been anxious to be treated as a respectable man in society. But one day, he says,

> It seemed all wrong, a senseless repetition of activities. . . . and I abruptly shed everything including (but for a bare minimum) clothes, and fled away from wife, children, home, possessions, all of which seemed intolerable. At midnight, I softly drew the bolt of our back door, opening on the sands of Sarayu behind our house at Ellaman Street, while others slept, and left very much in the manner of Siddhartha. (161)

Lost to mankind forever, he achieves complete anonymity, sheds his past and goes in search of attaining spirituality. After much hardship he attains his present state. His past no longer exists for him nor does his future. He lives for the moment, and would live that way as long as he is alive.

Together Raja and the ascetic pass their days in wise and philosophical discourse, particularly based on the teachings of the Bhagavad Gita, and then, nearing old age, they decide to part company. Before going to attain Samadhi the Master entrusts the old and infirm Raja to the professional care of a zoo, to save him from suffering starvation or attack from other creatures or hunters and to die in peace. They bid farewell to each other with the hope of meeting again in the next life.

There are plenty of stories based on the spiritual odysseys of ascetics in India. But the story of a tiger endowed with an intelligent, sensitive personality, spiritualized by the mysterious powers of his Master is not only new but also incredible. Vasu, in *The Man-Eater of Malgudi*, is a man metaphorically termed as the man-eater. But in *A Tiger for Malgudi*, we have a tiger behaving as human being. As J.K. Biswal says, "Raja has not only undergone humanization, but even looks forward to his salvation. He understands the master's spiritual discourses on Yoga, on 'life and existence and death,' on God and Bhagavad Gita and the like. . . . One may put the question—Is not Narayan asking too much of a tiger? . . . To a reader skeptic of such spiritual workings, this may also seem utterly absurd. Even the craziest behaviour in spiritual miracles would find it hard to accept a tiger repenting for his kills, understanding lessons on yoga, time and eternity." (1987: 111-12) Biswal, however, adds an explanation: "Perhaps that has been uppermost in the novelist's mind. That is why the tiger (narrator) adopts a persuasive stance throughout the course of narration. The reader is persuaded to suspend his disbelief almost in the beginning of the novel." (112)

The tiger's observation may be quoted in support of Biswal's comment. At the beginning of the novel he says, "You are not likely to understand that I am different from the tiger next door, that I possess a soul within this forbidding exterior" (12). Towards the end of the novel he makes it clear again, "I was feeling uncomfortable with some change coming inside me. I was beginning to understand. Don't ask me how. My Master never explained to me the mystery or the process of his influence on me" (146).

Taming wild animals was considered an art in ancient India. Though the art is diminished at present, it is not altogether impossible for an ascetic habituated to live alone in caves and deep forests to tame an aged tiger who has already lost its strengths. The tiger's capacity to understand human language may not be true, but its capacity to understand human gestures can be an acceptable idea. The strength of his youth vanished, the tiger also easily accepts the situation as he finds the ascetic's treatment is quite different from that of Captain. Man's aggression and hankering after more and more power over the world of nature explain the increasing violence of wild animals like tiger. Through the discourse of the ascetic and the tiger Narayan reveals some basic truths which should be remembered for keeping up balance in the environment. These truths are: a) Man is physically weaker than most of the animals and yet man reigns Supreme in the animal world because of his intelligence; b) but man does not know how to control his aggressive temperament; "drunk with authority," he forgets the natural rule of co-existence and invites danger for human civilization; c) ancient Indian civilization sought to arrive at a state of balanced co-existence with the natural world and this balance is destroyed because of the intrusion of materialistic trends that have made man more power-hankering than ever.

It is to be noted that while introducing the Hindu philosophy of Karma, rebirth and transmigration of soul, and meaning of life and death through the ascetic in his novel, Narayan does not depart from his concern with important worldly issues. He explores in the novel a new dimension of man-woman relationship and emphasizes on the change that has taken place due to the impact of the changing socio-cultural conditions. Narayan portrays a nagging wife, a modern-day reality, with his characteristic irony and pathos. The most real and authentic (flesh and blood) characters in the novel are Captain and his wife. Captain's wife is nagging, and argumentative, sometimes even jealous of the animals getting so much of her husband's attention. Disgusted, Captain reflects, "Women are impossible. Worse than twenty untamed jungle creatures on one's hand at a time" (38). But the ascetic is not of the same opinion. "Human ties cannot be defined in just black-and-white terms," he wisely says, "There can be no such thing as unmitigated hatred or unmitigated love. Those who are deeply attached sometimes deliberately present a rough exterior to each other and that is also one way of enjoying the married state" (69). In fact, Captain and his wife are a peculiar couple devoted to each other but dissatisfied with each other's ways. That is why Captain worries about his wife, and his wife commits suicide after his sudden death.

The reality of violent communal disharmony that leads to bloodshed has also been hinted at in the scene that describes the tiger and the ascetic passing through a rioting mob—groups of people engaged in bloody strife, attacking each other with stone, knife and iron rod, and screaming murderous challenges. The ascetic enumerates the flimsy grounds on which such strife begins—"a division of canal water in your field, two urchins of opposite camps slapping each other, rumours of molestation of some women, even the right to worship in a temple, anything may spark off a fight if you are inclined to nurture hatred" (165). It is further enunciated as the ascetic says, 'all causes of rivalry and clash are senseless and so need no defining or explanation,' and 'No cause is worth a clash' and that 'only the foolish waste their lives in fighting' (165). The authorial voice can be heard for the first time in the voice of the ascetic.

For the first time, Narayan touches upon an emerging contentious issue of the national policy of language—the three language formula consisting of the regional language, the national language and English. (However, there is also a mention of learning Sanskrit, the language of the gods, the language in which all Hindu scriptures are written). Captain, explains the reasons for making his speech in at least three languages,

> in Hindi since it is our National language and given to us by Mahatma Gandhi himself; also in English because as our beloved respected leader Nehru put it, it opens a window on the world. In Tamil, because it is, as, our mother tongue, in which our greatest poets like Kamban and Valluvar composed. (66)

Narayan also hints at another issue of national importance—rampant corruption in all walks of public life. The picture underlies Narayan's pungent irony. Alphonse offers a substantial bribe to the officers of the wildlife group of the Forest Department to be allowed to kill the tiger by certifying it as a man-eater and be waived the penalty prescribed for such offences as killing endangered species and exporting tiger skin as a part of his business. When Captain shifts his circus from Poona to Malgudi he liberally disperses money to "smooth out the passage of all kinds of transactions and favours" (36) and within a short period makes Malgudi more famous for its circus than for its mountains and rivers. When he starts the publicity for his special Jubilee show, he advises his men to stick the posters on the walls of the Albert Mission School, well over the stencilled warning that says 'BILL STICKERS WILL BE PROSECUTED' (70) and thus make it lawful. If they are questioned they would send complimentary passes to the principal and professors. He has also planned to reserve seats for all possible objectors and obstructions, from the sanitary department to the jail superintendent. All the walls are to be used for publicity and those who differ from him in the name of adorning the town are considered eccentrics who cramp the town's economic life and ultimate prosperity. And when complimentary tickets don't work, he would donate cash as 'Birthday Gifts.' This is just an instance of showing how the system in India works by money changing hands. He is a symbol of success in an age of capitalism and self-advertisement.

Narayan satirizes the cumbersome ways of the functioning of the bureaucracy and the law enforcing agencies. Narayan shows how difficult it is for the common men to move the bureaucracy to action. He shows with what difficulty the villagers persuade the collector to act in time for relief from a menacing tiger who is 'fattening' itself almost everyday on the village cattle. First a written petition has to be given even when the villagers have no notion of the 'world of letters.' "I can't take action unless there is a written petition" (30), he says. All the official formalities are to be completed first and then a date is to be fixed for inspection and taking action. "For all I know there may be no tiger whatever. You may be imagining," the Collector says and then assures, "However, it is my duty to look into it, if you have a grievance" (30). The villagers visit the Collector almost once a week, spend time and money for no purpose, and after much waiting could meet only the Collector's clerk to satisfy further official formalities. The desperate villagers adopt their own defensive measures such as keeping up a bonfire all night, and posting vigilant guards, armed with sharp weapons or even scatter poison meat for the tiger. And when they force the Collector's clerk for an early action in the matter they are only to be scolded and threatened of police action. Ultimately, the poor villagers are saved by Captain taking initiative to capture it, though for his own personal interest. There is another ironic reflection on red-tapism—on the laxity in the functioning of the government departments when the assistant tells: "Unless they sanction the budget, we can't even buy a pin" (127). When the headmaster is locked in a room with the tiger, the assistant headmaster thinks of the legality of his giving order for an action to be taken, in the process staking the interest of the school.

The speech on non-violence by Captain sets in sharp ironic contrast the violence practised in real life to tame animals. The entire episode relating to the shooting of the film from the beginning to the end is a satire on the fallacies of filmmaking. Raja's reflections on human behavioural patterns also draw attention. He observes how easily and blatantly men can tell lies and fabricate things for selfish interest, how thoughtlessly and purposelessly they can kill and torture animals or even their own species: "Tigers attack only when they feel hungry, unlike human beings who slaughter one another without purpose or hunger" (117). He describes human beings' habit of never being in 'a moment's silence or stillness of mind' (44), always talking or listening. He feels sick of human beings who are "everywhere, every inch of the earth seemed to be swarming with humanity" (146). He yearns to be in the grand silence of the jungles instead of being amidst the noisy affairs of humanity. He thinks "to be back in the world of bamboo shade and monkeys and jackals! Even the supercilious leopard and the owl I would not mind; compared to human company, they were pleasant, minding their own business, in spite of occasional moods to taunt and gossip"

(146), he cannot however return, as the Master has planned a different life for him.

Throughout the novel, Narayan's social criticism is blended with his personal brand of humour. It has all the characteristic features of Narayan's novel but rendered with maturity and confidence.

> Everything is so superbly done that Narayan remains an acknowledged master of his craft. One can hardly disagree with the verdict that Narayan is at the peak of his creative originality in *A Tiger For Malgudi*, which will be widely read and long remembered as a political allegory and social satire, for it possibly has not only all the merits of George Orwell's *Animal Farm* but also something more for those who are prepared to look for deeper meanings in it.[12]

Talkative Man

Talkative Man, Narayan's thirteenth novel, is the story of a wife's attempt to reclaim her errant and elusive husband, Dr. Rann, and Talkative Man's attempt at saving the honour of a young girl from Malgudi. Talkative Man, the narrator of the story, is so called because he cannot help talking when surrounded by others. His impulse to share an experience with others is irresistible (1). He belongs to one of the few rich families of Kabir Street of Malgudi who have inherited their riches from previous generations. They are all comfortably placed in life, mainly "occupied in eating, breeding, celebrating festivals, spending the afternoons in a prolonged siesta on the pyol, and playing cards all evening" (4). The women rarely come out, "being most of the time in the kitchen or in the safe-room scrutinizing their collection of diamonds and silks" (4). This sort of existence does not appeal to or suit Talkative Man who likes to be active and cherishes dreams of becoming a reputed journalist. Working as a reporter and journalist he has earned the name of 'Universal Correspondent' as he has no authority to represent any particular publication. He works hard all through the day, reports all kinds of activities, sends it for publication and feels pleased if a few lines written by him appear in print as a space-filler somewhere in the two morning papers coming from Madras to the Town Hall Library of Malgudi. It is when he is struggling to establish himself as a journalist that he gets involved in the affairs of Dr. Rann.

Talkative Man meets the mysterious Dr. Rann when he is on the lookout for a good story. Rann is actually Rangan, as he discovers later—a name trimmed and tailored to sound foreign and to hide the purely Indian origin—origin from a southernmost village named Maniyur. He looks unusual for an Indian—"blonde hair, a touch of greenish blue in his eyes, and borderline complexion" (3). Dressed in a blue suit, tie, shining shoes, a felt hat and with manners too grand for the simple Malgudians he overwhelms them, and at the same time is treated as an oddity. He claims to have come from Timbuctoo, a lovely place on the west coast of Africa. He also says that he is working on a project for the United Nations and has come to Malgudi only for collecting his material for research though he is critical and quite resentful of the ways and means of the Malgudians. He first makes his appearance at the Malgudi Station, occupies the waiting room and refuses to leave the place, to the confusion and embarrassment of the law-abiding station master. Talkative Man tries to find a house for him. Unable to find one of Rann's choices, Talkative Man takes him to his large house to give him shelter—a gesture, symbolic of "the lofty, patronizing hospitality" of the "Kabir Street Aristocracy" (26). But, here too, Rann extends his stay as a house-guest. Talkative Man's association with Rann generates mixed feelings in the former. His outlandish clothes and behaviour catch his imagination and provide him with enough material for a story or for an article. He enjoys his company. On the other hand, he dislikes Rann's secretive ways and his habit of keeping himself closed and confined to the room and making him feel like an intruder in his own house. However, the latter gradually gives up his outlandish habits to some extent in order to fit himself to the Malgudi climate especially when he is all set to woo the Malgudi girl. The blue Oxford suit is gradually replaced by shirt sleeves and trousers and later by the normal Malgudi executive costume—cotton pants and shirt sleeves.

Troubles for Rann start when his wife commandant Sarsa, a huge and dangerous looking woman, arrives at Malgudi on her husband hunting business. She brings a press-cutting of "Timbuctoo Man" which is written and published by Talkative Man. A photograph of Rann is published along with the article. Claiming Rann to be her husband she holds Talkative Man in her hypnotic narration of her early romance with Rann and her marriage with him against the will of her parents and all the legal troubles that followed the marriage. She tells him of Rann's bitterness that developed from those troubles, his dislike for his in-laws and attitude of indifference towards his wife that compelled him to leave his house. Since then he has been on the run from his wife who is frantically searching for him.

After initial indifference to, and disbelief in the story of Rann's wife, Talkative Man finds out the true nature of Rann. His realization comes as he observes Rann's clever attempts to impress Girija, the seventeen year old grand-daughter of the caretaker of the Town Hall Library of Malgudi. He plays the confidence trick also on her grandfather and grandmother. Talkative Man then learns, through local gossip, of Rann's secret meeting with the girl at different distant places of Malgudi with a purpose to seduce her. The girl was young enough to be his daughter. Talkative Man, now suspicious about Rann's background, decides to act as a spy and arm himself with facts, before tackling him. He soon discovers proof of Rann's misdeeds—the letters of the girls he has seduced and deserted, assuming thousand names and escaping to different towns and countries. They are all trying to pursue him but are unable to get at him. He is a wanderer, a philanderer on a global scale, abandoning women right and left (120).

So Talkative Man takes upon himself another responsibility—'to puncture this pompous fellow' and to rescue the Malgudi girl from this 'lecherous demon.' Just as Rann is secretly packing up to abduct the girl, Talkative Man makes elaborate arrangements to trap him and secretly invites his wife to claim him back without letting anyone have an inkling of the matter. His ultimate aim is not only to stop the young girl from being abducted but also to save the honour of the family. Rann's wife reveals that he has unsuspected depths of duplicity and that he is an expert in the art of deception (118). Talkative Man succeeds to send Rann out of Malgudi with his wife.

However, the reunion of Rann and his wife does not last more than six months. Talkative Man comes to know from Rann's wife the details of her husband's next escape with a nurse from Matilda, this time, perhaps to Rome under a new name again and manufacturing a new passport. Now with all hopes lost she prays to God that "some day he may be caught at least for his passport frauds and made to spend the rest of his life in some hellish prison" (119). A realistic portrait of a man without faith in the institution of marriage, and of a man who bothers only about his sexual gratification, is offered by Narayan.

Bruce King is quite critical of *Talkative Man* which he says 'ignores such traits of the western realistic novel as characterization, clothing, description, detail, probability, and uninterrupted continuity; instead the story telling seems increasingly oral, with emphasis on the narration, monologue, narration frames, myth and the wondrous"[13].Quite aware of such shortcomings, Narayan makes his excuses in the 'Postscript' to the novel. As he says, though he conceived *Talkative Man* as a full-length novel, it could not grow beyond 116 typewritten sheets, because after a point he had nothing more to say. He is not in favour of inflating stories with laboured detail and description of dress, deportment, facial features, furniture, food and drinks, things that obstruct the smooth reading of a novel. *Talkative Man*, could have been made longer if he had made the Commandant Sarsa, Rann's wife, pursue her husband on the run, across continents or societies. But in her present mood, it is impossible to make her do so. Apart from this, he says, on the basis of Graham Greene's advice received half a century ago, "I do not concern myself with quantity while writing" (122).

Talkative Man is short, and therefore, does not have enough scope for elaboration of details about characters and situations. Yet there is no denying that the fiction has its roots in real life situations and realistic characters. Narayan has concentrated on an outsider who seeks to corrupt the atmosphere of Malgudi.

The World of Nagaraj

Mohan Ramanan describes *The World of Nagaraj* as 'Narayan's last sustained piece of fiction' because 'it is in the familiar line of Malgudi Stories'[14]. Set up in Malgudi, the characters with all their actions and approaches to life are found to be familiar and recognizable. With his delightful powers of observation, Narayan focuses his attention on the protagonist, Nagaraj, a traditional middle-class man and his smooth, easy-going and apathetic world. He lives with his wife Sita in his family's vast and spacious house, which is his share of the family property. Later Tim, his nephew, and then, Saroja, his nephew's wife, come to stay with him. He has an ambitious elder brother Gopu who lives in the village with his wife Charu. Gopu prefers a nucleus family to a joint family.

Quiet and comfortable in his world, Nagaraj leads a routine life at home and outside. Any of his normal days includes an early rise from bed, morning coffee, a stroll along to wake up his friend Jayaraj, the photographer, who sleeps 'on a bench in front of his shop at the market archway' (1). This is followed by bath, prayers in the puja room putting on the ochre robes of a sadhu, and some time spent sitting on the pyol from where he could "watch the goings on in Kabir Street" (4) and brood. The last one is a favourite pastime of his. He could see from there the movements of Talkative Man, the busiest man in the street, a journalist and a good friend; Sambu, his immediate neighbour, who in contrast to Talkative Man, remains glued to a canvas deck chair, sitting all the time and reading. His daily wanderings also take him on a familiar route. A major part of the day is spent in doing book-keeping for Coomar at Boeing Sari Centre. He works free for Coomar, 'no pay packet at the beginning of a month' (24). This arrangement gives him a double benefit—it leaves him free to come and go as he likes and do the work without any feeling of compulsion, and secondly, it gives him a break from the monotony of home.

In this novel Narayan takes his readers round a particular area of Malgudi which further strengthens the geography of his fictional Malgudi, grown and developed through a period of more than fifty years. Some new members are introduced along with the old ones who have already made their appearances in the previous novels. As Nagaraj watches or visits his friends, particularly those who appear for the first time and as he encounters his relatives, mother, brother, sister-in-law, wife, nephew and nephew's wife at home, he analyses his experiences with them in detail and thus, opens up before our eyes a pleasant view of a multitude of men and manners.

Nagaraj remembers his mother (dead at present) and her relationship with him and other members of the family—his wife, brother and sister-in-law. Through his recollections one gets a glimpse of the interior of an Indian household in which complex human relationships grow, and survive in spite of conflicts and clash of interest. In the early days he found his wife "too timid and bashful,' and his mother a 'Commander-in-Chief.' His wife meekly accepted the role of a lackey at home, forever at the beck and call of her mother-in-law, trailing behind her all the time, hardly ever coming into his room (25). In her declining age, his mother had nothing to do but hobbled about with weak legs and minimal energy like a frail ghost asking inane questions of the two left at home (31). She would not rest, but would keep inspecting and watching every corner of the house and commenting, to the great annoyance of his wife who would burst out in anger against her. Her greatest ally against her daughter-in-law is the maid servant who has served them for years. His mother's decline started with his father's death, after which she had to take to her role as an Indian widow. Gopu's suggestion for a division of property, and the division that actually followed brought about further decline. His mother was too unhappy to be a witness to this sad occasion of her life. His mother's relationship with her elder daughter-in-law, Charu, had been tact and carefulness all through. From the beginning the latter had shown her preference for a separate living even while staying in one house. Whenever together, especially in the kitchen, Charu would mumble to a question of her mother-in-law without turning round, and as the mother-in-law repeated her question, she would mumble persistently. "After the first few days she ignored all queries and communicated only when it pleased her" (30). But his mother would give an elaborate answer to any query that was initiated from Charu, the 'imperious and self-assertive' elder daughter-in-law of the house.

Nagaraj's elder brother Gopu had always intimidated him. Their father used to compare their relation to that of Lakshmana to Rama. True to his role, Nagaraj continued to be a devoted younger brother. But Gopu was selfish and arbitrary. He insisted first on a division, immediately after his father's death, and then insisted on a proper division of the property. "Nagaraj's own inclination was to accept whatever came in his share, but his brother was aggressive and demanding" (33). Gopu always supported his wife without the slightest dissent to any of her wishes and desires. She was the prompter behind the scene of partition, planning to get away from the mother-in-law (34). However, Gopu being a man of action and moving to the village, prospered in his rural life with his expanding coconut groves, guava orchards and fields of rice and millet. Nagaraj reflects upon the Government's efforts to modernize rural life by making mechanical gadgets available for threshing, for slicing and mashing cattle fields and also by giving subsidy, content and technical staff for the success of the cement gas plant. This is an instance of Narayan's touching upon social and political programmes undertaken in post-independent India.

Narayan is best at the delineation of family relationships. In the traditional set-up of an Indian family, it is generally the man or the husband who dominates over all and dictates the affairs. But it is the woman or the wife who has an indirect control of family affairs with such exceptions as Savitri in *The Dark Room.* And when the wife has a strong personality, and ability to think, judge and decide, the control becomes stronger and more effective. Nagaraj's wife Sita is a traditional Indian woman who accepts her subjugation, but because of her personality acquires great natural authority over the members of the family. After her initial surrender to her mother-in-law's authority she has taken over. She slaves her husband and his family as long as it is necessary. When she is in a bad mood, she would complain about becoming 'a prisoner in the house' having to guard her mother-in-law's restlessness (14). But in her limited sphere at home and busy family schedule she enjoys the real power, though the real power is never translated into any real action. She nags and forces her husband to act in a crisis but does not take stock of the situation in case of her husband's failure.

Nagaraj is portrayed as a weak person who considers himself "a prisoner of domesticity" (5). Narayan has shown that the actual reason behind Nagaraj's lack of power is his inaction, his indecision and his procrastination. In a traditional Indian marriage, as is shown in Narayan's novels, it is not so much a relationship of love between husband and wife, as it is of duty and necessity. Yet it makes a marriage happy and successful. Nagaraj has enough money for a decent living and is happy that he does not have to think of money for living. His only concern is the book he intends to write about the life of the great sage Narada—a work which, he imagines, will lift him out of the mundane world of trivialities and will give him his own identity. His obsession with the topic is the source of all humour and satire in the novel. In his own lingering ways, he continues his literary struggle, but never abandons the idea. He meets Kavu Pundit, an expert in literature to know more about Narada. With him he has a bitter and disappointing experience, first for not knowing Sanskrit and second for the Pundit's attitude of procrastination. The next man he hopes to get some aid from is a businessman Bari, who makes him buy notebooks from his shop alluring him with the promise that he would explain the events about the sage Narada from a book 'Narada Purana' that he has with him. But his promises prove futile too. Then he decides to write on Narada at home without any help, at the early hours of morning, but this time his plan is thwarted by the disturbance caused by the ear-shattering noise of Saroja's harmonium as she goes through her music practice from early morning and all through the day. He is relieved when Tim leaves home with his wife in protest against Nagaraj's unwillingness to appreciate her art. But the relief is short-lived as they come back soon and Nagaraj's hope for writing in peace is again postponed or is kept in abeyance.

Nagaraj, himself childless, is fond of his nephew Tim. But he is not accustomed to taking responsibilities. Hence, he is puzzled by his activities from the start. His days are filled with unwelcome complication and turbulence by Tim's secret late-night activities. Tim leaves college in the middle without letting anyone guess, and works in a Bar/Restaurant called Kismet. He marries Saroja and is happy with her. He leaves home with his wife without much careful thought and after a few days comes back without any fuss or fanfare. As Nagaraj reflects, they come back in the same manner as they leave—"no explanation or any elaborate discussion—not in his nature" (183). So Nagaraj must accept everything about Tim as it is. He prepares himself to sacrifice his quest for peace, silence and isolation needed to accomplish his mission. Sita is happy to get them back. What is noise to Nagaraj, is normalcy for Sita, 'Now our home is back to normal,' she feels (183). Nagaraj cannot take any risk of upsetting the children and driving them out again. The only way out for him is to forget about his book, wear the ochre robe that would force him to remain silent and to acquire a lot of cotton wool and try and pack it all in his ear that even a thunderclap may sound like a whisper (185). The comic hero of Narayan finds a comic solution to the tension of his life. "Growth does not characterize Nagaraj; he is finally a thin, static creature"[15], says Robert E. McDowell. Like all Narayan's major characters, Nagaraj is eccentric and so is the centre of his human comedy, and it is by him or through him that the comedy is to come to a meaningful end—an end that is supposed to give stability to the world and avoid any disruption of the routine. Nothing beyond the routine can be allowed to happen in this world. The crisis of the self ends as a crisis without angst. There lies the essential pathos of everyday human condition.

As a modern trend the later novels of Narayan put greater emphasis on individual existence. Though Malgudi has nothing to do with the greater issues troubling India yet it shows an awareness of the new and real challenges it faces as a growing town. One such challenge is the problem of garbage disposal. The municipality is lazy and indifferent to the garbage that develops into a hillock anywhere around with pigs and goats to rummage. Ministers make speeches but don't act. Similarly the old man who meets Nagaraj at the Boardless talks of the reckless behaviour of the mass at the level crossing. He is always there to hold a flag and warn the people. Still the people get run over sometimes. "Before the signal comes up people want to dash across and reach the other side in a hurry. . . . oh, after that the crowd and police and the wailing of relatives!" (160), says the old man. Nagaraj wants level crossings to be set up to save men and animals. He wants Talkative Man to write about this to draw the attention of the authorities. Even almost after forty years of the growth and development of Malgudi the problem has not been addressed. On the other hand, Narayan's account of Dr. Velu, the doctor of the poor, and of Dr. Natawar whose polyclinic, equipped with modern gadgets, provides expensive treatment to Malgudians, show that the state of health services has improved since the time of Krishna of *The English Teacher*. To conclude in agreement with Ralph J. Crane, the novel is a part of Narayan's formula—a case of old wine in new bottles perhaps—yet "it is always pleasant to revisit well-loved territory, and for this reason as much as for any other, Narayan's latest novel is a welcome addition to the world of Malgudi."'[16]

Grandmother's Tale

Grandmother's Tale, the last one of Narayan's novels, is the story of his great-grandmother who lived in the later period of the East India Company's reign in India. The novel has a purely autobiographical tone. In the forewords to the novel called 'Explanation,' Narayan clarifies that the composition grew as he wrote it from his grandmother's narration, in daily installments, of her mother's search for her errant husband, a story which has already been mentioned in another of Narayan's novels, *The Painter of Signs*. Narayan cannot tell for sure how much of it is history and how much is fiction. "The borderline between fact and fiction, between biography and tale wears thin and ultimately vanishes in the following chronicle" (Explanation, *The Grandmother's Tale*)—he says. To convey that it might not all be imaginary, Narayan incorporates into it interlocutions, interpolations and interruptions that take place between him and his grandmother—the two narrators in the novel. Moreover, he testifies the truth of the narration, at least some parts of it, citing what he believes to be evidence of the family history.

The novel begins with a brief and abridged account of Narayan's early days spent with Ammani—his grandmother, who eventually ends up telling him the story of her mother. Thus supported by some real events of his own life at the beginning, the novel sets its foothold in reality. The story goes like this—Narayan's great-grandmother Bala, married at an early age of seven to Viswa a boy of ten, "as those were days of child marriages" (18). The innocent couple were confused while going through the entire process of the marriage ceremony and the rituals that followed, as they were too young to understand the meaning of all this. As they were not supposed to live as husband and wife at that age, Bala had to stay in her parents' house for some time. Therefore, they hardly got any chance to know each other, except for the special occasions when the boy was invited to spend some time with his wife and for a few glimpses they had of each other during the boy's secret visits to his wife's house.

But suddenly one day, Viswa left the village bidding Bala good-bye, joining a group of pilgrims going to Pandharpur in Pune. He was gone before she or anyone else could realize what had happened. Time passed and the small girl of seven grew to 'full-blown womanhood.' Being in an orthodox society it became difficult for her to pass down the Agraharam Street without people staring at her and whispering comments behind her back and sometimes, asking questions about her husband. Sometimes she answered and satisfied her questioners, and sometimes situations were beyond her control. But it is when the priest started questioning her married state and suggested to accept widowhood that Bala left home, determined to find her husband and come back with him.

Bala undertook a long and arduous journey to Poona. How she reached there, how she survived the hardships faced on her way, what happened to her parents and also to Viswa's parents, all remained a mystery. On this matter, Narayan's grandmother had no answer. However, in Poona she was exhausted of all her gold and cash and was left with nothing, and therefore felt terrified and lonely. Luckily she came across an elderly Marathi lady who took her to give shelter. Unable to understand her language, Bala explained in gesticulation her miserable situation in life. Coming to know that she was from Madras, the lady sent her to the only 'Madrasi' she knew. That man turned out to be her husband, Viswa who now known as Bhatji and married to a lady of means Surma Bai, had established himself as a respected and prospering diamond merchant and an official at the Peswa's Court. Using her shrewdness Bala got an entry into his house, in fact, with the help of Surma who was kind-hearted and had no inkling of the matter relating to her husband and Bala. They had become good friends, but Bala took advantage of this intimacy and reached Viswa, who, at first, refused to recognize her, but could not do so for long. Bala put pressure on him to go back home with her. Biswa was not ready to leave either Surma or his business after all those years. Bala then adopted means of deceit and coercive tactics and finally succeeded to take him back to her village, without ever condescending to Surma's pleas to let her accompany them and live with them. This was followed by a long and happy married life for Biswa and Bala in Kumbakonam, a place near the village, where Biswa established himself as a gem expert and where five children were born to them. The next few pages describe Bala's death, Biswa's next marriage to the seventeen year old daughter of a woman appointed as the caretaker of their house at Kumbakonam, and finally his death under mysterious circumstances.

In the last phase of Biswa's life, when he was seventy-five, he was living in Kolar with his son and his family. He was happy as long as things continued to his satisfaction. But when for some practical reasons arrangements among them were altered, he became resentful. He went back to Kumbakonam and then married the caretaker's daughter in a quiet simple ceremony conducted by the woman who managed to get a priest from her village. "It was a culmination of his rage against his son. He could think of no better way to assert his independence" (91). But soon he found himself under the control of the caretaker woman who wanted to be the owner of the house. The old man had some sense left and so did not succumb to her pressure. The greedy and wicked woman, on the advice of the wiseacre of the village, gave him two pills with his food to have full control over him. But that brought an end to his life. His son came to take charge of the situation and his father's assets. They could not know what happened to the caretaker's daughter. Only after speaking to the neighbours, they came to know of the woman's schemes to grab the old man's wealth and property.

In the novel the emphasis is on the tale of Bala and Biswa and not on the set-up in which they lived. Yet, a real and true picture of the social life of the people of the time emerges. The system of child marriage that prevailed at the time, affected adversely the life of young, innocent boys and girls. Both were victims of the system, but the women were wretched. As a reasonable man Narayan had one reservation expressed about his great-grandmother. He would not approve of Bala's manoeuvers to get rid of the other woman, Surma. She was "deep and devious for the poor lady, who had shown so much trust in her, whom she had sheltered and nourished when she was in desperate state, not to mention the years she cared for and protected Viswa who had after all strayed his way to Poona and was literally a tramp at the start " (65). But to an orthodox psyche, like that of his grandmother, all means are justified when a woman's husband is concerned—"To a woman her husband is everything. She can't lose him" (65), says his grandmother. She alludes to the myth of Savitri, for support of her view—Savitri who conquers Yama trapping him to bless her with her husband's life and children, by using her tricks. "You could not imagine a greater woman than Savitri for austerity and purity of mind," (66) she argues.

Narayan shows how a woman's honour depended on her marital status at that time and so she was allowed to adopt any means to ensure her husband's loyalty, sometimes even at the cost of being unjust and inhuman. People turned to myths and legends for support and justification and in the process twisted and misinterpreted them to suit their purpose. Attitude to men was liberal. A man could remarry; even a seventy year old man could marry a girl. However, while most of Narayan's contemporaries throw light on the plight of women in the male dominated society, Narayan shows that women were also the causes of suffering of other women. To do justice to herself and prove her worth as a woman in terms of the norms prescribed by the society, Bala could knowingly deceive Surma and put her to harrowing experiences.

The writer, being a modern and educated person, questions the old values that his grandmother held precious. He could not understand why Surama was punished and humiliated for no fault of hers and why a woman could not behave more humanly and why there should be separate values for men and women. Narayan also shows a geographical reality of the time. Bala, a South Indian girl, finds herself in the strange world among strange people of the Western part of India at a time when massive progress and advancement were not thought of. Narayan also renders Bala's growth from innocent school girl to a firm, determined, aggressive young woman, and in the end, to a quiet, docile, orthodox Hindu wife—her deliberate transition from one phase to another according to the demands of her life.

According to Narayan Chandran, "In refreshing contrast to his Malgudi "characters," the real men and women of Madras, Kumbakonam or Kolar seem as inscrutable and intriguing as those whom we meet and part with in our daily lives."[17] However, Narayan is unable to fix the historical background by any clue or internal evidence for this autobiographical novel. Nor were there particulars of location. The location might be anywhere in the Southern Peninsula. It was just any village having a familiar pattern: a hundred houses scattered in four or five narrow streets, with pillared *verandas* and *pyols*, massive front doors, inner courtyards, situated at the bend of a river or its tributary and the like. No chronological particulars are provided by his grandmother either, except for assuming an arbitrary period—the later period of the East India Company, before the Sepoy Mutiny (8). With these details the story of the Grandmother is set in space and time. Its status lying between the tautness of the short story and the expansiveness of the novel, *Grand Mother's Tale* is more a novelette than a novel, but written towards the end of his career, it is no small achievement.

NOTES

1. K. Venkatachari, 'R.K. Narayan's Novels: Acceptance of Life,' *Indian Literature*, March, 1970: 84-85.
2. C.D Narasimhaiah, 'R.K. Narayan's *The Guide*,' *Aspects of Indian Writing in English*, ed. M.K. Naik. New Delhi: Macmillan, 2007: 177.
3. *Loc. cit.*
4. In this context one remembers that during the making of an English film based on *The Guide*, Narayan, protesting against the distortion of the geography and sociology of his novel, cries, "Although it is a world of fiction, there are certain inner veracities." *The Writerly Life*, 2001: 91. Truly, the inner veracities give credence to his realistic art.
5. It is Graham Greene who suggested to Narayan that the hero of the novel should die at the end. Narayan explains his predicament in *My Days*: "Graham Greene liked the story when I narrated it to him in London. While I was hesitating whether to leave my hero

alive or dead at the end of the story, Graham was definite that he should die. So I have on my hands the life of a man condemned to death before he is born and I have to plan my narrative to lead to it. This becomes a major obsession with me." (2006: 190-91)

Death is the only absolute truth of life. But generally Narayan's works never deal with death as a theme, except for Susila's untimely death in T*he English Teacher* which echoes the poignancy and pain of real life experience and which is rendered quite in detail in the novel. In *The Vendor of Sweets*, however, the death of Jagan's wife is treated as an important event in his life, as it leaves a deep impact on his young son's mind. Otherwise, death does not find a place in his scheme of things. Perhaps, due to that, Narayan has not been able to compromise with the idea to end *The Guide* prescribing death for Raju and rain as its outcome. The novel ends with an ambivalence leaving it for the readers to decide according to their faith and belief.

There is also a reflection of the traditional Indian belief, though not confined to India alone, that prayer or particularly collective prayer can move the gods and bring about rain for the relief of the humanity suffering without rain. In the particular case the belief is that it is the Rain God on whom these activities of nature. A big Indian mass doesn't attribute the phenomena of drought and rain to any scientific cause.

6. Revealing the irony of character and the irony of the situation in the novel L.N. Murty observes: "This has a similitude with the ancient Bhasmasura who killed himself or was made to kill himself by laying his hands on his head in the posture of dance under the supervision of Mohini. In the novel also Rangi acts as an instrument, not intentionally, for the death of Vasu. Just as Bhasmasura wanted to taste the authenticity of the boon on Lord Shiva himself, Vasu, the Bhasmasura of Malgudi, harasses, tantalizes and humiliates Nataraj, oblivious of the fact that he has given him shelter. Most surprisingly, Nataraj is another name for Lord Shiva. Thus this novel has an impeccable affinity to the ancient mythological episode of Bhasmasura. The title suggests a haunting yarn but presents a moral tableau instead. There is irony in this aspect also." 'R.K. Narayan's—*The Man-Eater of Malgudi*,' *Critical Response*

to R.K. Narayan, ed. Amarnath Prasad, New Delhi: Sarup, 2003: 111. Murty fails to note that Nataraj is projected as a typical Malgudian who is afraid to take any responsibility. He is even afraid of his wife who does not like that he will talk to Rangi. Nataraj's inability to take any decisive step shows that he is comfortable only in following the beaten track.

7. P.S. Sundaram appreciates the real world projected in the novel. But he does not make Vasu a citizen of this world. He thinks Vasu belongs to the mythical world. "The pretty tyranny of a Circle Inspector; the way the driver and the bus conductor of the bus can make quick money at the expense of the public obliging them practically to sit on each other, and wasting their time hunting for passengers in by-ways; lawyers arguing irrelevantly till the court rose adding to the law's delay because they earned their fees on a daily basis—these things are certainly bad, and Narayan deals with them in his inimitable fashion. But the way Vasu sets about making himself important and comfortable is of a different order altogether. Only God can deal with such wickedness. And as he came to rescue the elephant caught by crocodile in *Bhagavata Purana* so, when Nataraj calls on Him in the Temple, He comes to the rescue of the temple elephant. The incubus sitting heavily on man, beast and bird is suddenly no more. Malgudi can breathe again." P.S. Sundaram, 1988: 88. Sundaram ignores the ironic twist in Narayan's novel which implies that Vasu cannot be punished by the Malgudians because they are by nature inactive, apathetic and corrupt.
8. Richard Cronin finds in *The Man-Eater of Malgudi* "the most powerful myth of nationhood that India has yet created." He continues, "Indian history is a sequence of invasions—Moghul, British, Chinese. In the face of every invader India seems helpless, and yet it is Indian, apparently so disorganized and so passive that survives, and the invader that somehow or other destroys himself" (*Imagining India*: 26). He further observes that Vasu's entrance—"tearing aside the curtain, an act which violated the saved traditions (of the press)" is suggestive of "a vision of a new India, a vision that violates traditions that Narayan holds sacred" (*Imagining India*: 27). Cronin finds in Vasu an embodiment of a new order

that Narayan associates with Nehru. "With his energy, his disregard for traditional restraints, and his capacity for hard work he builds up his taxidermy business into a thriving international concern. Vasu is the beneficiary of Nehru's Ram Raj, of the new India that Nehru envisages" (28). 'The Indian English Novel: Nations of Fools and *The Man-Eater of Malgudi*,' *Imagining India*, London: Macmillan, 1989: 18-33. Vasu's secular attitude fits in well with Nehru's, but the comparison may not be stretched far. Vasu is projected as an embodiment of materialistic evil.

9. Ved Mehta, 'The Train Had Just Arrived at Malgudi Station,' *The New Yorker, Digital Edition*, September 15, 1962: 70.
10. Mali represents the Western-influenced younger generation and his view on beef-eating is based on what a friend of Narayan's (whom he calls Govind in his *My Dateless Diary*) actually wrote to his political leader, "an austere associate of Mahatma Gandhi." The letter "made it impossible for Govind to look to his master for support if ever he should return to India." *The Writerly Life*, 2001:124-26.
11. Narayan to S. Krishnan, 'A Day With R.K. Narayan,' *Span*, vol.xvi, No.4, Apr., 1975: 40.
12. 'A Thematic Study of *A Tiger for Malgudi*,' *Glimpses of Indo-English Fiction*: *Vol. II*, ed. O.P. Saxena, New Delhi: Jainous, 1985: 173.
13. Bruce King, 'R.K. Narayan, Rev. of *Talkative Man*: A Novel of Malgudi,' *World Literature Today*, Vol.61, No.3, Sum, 1987: 491-92.
14. Mohan Ramanan, R.K. Narayan's World-View in *The World of Nagaraj*, *The Indian Novel with a Social Purpose*, ed. K.Venkata Reddy and P. Bayapa Reddy, New Delhi: Atlantic, 1999: 61.
15. Robert E. McDowell, Rev. of *The World of Nagaraj*, *World Literature Today*, Vol. 65, No.2, Apr., 1991: 367.
16. Ralph J. Crane, Novel No. 14, Rev. of *The World of Nagaraj*, *CRNLE Reviews Journal*, No.1, 1991: 14.
17. K. Narayana Chandran, Rev. of *Grandmother's Tale*, *Studies in Short Fiction*, Vol. 30, No. 4, Fall, 1993: 613.

Narayan's Narrative Art: Technique behind the Tale

It is important to note that the narrative techniques used in R.K. Narayan's novels help him to unmask social reality. The extraordinary charm of the stories told in R.K. Narayan's fictional writings are widely acclaimed, though critics vary in their opinions about his art of storytelling. Most of the critics tend to accept Narayan as a plain storyteller for whom only the story matters. Quoting Graham Greene who describes Narayan's art of fiction-writing as of the 'riskiest kind' holding out no message to be preached and no causes to be promoted, M.N. Srinivas observes, "Everything rested on the kind of characters that were created, and above all, the story itself."[1] Ved Mehta speaks of the magic of his unpretentious, almost unliterary novels[2]. For H.M. Williams is a 'plain storyteller'[3] who hides subtle irony beneath a simple exterior and for Uma Parameswaran he is a storyteller, "nothing less and seldom more."[4] According to R.M. Varma, Narayan's art as a novelist is largely limited to storytelling—as a genial storyteller, Narayan holds his listeners simply spellbound."[5] Interestingly, most of these critics cite Narayan's opinion on his own art to substantiate their views on Narayan. Narayan says, "I'd be quite happy if no more is claimed for me than being just a storyteller. Only the story matters, that's all."[6] In an interview to Ved Mehta, he describes himself as an "inattentive, quick writer who has little sense of style"[7]. In another interview with Stephen R. Graubard, Narayan makes clear that he does not read criticism because he does not want to be self-conscious and does not read much lest he be influenced. He says to convince the interviewer, when he writes he does not know what is coming next. He even does not know the details when he sits down to write, but the details come only when the writing is in progress. "They well up from some depth within me," he says.[8] More than once he has said that with him characters come first and plot only second.[9] In an interview to Naseem Khan, he states that to him the idea of planning a book is abhorrent. "I wouldn't know what is coming ahead, not only where they will end but also how they will progress, until I actually write."[10] To a question of Susan E. Croft as to if he was a very methodical writer, constructing a plan and sketching the characters before beginning, he explains, "I don't have a complete plan, just a broad outline, and the book simply grows."[11]

Some critics are not however deluded into this myth of writing simple stories without bothering about narrative technique. Hence, in their analysis of Narayan they emphasize on Narayan's conscious narrative art. Fakrul Alam, for example, regards Narayan as "a consummate artist who, at his best, displays his mastery over a wide range of narrative devices" (McLeod: 9). According to Rama Kundu, Narayan takes his craft seriously. He uses autobiographical elements following the process of selection, organization and transmutation, and turns those elements into a kind of leitmotifs of art. She further claims that to attain a balance, between reality and art, fact and fiction, he makes conscious use of various devices. She asserts that Narayan's unassuming style, the overtly realistic mode of genial narration flavoured by fine humour conceal his serious use of mythical method[12]. According to Meena Sodhi, Narayan makes use of various devices to co-relate 'the air of reality' with art, to validate the dissimilarity between art and life. Though Narayan appears seemingly innocent of literary technique, he carefully mingles the comic with the sad, providing a philosophical insight into life, and employs a lean, lucid and wonderfully expressive style of writing typically characterized by a lightness of touch[13].

Neither by saying that he is a plain storyteller nor by saying that he is a consummate artist, Narayan's narrative art can be described precisely. His writing is, indeed, not knotted with obscurity, and his plotting uncomplicated, but his craftsmanship as a storyteller is in no way negligible. He is an artist, as Iyengar rightly says, "pure and simple whose canon is of modest bulk"[14]. To quote Cynthia vanden Driesen, "In comparison with the allusive, complex works of some of the acknowledged masters of the modern novel, the novels of R.K. Narayan might not be seen profoundly impressive, particularly at a cursory glance. Their simplicity, however, is more apparent than real."[15] He is, in fact, an artist careful of his craft—an artist who uses narrative techniques according to the demand of the theme of his stories and sees that it does not affect the smooth reading of his work. His art recalls one to Dryden's Maxim—it is an art to conceal art. According to Keith Garebian, Narayan has a special way of making techniques serve content.[16] In fact, Narayan's narrative art is greatly determined by the content in his writings and by his belief that readability is the supreme test for a good novel. The content in Narayan's fictional writings is engagingly realistic. He shows a great deal of courage and self-possession in choosing ordinary, everyday occurrences in the lives of ordinary people as the theme of his stories. He also shows a great deal of talent and truth in keeping his readers interested in and enthralled by such writings. Narayan's preoccupation is with a wide range of human experiences covering all walks of life. He shows a profound awareness of the opposite and complementary facets of such experience—joy and sorrow, success and failure, hopes and frustrations, tradition and modernity etc. The odd and the incongruous, the follies and the nonsense, the tragic and the painful in human life draw his attention too. All these he renders with irony, satire and humour. But his irony is devoid of any derisive sting or harsh indictment. It is not cut-and-dry, but kind and compassionate.

Narayan's art of characterization is significant because, in Narayan, specific characters inspire the telling of the story. Narayan maintains an objectivity and psychological truthfulness in his character portrayal. Operating amidst all contradicting forces of life—tradition and modernity, change and stability—his characters maintain their identity and individuality. Narayan portrays incongruities, follies and vices of human nature with his characteristic irony and produces comic figures, but seldom creates villains. He discovers individual idiosyncrasies but does not invent the absurd. In the vast and teeming population of his world, there appear both saints and scoundrels. Sometimes the scoundrels like Raju (*The Guide*) change to become saints but there are others like Dr. Rann and Ramani who remain incorrigibly corrupt and habitually deceptive. The minor characters like the Adjournment Lawyer in *The Man-Eater of Malgudi*, the old landlord in *Mr. Sampath*, the small shopkeeper in *The Guide* exhibit the incongruities and follies in an exaggerated way. Such exaggeration turns the characters into grotesque figures or caricatures. Narayan's art brings out the characters—both major and minor—vividly in their oddities and angularities. The apparent simplicity and innocence of these characters are due to the human indulgence he extends to them. More significantly however, these characters, despite their distinct identity, are true representatives of their time.

Narayan's use of irony as a literary device enables him to combine seriousness and levity, and thus makes his style different from that of his contemporary realists Mulk Raj Anand and Raja Rao. Anand wrote with all seriousness to provoke pity for the Indian poor, denounce the evils of British rule and capitalist exploitation, to show his indignation at human deprivation and social cruelty, his hatred for class-oppression and caste discrimination in India. He continued with his satirical lash, when he wrote in the post-colonial backdrop, aiming at feudal survivals, corrupt politicians and capitalists, at sexual and social decadence. Anand's narrative technique is full of vitality, thanks to what Iyengar calls the "purposive energy of his narratives" (1983: 357), but there is hardly any humour that makes the story interesting. Raja Rao's serious tone in his novels and short stories, and his idealistic view of life were so much a matter of concern for him that he hardly thought about a narrative style blended with irony and humour. Even the comic elements in his short stories in *Cat and Shakespeare* bear a metaphysical undertone. Narayan, on the other hand, patently shapes his material into a tightly wrought ironic pattern quite in the manner of Fielding and Jane Austen. In fact, irony is ingrained into Narayan's perception. Hence he employs subtle shades of irony as a device, sometimes to dissimulate, sometimes to differentiate between what is asserted and what actually is the case, and sometimes to set the innumerable varieties of life's experiences into ironic contrast. Still "quite often," as Meenakshi Mukherjee rightly puts it, "his irony is nothing but an honest recording of facts, without any colouring of conventional sentiment" (2001: 181). This is clearly seen in his ironic treatment of romantic love—be it Sriram's love for Bharati or Chandran's for Malathi who could fall in love merely by seeing the girls from a distance. Whatever the purpose with which irony is employed in Narayan, it eventually affects satire and humour.

Narayan's mild and harmless satire does not affect the flow of his narrative. It occurs in flashes in a novel or a story to expose a particular trait in a character or situation, or in interpolated passages serving as ironic commentary on some aspects of human conditions or contemporary milieu, and evokes sympathetic laughter which is an end in itself. It does not bear the satiric venom of Swift but combines the good humour of Fielding and P.G. Wodehouse, the wit of Jane Austin, and Chekhov's sense of the tragi-comic. The protagonists in his novels struggle to extricate themselves from the "habitual, dreamy automatism" (Walsh 1992: 38) of their past which in a country like India with its inherited and established system turns out to be an arduous and intense effort. Walsh sees Narayan's comic talent in the portrayal of the various solutions adopted by them in their search for another more conscious life. Yet, he correctly points out that there is no logical division between the serious and the comic in Narayan, for, they flow "in and out of one another throughout in an intricate, inseparable alliance" (1992: 38). Commenting on irony and humour as integral parts of Narayan's narrative technique, William Walsh rightly observes that "Tracts of human experience are looked at with an affectionately ridiculing eye" bringing out the note of the bizarre, of human queerness, in the activities of many sorts of people, and that "At our most commonplace we are all exotic if scrutinized by a fresh eye" (1992: 38).

Narayan does not make any attempt at promoting any social theory (not even in *The Dark Room* or *The Painter of Signs*) or seek any sensational subject or delve into abnormal psychology to make his art distinct and recognizable. However, touching upon a variety of issues—modernization, westernization, caste, prejudice, communalism, injustice to women, gross materialism, corruption and such others—he only shows his awareness of the state of affairs in the society he lives in. Religion is not also obliquely presented through his characters or zealously debated by them. Narayan only depicts ironically the religious attitude of the common Indian mass. He does not share their religious ethos or behaviour although in certain cases as in *The Guide, A Man-Eater of Malgudi, The Vendor of Sweets* and *A Tiger for Malgudi*, his reverence for spirituality or Hindu awareness are impressed upon his readers. For Narayan everything in real life is interrelated: stories, scriptures, ethics, philosophy, grammar, astronomy, semantics, mysticism and moral codes—each is a part and parcel of total life—and therefore, is indispensable for the attainment of a four-square understanding of existence[17]. A detached observer of this life Narayan wishes his work of art to have 'a life of its own independent of its creator' and to keep himself free from the responsibility of his fictional characters[18]. Hence, when he apprehends his characters and their lives, he does not speak—he lets his characters speak for themselves.

In the novels, there are two basic modes in which Narayan's characters speak—the first person and the third person. The first person speaker or narrator is intimate, confiding, explicating, ironic and self-indulgent. The third person speaker or narrator, with the usual intellectual and emotional difference, is objective, ironic, mostly omniscient, wise, bright and sophisticated, but "nonetheless just as indulgent, tolerant of human weakness and individual peculiarities as any self-aware and self-absolving first-person narrator," as says Sita Kapadia (McLeod 1994: 72). In *The English Teacher, The Man-Eater of Malgudi, A Tiger for Malgudi* and *Talkative Man* the first person narrative voice is heard. In *The English Teacher* Narayan uses for the first time the first person narration. It suits his purpose best as the novel is mostly autobiographical. It fictionalized the facts of his life—his blissful married life with Rajam, the tragedy of her untimely death, the responsibility of looking after his only daughter Hema and the final reconciliation with the unmitigated loneliness of life. The beauty of the novel lies in the balance Narayan draws between poignant and sombre recollections and a mildly ironic tone. Krishna, drawn after Narayan, shares his humorous disposition. His ironic comments on Brown, the Principal of his college, his colleagues, and other acquaintances flash his wit and sense of humour. He directs his ironic view even to a chance character, the old woman, who while travelling with his mother, holds out her opinion about marriage and conjugal life: A man must marry within fifteen days of losing his wife. Otherwise he will be ruined. "I was the fourth wife to my husband and he always married within three weeks. All the fourteen children are happy" (99), she says. The indifferent, insensitive remark of outsiders on tragedies of others and the social custom laid down for convenience are brought to sharp ironic focus. In *My Days* he says, "I have described this part of my experience of her (his wife's) sickness and death in *The English Teacher* so fully that I do not, and perhaps cannot, go over it again." (2006: 150)

Yet, he does not agree to the suggestion that Krishna, the hero of the novel, could be identified with him. He is of the opinion that the author and the character were not necessarily in accordance with each other. "Even if it is in the first person, the author assumes the role of a character but remains personally detached."[19] Once the book is completed the author becomes irrelevant. The fact that Narayan had the ability to universalize in his fiction an experience so personal and of such intensity and magnitude, and thereby qualify it as a full-fledged fiction, speaks immensely of his craft as a novelist.

Almost fifteen years after the publication of *The English Teacher* Narayan again used the first person narrative in *The Man-Eater of Malgudi*. The novel shows Narayan's maturing excellence in the use of narrative technique. Though Narayan claims that he has never carefully plotted his novel, this novel is certainly an exception. Everything is wonderfully put together here. Critics like K.R.S. Iyengar, Meenakshi Mukherjee, Edwin Gerow, P.S. Sundaram and William Walsh have pointed out, and rightly too, that *The Man-Eater of Malgudi* has a definite sustained mythical structure, and is allegorical in nature. Narayan introduces the Bhasmasura myth to the novel and draws a broad mythical parallel to the plot involving Nataraj and Vasu. The mythical design is used to create a world which seemingly moves around a pattern of order, dislocation of order and restoration of order. The character of Vasu runs parallel to the character of Bhasmasura, the rakshasa of the myth. Vasu, the modern-day Rakshasa, brings in disorder to the ordered world of Malgudi. At the end, he is destroyed by his own arrogant power: like a typical demon he carries the seed of his own destruction. His death is supposed to bring back order in Malgudi. Critics often emphasize upon 'the undercurrent of serious intention' in the employment of the mythical structure. As P.S. Sundaram says, Narayan is concerned in this novel with cosmic issues: good, evil, man, demon and God (1988: 83). Meenakshi Mukherjee even argues that the puranic or archetypal pattern of order-disorder-order that is established through this novel is actually repeated in all his novels, and she surmises that it operates unconsciously because it is a part of his world-view (2001: 143-44). It is true that the mythic parallel serves to anticipate Vasu's ultimate destiny. But it is wrong to read the story as a moral fable reinforcing a world-view that is rigidly Hindu. On the contrary, Narayan's perception of a discrepancy between the ludicrous realm of *The Man-Eater of Malgudi* and the sublime realm of the Bhasmasura myth is the basis of this comedy. Vasu's self-annihilation is accidental and ironic, unlike that of Bhasmasura which is manoeuvered by no less than Lord Vishnu. Even P.S. Sundaram acknowledges, "This is not only philosophically right but also artistically satisfying. It is well contrived and carefully prepared" (1988: 88). It is curious to note that order is not restored to Malgudi immediately after the destruction of Vasu, though it is supposed to be so in a story based on myth where the destruction of the demon presupposes restoration of peace and order. Ironically enough, the Malgudians are not relieved that Vasu who disturbed the environment so much is dead, but are disturbed with the thought that Nataraj might have killed Vasu. As long as Nataraj is suspected to have murdered Vasu, the Malgudians are ill at ease, because murder as a means to an end is not accepted in the world of Malgudi. Only after the real cause of Vasu's death comes to light—Sastri discloses the fact that he was killed while slapping with his iron-fist mosquitoes that sat on his forehead—order is believed to be back in Malgudi. Until then Nataraj suffers isolation and humiliation. Narayan's characteristic irony is directed at this typical Indian attitude—the attitude of interpreting everything as work of fate and of avoiding individual responsibility. Indians live their entire life with the philosophy that whatever is fated must be endured, and that life would take its own course. Moreover the Malgudians take for granted the maladies that affect the society—corruption, greed, human exploitation, loss of moral value etc.—because these form a part of their ordered existence. Vasu's wickedness is new to them and so they are unable to handle it. Only God can deal with such wickedness, they believe. This world is the source of all Narayan's irony, satire and humour[20].

Irony also operates through Narayan's delineation of individual characters and their life in Malgudi. The first person narrator Nataraj sets the comic tone as he describes the nature of his profession, his ablutionary routine, his indolent friends, Sastri, Sen and the Poet—all who set the so-called order in Malgudi and his demonic foe, Vasu, who breaks that order. He is meek, passive and has little power to influence events. Everyone takes advantage of him and Vasu sneers at his circumscribed outlook. He is frightened to deal ruthlessly with complications that arise due to his indecision, procrastination and misplaced benevolence. He cannot even think of anything substantial to get rid of Vasu. Narayan's comic vision exposes the gap between what is expected from a reasonable person and what exactly is done by Nataraj. For instance, Nataraj asserts that he has all sorts of wonderful and effective plans in his mind but cannot show them as the 'blue-prints' of these plans are not yet ready. He thinks of going stealthily to Vasu's room and shoots him from behind and 'save everyone all the worry and trouble of argument.' But the next moment he retracts:

> Not practicable. One might talk of finishing off a cobra with a staff of bamboo, but it was always more likely that the cobra would prove smarter. Vasu might after all not be facing the window, but facing the door. Non-violence would be the safest policy with him. Mahatma Gandhi was right in asking people to carry on their fight

> with the weapon of non-violence; the chances of getting hurt were much less. (163)

His observation makes a mockery of Gandhiji's non-violence theory which is used by a spineless and non-decisive man for justifying his own weakness and timidity.

During the temple festival, instead of taking any step to protect the animal, Nataraj makes a loud appeal to the God to save the temple elephant, Kumar from Vasu's vicious plan to kill him. Amidst the noisy celebration he creates a scene by letting out a terrific cry:

> 'Oh, Vishnu'! I howled. 'Save our elephant, and save all the men and women who are going to pull the chariot. You must come to our rescue.' (139)

Nataraj evades reality by taking refuge in the world of myth. In his final encounter with Vasu, Nataraj is shown in a funnier light. He begins his journey to Vasu's place with courageous plans to confront him but ends up guarding the whole night only a dead Vasu from doing anything. He knows that he has not killed Vasu. But when he is suspected for the murder he even begins to imagine it as true. "If I have rid the world of Vasu, I have achieved something," he says, "I hardened myself with such reflections, and suffered at the same time" (179).

Narayan's skill lies in making such a person the narrator protagonist of his novel. Everything in the novel is seen through the dubious eyes of this narrating character. He is very different from the author-narrator of *The English Teacher*. He is rather close to what is called 'the fallible or unreliable narrator'—a narrative tactic used to cut across diverse points of view. His interpretation and evaluation of matters do not coincide with the implicit belief and values held by the author which the author expects to share with his readers. One cannot agree with Keith Garebian when she says that with "Vasu's death by a blow aimed at mosquitoes sitting on his forehead the story loses its force and shrivels to the level of a melodramatic recreation of the Bhasmasura legend. It is as if Narayan felt compelled to squeeze his story into a mould pre-established by mythology "21. She finds in the plot a collision between realism and fabulism and observes a mechanical design of a mythical formula which the plot cannot support. But in reality the Bhasmasura myth serves the purpose of structural irony and makes the novel persistently or even totally ironic. An analysis of the structural irony used in the novel helps one to see the 'melodramatic' happenings from Narayan's comic-ironic vision.

In *A Tiger for Malgudi* the first person narrator is the tiger named Raja. The novel is about the spiritual journey of his life starting from his wild days at the jungle to the humiliating and rigorous training at the hands of the captain of Grand Malgudi Circus and then to the spiritual care of his Master, an ascetic, and finally to the protective retirement of the zoo. Raja is intelligent, sensitive like human beings. And spiritualized by the mysterious powers of his Master, he is able to communicate on human level. Though written apparently on the model of fables, Narayan's choice of a tiger as the narrator-protagonist unfolds a unique design of irony and comedy that commands the readers' attention till the end of the story. Narayan prepares his readers with a solemn note to accept the miracle of the spiritual transformation of a tiger as the central theme. Keeping in mind the Indian psyche that is reared in a tradition of the *Vedanta*, the *Upanishads*, the *Panchatantra* and the *Jataka tales*, Narayan prepares the ground to establish credibility. The tiger unfolds the drama dealing with the manager, a film shooter and the Swamiji, and simultaneously opens up the old comic but real world of Malgudi—the world inhabited by people like the Headmaster, the Assistant Headmaster, and Alphonse who expose issues of bribery, corruption, redtapism etc. This world, however, is confined to the periphery of the narrative, only tangential to the central theme.

The tiger shares the author's comic vision, and, therefore, as he sees the world of men and animals in hindsight he assumes an ironic and satiric tone. He sees how both men and animals enjoy power frenziedly and indiscreetly without ever realizing their own vulnerability and fragility. At the circus, the Captain, drunk with authority, poses as invincible to a tiger, caged and famished. Inside the circus the tiger sees men from one angle. But outside the circus, when the tiger runs through the market he sees another face of the truth. "I got a totally wrong notion of human beings at that angle. I had thought that they were sturdy and fearless. But now I found them fleeting before me like a herd of deer, although I had no intention of attacking them," he says (116). He notices how greed and gradual corruption come over the Captain during his association with the film world. The shallow and frivolous film world comes under his satiric observation too.

The film-maker's views on aesthetics actually reveal his commercial outlook and the shallowness of the film world. He says that "I always take care to see that when my picture goes up for the censor's certificate it is seen only by the male members on the panel" (81) because women are likely to be squeamish. "All the sentimentalists' outcry against the so-called sex and violence must be ignored. They make too much out of it. Life is created and made possible only through sex and violence, no use fighting against it, shutting one's eyes to the facts of life" (8), he says and reveals the attitude of sensationalizing the theme of sex and violence for pure commercial purposes. There is no story or an outline of a story on which the film on the tiger is to be based. The filmmaker first decides the ingredients to be incorporated in the story and the script is written accordingly. The tiger records the entire ridiculous incident telling how the hero, Jaggu, comes out ready for the shot—"properly painted and costumed, his hair done up in proper style" (93). A satisfied filmmaker comments,

> An hour or more wasted because of the moustache. I don't know where they got the idea from—our mythology, I suppose! Jaggu is not a demon. . . . We must establish him as a normal human being. Any character with whiskers repels—particularly women and children. . . . the audience's sympathy must be established first—and he (Polanski) has statistics to show that between a character with hair on his lip and one clean-shaven, the latter gains more sympathy." (94)

Through the observations of the tiger Narayan ridicules the way films are made. The real factors that inspire the film-makers ultimately end up in creating an unreal world with unreal happenings.

In the novel there is a long and dragging scene describing the funny and vain attempts of the gunman Alphonse to save the Malgudians from the tiger. Alphonse is the symbol of corruption, vanity, falsehood and frivolity. With Narayan's personal brand of humour and satire, not only the follies of Alphonse but also maladies like bribery, red-tapism, and lack of understanding in man-woman relationships come under scrutiny. Verbal irony is used to expose hypocrisy and manipulative nature of man. The novel is more in tune with Orwell's political and social satire than Aesop's fable. Critics read deeper meaning into it, yet the irony and humour is not lost at any point in this political and social satire.

Narayan's archetypal Indian Talker reappears after a long time in *Talkative Man* and talks with a reassuring sense of familiarity and makes the readers feel happy. He says honestly 'I cannot contain myself.' He is a compulsive, born storyteller.

> My impulse to share an experience with others is irresistible, even if they sneer at my back. I don't care. I'd choke if I don't talk, perhaps like sage Narada of our epics, who for all his brilliance and accomplishments carried a curse on his back that unless he spread a gossip a day, his skull would burst. (1)

The author performs the difficult task of maintaining objectivity while exposing the follies and vices of the society through the protagonist. At the same time the narrator is also ridiculed and laughed at, thanks to the writer's comic vision. Sharing the author's sense of humour the protagonist draws the odd and eccentric in the characters of his stories. For example, he tells the story of Dr. Rann, emphasizes his odd looks, outlandish habits and his philandering, and he also tells of his odd-looking wife and her funny husband-hunting acts. Just as Rann installs himself as Talkative Man's non-paying tenant, his wife, another intruder in the world of Malgudi, arrives to create flutter with her menacing looks—a six-foot woman as it seems at first sight, dark-complexioned, cropped head, and in jeans and a T-shirt with bulging breasts, the first of her kind in the Malgudi area (39), and "commanding manner" (40). Deciding to protect Rann from wifely intrusions, Talkative Man first denies her any knowledge of the whereabouts of her deserter and errant husband, and suggests that she must look for him in Madras. At the same time he enjoys Rann's discomfiture in hiding. He desires a kind of self-satisfaction for being his benefactor and is happy to get a flattering promise to have his patronage acknowledged in the book Rann is writing. But very soon the situation is reversed. Rann's wife arrives at his house on the Kabir Street and reduces him to a silenced listener and raises herself to be the talker—Rann's wife the Ancient Mariner and him the waylaid Wedding Guest. This provides the biggest irony to the novel. Talkative Man is found in a situation that is strangely ambivalent—on the one hand he has his autonomy, authority, routine, independence undermined and compromised by Rann and his wife and he resents their arrogance, but on the other hand his association with them gives him a welcome sense of self-satisfaction. The confusion that arises from this becomes the source of humour and fun. Humour also arises from the ironic clash between the conventional elements and the ultra modern ones.

Grandmother's Tale is the tale of how the storyteller gets his grandmother to tell him the story of her mother. It begins with first person narration echoing the content of *My Days*. The story told by his grandmother, however, is related in the third person. A blending of the first person and the third person narratives offers a unique charm to the narrative technique. The details of his great grandmother's marriage in her childhood, the short meetings with her husband who was then a schoolboy, his sudden disappearance after telling his girl wife that he was leaving, the gossip that he must be dead and she must behave as a widow, the priest's advice to her mother in regard to her daughter's behaviour and finally the search of her husband are recorded through third person narrator, who takes the liberty of putting direct speech on the mouth of the characters concerned. The dramatic presentation is followed by the grandmother's observation,

> Bala must have gone to the village cart-stand in the field beyond the last street, where travellers and bullock carts assembled. Bala must have paid for a seat in a carriage, travelled all night and reached a nearby town. Even in her hurry, before leaving home she did not forget to pack a small bag with a change of clothes, some money she had saved out of her birthday and other gifts, a few gold ornaments, and above all a knife in case she had to protect her honour and end her life. At the town she stayed in a choultry where an assortment of travellers and pilgrims was lodged. Her mind harped on a single word: Pandharpur. She made constant enquiries of everyone she came across and set forth in that direction. After many false starts, she got on the right track and joined travellers going on foot or by some mode of transport and reached Poona about a year later. (34)

Then there comes an interruption through the writer's conversation with his grandmother.

> My grandmother's account had many gaps from this point onward. How Bala survived, what happened to her mother and where was her father all the while? What happened to Viswa's parents?

> Above all, why did she go to Poona to search for her husband? What led her steps to Poona? These questions never got an answer. My grandmother only snapped: "Why do you ask me? Am I a wizard to see the past? If you interrupt me like this, I'll never be able to complete the story. I can only tell you what I have heard from my mother. I just listened, without interrupting her as you do now. If you don't shut your mouth and keep only your ears open. I'll never tell you anything more. You can't expect me to know everything. If you want all sorts of useless information about the past, I cannot help you." (34-35)

The interlocutions and interruptions between the two narrators as well as the author's comments in between to establish the truth of the events narrated by his grandmother provide another paradigm for Narayan's poetics, so to say. Most importantly, the Grandmother, like Talkative Man, as a storyteller exemplifies Narayan's own ideals of storytelling. There is a novelty about the narrative technique that establishes him as a modern craftsman.

In a fiction the first person narrator could either be the central character in the story taking part in the action or a fortuitous witness of the matters he relates or a minor peripheral participant in the story. Narayan uses the first person narrator as the central character speaking for himself as well as for others from his point of view. His point of view is naturally limited to what he knows, experiences, infers, or finds out through his interaction with other characters. The third person narrator on the other hand is wise and omniscient, understanding and indulgent. He is someone outside the story speaking about one character or all the characters. He knows everything about the characters—their thoughts and actions, their overt speech and inner feelings. He is entirely free to move in time and place, to shift from character to character as he pleases. Narayan's omniscient third person narrator is not intrusive and is impersonal who withholds his comments, and judgements. He is witty and ironic, detached and impartial. In Narayan's early novels, narrative mode is more or less traditional—straight and chronological. The story of irresponsible boyhood in *Swami and Friends* or of romantic love in *The Bachelor of Arts* or of an ill-fated marriage in *The Dark Room* is told with remarkable ease, objectivity and restraint. Narayan portrays Indian sensibilities with all fidelity. Pathos and poignant emotion are combined with irony and humour. These novels are marked by their quality of concentration that allows no digression or diversion from the central theme. *Swami and Friends*—consisting of a series of episodes, fastened by a single thread that establishes a logical connection from the first line to the last—is a bright example of Narayan's mastery over his art. The comic sets the tone of the entire novel.

In the novel Swami shares the instinctive comic attitude of the writer and sees the absurdities and incongruities in things and even the most trivial and unnoticeable things tickle him to death. Seen through his eyes all characters and all events assume comic proportions. To Swami, both his teachers—the fire-eyed Vedanayagam, and the fanatical scripture teacher, Ebenzer—appear ridiculous and grotesque. Vedanayagam's face appears peculiar with his eyes too near each other, and there is much hair on his chin than one sees from the bench. Ebenzer makes himself a comic figure when he discharges his job as a scripture teacher: "Tears rolled down Ebenzer's cheeks—when he pictured Jesus before him. Next moment his face became purple with rage as he thought of Sri Krishna." (4)

The tyranny of Swami's father, Swami's passionate involvement in the game of cricket, the adult-seriousness with which he and his friends launch their cricket club, a child's dismay at his grandmother's 'appalling ignorance' about the game of cricket—all this is narrated with Narayan's characteristic irony and humour. Narayan uses frequent verbal irony to bring out the genial humour and irresistible fun involved in the simple and innocent world of the children. The episode relating to the protest against the arrest of some Gouri Shankar leading to the burning of foreign goods, the pelting of stones at school building by the students has a lot to say about the mood of the public towards colonial rule, yet the vain protest carries in it a strong element of the comic.

Chandran's observation of his professors at the Albert Mission College, in *The Bachelor of Arts*, is as funny and amusing as that of Swami. Mr. Gajapathi, 'the Elephant Master,' has earned the hatred of the students by his teaching and of his colleagues by his conceits (24). Chandran is amused to imagine the formidable Mr. Raghabachar without his spectacles, the turban, and the long-coat, but with his loin-cloth only, in which he "would lose three quarters of his appearance" (26). Though Chandran has a good sense of humour to see the funny and amusing traits in others, he, being a young romantic lover, undergoes the ironic treatment of the author. The entire episode of the one-sided love affair of Chandran with Malathi leading to frustration and temporary sanyasi hood, followed by the ecstasy and bliss of marriage with Susila, ridicules the fanciful and volatile romantic love. When his one-sided love affair with Malathi ends in despair as his marriage plans never materializes, he feels, "It would be impossible for him to live again in that hell" (102). He leaves home for Madras where he takes recourse to sanyasi hood. But, ironically, soon he outgrows his infatuation only to fall in love again with Susila with similar passion and impatience.

> For the rest of the journey the music of the word "Susila" rang in his ears. Susila, Susila, Susila. Her name, music, figure, face and everything about her was divine. Susila, Susila—Malathi not a sport beside Susila; it was a tongue-twister; he wondered why people liked that name. (162)

Apart from romantic love, Chandran's futile and temporary rebellion against social customs and beliefs, parental authority, the whimsical ways of his teachers etc.—all natural for a boy of his age—become the butt of Narayan's irony. The most ironic is Chandran wearing a shaven pate and ochre loin cloth and declaring himself a sanyasi—one who has "renounced the world," "untouched by its joys and sorrows" (107). The villagers at the Kopal village welcome him reverently to whom it never occurs to doubt. "They were innocent and unsophisticated, in most matters (excepting their factions and fights), and took on ascetic's make-up at its face value" (110). They force him to stay with them, supplying him with food and gifts. Chandran, however, leaves the place silently and comes back home in his natural self feeling like "a cad and a fraud, a confidence trickster" who has neither earned nor by virtue of spiritual worth, deserved" anything (111). The irony and humour, aimed at asceticism which is most often superficial and meant to dupe others' credulity, is sharp and pungent.

The Dark Room which follows a simple, straightforward third person narrative is essentially a tragic story. Yet it has its moments of lively humour. The darker shades of life, the sombre and the pathetic, centre mostly on Savitri. The other characters like Ramani, Gangu, Janamma, Shanta Bai, Mari and Ponni are treated with Narayan's obvious and well-defined irony. The pomp, vanity, immorality, and male chauvinism of Ramani, even his show of love for Savitri and his attempt to seduce Shanta Bai are caricatured to be disapproved of. The episode involving Mari, Ponni and Savitri is not only the most hilarious part of the novel but also the most redeeming one. Mari, the burglar with his innocence and simplicity, follows his own code of conduct—"Opening a lock in the correct manner, and locking a house again when leaving it, was, Mari felt a piece of courtesy which a man owed the absent householder" (99). The scene describing Savitri's rescue by Mari and the kind-hearted, straight-forward, strong but uncouth Ponni's handling of her husband provides the much needed comic relief in this serious story of Narayan. However, Saviri's plight due to her husband's betrayal, her helplessness and utter dependence on her husband, her struggle to be self-sufficient and the final realization of her limitations as a woman are poignantly but ironically rendered—the irony giving out a sense of the tragic.

Narayan's irony is seen to have grown sharper and subtler with time. Hence M.K. Naik observes that in later novels that Narayan's irony makes "a giant leap from irony as weapon to irony as vision, from irony of brief moment to irony of the great occasion, from ironic filigree to ironic architectonics, from intermittent irony to integral irony, from local irony arising desultory out of amused superior insight to universal irony informing the entire action as a total serio-comic vision of a man's fate."[23]

As a result Narayan's later novels use complex narrative mode built up to support his maturing comic genius and deepening ironic vision. As an example, the technique of more or less immediate transmission of autobiographical and biographical events and characters becomes a new method which throws these elements into new combinations, refashioning them according to the novel's theme and modifying them to fit the particular context. With the exception of *Mr. Sampath* which has two central characters, other novels of Narayan are marked by the dominance of one central character. Nearly all his books designate the 'hero' in the title—either by name—*Swami and Friends, Mr. Sampath, The World of Nagaraj,*—or by his profession—*The Bachelor of Arts, The English Teacher, The Financial Expert, The Guide, The Vendor of Sweets, The Painter of Signs, Talkative Man* etc. The definite article in the second category particularized the character. Hence, Raju is not a stereotyped representative of guide in general, but an individual. In the later novels, the situations, which the characters find themselves in, emerge under the impact of some uncontrollable forces like craving for money, power and indulgence in lustful sex etc. In such situations "farces and tragic-comedies are played without end" (Iyengar 1983: 373). Narayan brings into sharper focus these realities by subtle and complicated use of the devices of comic irony, and makes a holistic approach to life

Mr. Sampath witnesses the hallmark of Narayan's narrative art—the metamorphosis of facts from real life into a fictitious form. Narayan's experience as an editor undergoes a metamorphosis to describe the experiences of his protagonist, Srinivas. Srinivas's 'The Banner' is shown to be as unsuccessful and baffling as Narayan's 'Indian Thought.' The model for the comic villain in this novel is a real life person from Mysore with the same name, Sampath. The novel falls sharply into two parts which are described by Walsh as the novel's 'double structure' (1992: 62). The first part revolves around Srinivas and his life as the editor of *The Banner*. Sampath is the central character of the second part. Sampath appears in the first part and Srinivas continues to be there in the second part and thus, the link is established to make the two parts an organic whole. However, they have their roles reversed in the two parts. Comparisons and contrasts in respect of characters and context give rise to a variety of tones in the novel, intensely serious to the deliriously comic. The novel is about the comic involvements of Srinivas in the affairs of Sampath. And there is drawn into it the story of Ravi and his sad infatuation, with an undertone of the tragi-comic. Srinivas edits 'The Banner,' while Sampath prints it. Srinivas puzzles over the futility of human existence as he writes the editorial and Sampath good-naturedly shoulders all the financial burdens. Suddenly the newspaper folds cover. But circumstances do not foil Sampath's spirit. Soon he gets involved with Sunrise Film Productions and makes Srinivas write film scripts. But Sampath's unwise handling of the glamorous life leads to absurd and hilarious confusion and chaos. The inaugural ceremony of the film studio, and the shooting of song and dance sequence, and the distortion of myth in the film script—many such authentically drawn comic incidents stuff the story. After much deliberation Sampath and his team pick "the mythological story of "The

Burning to Ashes of Kama—God of Love" for their film script. They prefer a mythological story with romance in it to a story based on a social issue like caste discrimination with a message of Gandhi. Romance, according to them, has the scope for engaging a lady as the leading actor. Srinivas reads a 'symbolic meaning' in 'the representation of the power of love, its equipment, its limitations'—and sees in the burning of Kama, an act of sublimation whereas Somu, a member of Sampath's team, sees a different advantage in the story. As he says, "there is any amount of love in the story, and people will like it. Personally, also, I never like to read any story if it has no love in it" (101). Sampath being practical in this business chooses to "move on safe ground" (99). Srinivas's dilemma is whether to treat the story as a story of normal human beings or of mythological characters. The end result is the mangling of the ancient story beyond recognition. The ridiculous way in which Sampath and his friends attempt to make a film ends disastrously for all during the shooting of the dance act with its peculiar and funny mixture of Indian and Western elements.

Narayan's skill as a narrator is perceived in his rendering of his protagonist as unaware of the long term consequences of his action. Sometimes the protagonist fails to apprehend a real object which is known to the readers. Laughter arises out of a sudden perception of the incongruity between a concept and a real object. With his set of new techniques Narayan delves beneath the surface realism to have an access to his characters' inner life. His later novels especially *The Financial Expert, The Guide, The Vendor of Sweets, The Painter of Signs, The World of Nagaraj* reflect the use of such techniques. In these novels the story is presented by omniscient narrators while focalization is done through the central characters like Margayya, Jagan, Raman, Nagaraj and the like.

In all these cases the narrator is different from the character whose point of view orients the narrative-perspective. Therefore,

Fakrul Alam says, "Narayan takes full advantage of the infinite flexibility enjoyed by an omniscient narrator while retaining many of the privileges of the first person narrator" (McLeod 1994: 11). Narayan uses 'impersonalized dramatic projection' (McLeod: 11), preferring not to come between the narrative and the reader. He presents the events dramatically, so that a sense of immediacy is created, and the readers get personally involved in the stories. Thus, *Mr. Sampath* starts with "Unless you had an expert knowledge of the locality you could not reach the offices of 'The Banner'" (1), and continues with a full picture of the locality in which it is situated. Similarly, *The World of Nagaraj* begins with, "Nagaraj fancied himself a man with a mission. If you asked 'What is your mission' he would look away and pretend not to have heard your query" (1). *The Financial Expert* begins with "The emergence of Margayya was an unexpected and incalculable offshoot of a co-operator's zeal. This statement will be better understood if we watch him in his setting a little more closely" (1). *The Vendor of Sweets* begins with a dramatic note, "Conquer taste, and you will have conquered the self," said Jagan to his listener, . . . The listener lost interest in the question; his aim was only to stimulate conversation" (7). The third person narrator offers descriptions of the background or information about a character's life to show things in their true light. For instance, *The Financial Expert* begins with an introduction to Margayya and his money-making business—"From time immemorial people seemed to have been calling him 'Margayya'"; *The Vendor of Sweets* after a dramatic beginning describes Jagan—"He had an outlook of a disembodied soul floating above the grime of this earth. At fifty-five his appearance was slight and elfish, his broken skin was translucent, his brow receded gently into a walnut shade of baldness, and beyond the fringe his hair fell in a couple of speckled waves on his nape" (8-9), and so it continues. Even in these occasions Narayan attempts to involve readers in the action, and provides those details which enable them to 'watch him in his setting a little more closely.'

Narayan's narrative style compels the readers to develop sympathy and understanding for the man in question. He adopts a technique which Fakrul Alam calls 'internal focalization' (McLeod 1994: 12). For 'internal focalization, Narayan employs devices like free indirect speech, direct speech and something resembling interior monologue or stream-of-consciousness technique, and flashbacks, flash forwards. Sometimes there are a number of passages which employ all these devices together. It seems that Narayan's goal in such passages is to capture the flow of a character's mental process and to stimulate the mixture of memories, expectations, feelings, obligations, and random associations that constitute man's working consciousness.

In *The Vendor of Sweets*, one comes across Jagan's frequent and long internal discourses. After he decides to leave everything behind for Mali and retire and go in search of peace, he is assailed by a variety of thoughts and feelings. For instance, he thinks of Grace whom Mali may send back if he spurns his father's suggestion and decides not to marry her. Other thoughts also force themselves in.

> He felt hurt at the recollection as if a needle had probed a wound. "I have probably outlived my purpose in this house. If I live for ten or fifteen years more, it will have to be on a different plane. At sixty, one is reborn and enters a new janma." That was the reason why people celebrated their sixtieth birthdays. He remembered his father and mother, his uncle and aunt, and a score of other couples celebrating a man's sixtieth year like a wedding, with pipe, drum and feasting. People loved to celebrate one thing or another all the time. He had had his fill of these festivals, and had nothing to complain of. Mali had proved that there was no need for ceremonials, not even the business of knotting the thali around the bride's neck. Nothing, no bonds or links or responsibility. Come together, live together, and kick each other away when it suited them. Whoever kicked harder got away first kick? Where was the kick? They

> sat in a green car with their legs intertwined in spite of what they had said of each other. (175)

Almost in a similar way, in *The Painter of Signs* one gets a glimpse of Raman's overactive imagination when he is imagining Daisy going to the Superintendent of Police to lodge complaint against him:

> He was, of course, familiar with the superintendent of police, a friendly man who gave him a nod when they met at the market fountain, where he sometimes came to watch a procession or a political demonstration. Couldn't call him his friend, but knew him. Would that man entertain any complaint from Daisy? On the other hand it was possible there would be a knock on the door, and he'd be marched down Ellaman Street in handcuffs, the neighbours and the customers at the Chettiar shop standing around, gaping and nudging each other and commenting, "A sign-board painter, after all, should have known his place."
>
> "What a woman to pick up a fellow like that and encourages him and now goes and complains to the police? She can't be all that innocent." (107-8)

The central characters of Narayan's novels are not necessarily the only centre of attention. Other characters, though minor, are found in the background of action, and they play their roles in revealing the minds and motives of other important characters. In *The Financial Expert*, Margayya's wife Meenakshi is also provided with Narayan's variant of the interior monologue letting readers enter into her consciousness and letting her opinions of Margayya or of Balu be unravelled.

> 'Don't abuse me father,' said the boy, whose voice had recently become gruff. It had lost, as his mother noticed, much of the original softness. The more she saw him, the more she was reminded of her own father in his younger days; exactly the same features, the same gruffness, and the same severity. People had been afraid to speak to his father even when he was in the sweetest temper, for his face had a severity without any relation to his mood. She saw

> the same expression in the boy's face now. The boy's look was set and grim. His lips were black with cigarettes which she knew he smoked; he often smelt of them when he came home. . . . But she kept this secret knowledge to herself since she didn't like to set up her husband against him. She understood that the best way to attain some peace of mind in life was to maintain silence. (112)

Similarly, in *The World of Nagaraj*, Nagaraj is seen through his wife's point of view.

> She felt disturbed, having mostly known him as vivacious and talkative. Now his silence seemed unnatural. The only other occasion on which he remained moody was when his mother was laid up, years ago, with a fractured hip; and another time, earlier, when Tim was carried away in the tempo van on the day the brothers separated. Of course, other occasions were minor ones when they had arguments on domestic matters. But today, thinking back, Sita felt she had done nothing to upset him. In her turn she became introspective while cutting some vegetables for dinner. (77)

Narayan's narrator moves deftly in and out of the mind of his characters. He skillfully manipulates narrative perspectives and utilizes techniques to suit his thematic concern. It is done so effortlessly and naturally that he seems to have taken no trouble in devising such technique.

The Financial Expert is a real achievement as a comic fiction. There is a concentration of comic effect in this novel achieved through a strange mixture of the sad and the solemn with the light and the joyful. The irony and satire is directed mainly at the gross materialism of the new age which has made its mark in the idyllic Malgudi. Margayya belongs to a time when everyone is busy making money in all sorts of ways. There is the rice merchant who black-markets the hoarded rice in a secret godown, "whose frontage was stuffed with innocent looking rag and old paper collected from the paper mills' ' (158). There is the man who supplies office ghee to the army and hoards enough cash by showing a joint stock firm with imaginary partners. Another merchant supplies screws in cartons only half-filled, a contractor who builds huts and gets enormous bills passed by bribing the friendly Garrison Engineer. There are the drug stockists who bargain even when it is a matter of life and death to a customer. There are military men with pensions and go-betweens and busy-bodies who could secure contact at New Delhi for a consideration, and there are people who could manage export and import priority. There are people who disclose a small part of their earnings to pay income-tax returns and keep the rest hidden. The town is raking with such people and Margayya is to attract their money for deposits. Like others of his generation he is mean, ignoble, bullying and superstitious, and has a mad craving for money.

The picture of Margayya under a banyan tree with his entire business equipment contained in a grey, discoloured tin box stands in complete contrast to the proudest building in Malgudi known as the Central Cooperative Land Mortgage Bank. The Bank with its strong Victorian-British emphasis on self-help and thrift on one hand, and Margayya with his money-lending business to those sitting before him as supplicants on the other, set the ironic tone from the very beginning. His strange drive for money—his God, his religion, his worship—makes him look a little better than a caricature. Graham Greene describes him as the sad ambitious absurd financial expert (Introduction) and Iyengar describes him as well as the other characters of the novel as 'a little better than caricatures.' His character and action comes under sharp ironic scrutiny when in his desperate desire to amass quick wealth, he tries to propitiate the Goddess of wealth, and when he comes under the spell of Dr. Pal by agreeing to publish his 'Bed Life' and earn huge money. This is followed by a sequence of comic involvements with Madan Lal, the printer, and Guru Raj, the fly chasing blanket man. The element of irony grows, as his obsession for money grows and with it grows his illusion that money is the source of all happiness. He undertakes various ambitious and successful ventures and fulfils the dreams of his life. But in a moment of honest indignation he makes an enemy of Dr. Pal, his only accomplice on his way to opulence. Ironically the same person becomes the cause of his ruins. Life takes a full circle for Margayya. His last act of ironic importance is to rehearse his son in the act of luring peasants into borrowing outside the Central Co-operative Land Mortgage Bank. His reduction to penury does not alter or refine him just as his elevation to wealth has not altered or improved him.

Margayya is absurdly ambitious about his son too. He wants his son to be a doctor. But to his utter despair Balu fails in S.S.L.C. Examination. He is as much shocked by Balu's ill-mannered way as he is flattered by it.

> Margayya felt that failing the Matric seemed to have conferred a new status on his son, and unloosened his tongue. He felt in all this medley a little pride at the fact that his son had acquired so much independence of thought and assertiveness. (114)

He manipulates the horoscope of his son bribing the astrologer, to match it with that of Brinda because the girl is the most eligible to be his son's bride. Margayya consults astrology 'purely as a formality.' He thinks the days of waiting anxiously 'on the verdict of stars' are gone. He believes man could 'make his own present and future,' provided he works hard and remains watchful.

Certain parts of the novel render exceptionally accurate pictures of Indian domestic life. But when seen through the author's ironic perspective, the picture, even if sad and serious, turns out to be funny and hilarious. The incident in which a postcard arrives announcing the death of the vanished Balu (which later proves to be false), shows the turmoil and hysterics with which the news is received by the entire family and the way Margayya's thoughts under the circumstances flow in many directions corresponding to his basic nature. At one moment he condemns himself, laments at the news of his son's death; at another through all his grief a ridiculous question keeps coming to his mind relating to his failing relationship with his brother. He shouts at the crowd gathered by his house with deadly irony in his tone—"How can they leave? How can they afford to ignore all this fun and go?" (129). When he is asked to go to Madras to know the truth about Balu, he feels unhappy: "The duties of a father seemed to be unshakable" (130). His reactions to the words of wisdom coming from his neighbours at the time of this crisis, and his experience of a journey to Madras by train in a third-class compartment leading to his baffling experiences as a small town man in the big world of Madras are beautiful instances of Narayan's narrative technique, one that helps the author render small details of life ironically.

Irony in *The Vendor of Sweets* arises due to the wide gap between what the characters say and do, and what actually is the case or what actually happens. Jagan's statements in the novel normally involve explicit expression of one attitude or evaluation, but with the implication of a very different attitude or evaluation. Jagan is a strange mixture of Indian traditional outlook and modern materialism. He appears absurd and ludicrous in his attempt to combine handsome profits with high-minded Gandhian principles, and deep attachment to his family life with the Hindu philosophy of renunciation preached in the Bhagavad Gita. His abstemious lifestyle is more an example of his religious obscurantism than about his faith in Gandhi's principles. He obeys Gandhi by the letter of his principle but not by the spirit of it. That is why he so vehemently opposes the idea of charity. He claims to be against adulteration and uses pure ghee made from cow's milk in his sweetmeat shop. Yet he readily agrees to the head cook's suggestion of trying a new sweet—there would be no problem of leftovers as everything could be pulped back and fried afresh in a new shape. Jagan's argument in favour of it is "after all, one had to take a practical view, with the price of foodstuff going up" (13). Like a typical money-minded businessman he maintains two accounts—one for his knowledge and the other for that of the tax collector.

Following the preaching of the *Gita*, Jagan talks of conquering the self. As a first step towards it he conquers taste—gives up eating salt, sugar or rice. But he is in a business that exploits the gluttony of others. Moreover, he has not conquered what he should certainly have done—that is, his excessive affection for his son, Mali which is the root of all the troubles of his life. His attempts to put straight the relationship pathetically fail. As the boy grows, the split becomes wide open. He distrusts all that his son says about his grandiose scheme of manufacturing novel-writing machines but still cherishes a secret and absurd affection and admiration for him. The scheme is in itself an ironic proposition because it conveys how with the change of time, attitude to creativity is gradually falling low. Secondly, the mechanization of human life, human emotions and experiences has also been hinted at. Unable to say an outright 'no' to Mali's absurd schemes, Jagan plans to meet the whole situation by ignoring the whole business, which he calls 'a sort of non-violent non-cooperation' (86). In that too he miserably fails. He is not strong enough to survive his son's unshakable determination and pestering attitude to extort money from him. Then with the shocking revelation of the actual relation between his son and the half-Korean, half-American girl, Grace, Jagan is confronted by the new world where his cherished notions of marriage and morals seem to count for nothing.

The irony grows to be sharper and clearer as more of the changing realities of the time are revealed. In a state of total hopelessness about his son's irredeemable ways Jagan takes the first step to do away with the evil of money in which is rooted his ruin and takes to a bit of charity. He sells sweets at a much reduced price so that children and the poor could buy it, and less money would flow in. Still failing to contain Mali, he makes up his mind to retire and renounce his worldly worries. He is firm in his resolution. But ironically, as he is leaving and renouncing the world and thinking of a new birth, he takes his bank book and the key of backdoor lock with him and leaves his business in the safe hands of the cousin with a hope of saving it for the future use of Mali. If Jagan's mind is ready for renunciation is a topic of debate. Scriptures and Gandhi's philosophy have not changed the elemental human being in him. But evidently being cornered by circumstances he realizes that there is wisdom in renunciation. Narayan appreciates the strength of religious feelings in India. But religion without actual illumination of the mind is rendered ironically in the novels of Narayan. At the same time ultra-modern ideas and ventures such as Mali's—his disrespect for age-old values and faith of a race in the name of modernity and advancement—are rendered absurd and ludicrous, too. Narayan's skill lies in delineating the actual situation in his moving style without being pedantic: the blending of irony and humour saves the narrative from lapsing into serious discourse on tradition, modernity and Gandhian philosophy.

According to I.A. Richards, irony is equilibrium of oppositions. In this sense all Narayan's novels are ironic because they bring in the opposite and the complementary impulses in the characters—in their action, thought or in situations cropped up accidentally or co-incidentally. *The Painter of Signs* and *The Man-Eater of Malgudi* are no exception. In *The Painter of Signs*, Raman, the central character, himself is a juxtaposition of the opposites—the modern and the traditional, the romantic and the rationalistic. He belongs to the Malgudi of the 1970s that is undergoing rapid changes under the impact of modern trends like the growth of scientific temperament, quest for logic or reason behind human action, arrival of feminism and sexual permissiveness. With his roots in the age-old traditional and socio-cultural values of India, Raman claims to be keen on establishing the Age of Reason in the world. He is a self-proclaimed rationalist seeking logical explanation from everybody. This is challenged by the lawyer whose action is controlled by astrology and superstitions. Raman's rationalism is also challenged by the centenarian priest in the temple who, it is believed, can read people's past, present and future. It is ironic that Raman's curiosity is aroused even though he does not see any logical explanation behind the belief. Daisy, the modern, pragmatic, super-rationalist, also poses a challenge to his rationalist temperament, and she regards him as an incurable romantic.

Raman's morbid attitude to sex is a source of humour and irony in the novel. On the one hand, he is obsessed with sex, and on the other, he considers it unholy and so makes futile attempts to banish it from his mind. According to him 'money and sex' are modern trends found 'too much everywhere'—literature, magazines, drama or cinema. But there is no doubt that the water-soaked female figure enchants him, and Daisy comes to his dreams with no clothes on. All his funny attempts to discipline his mind fail. It is funny that he draws similarities between his situation and that of the sages of the Purana whose attempts at deep meditation are foiled by attractive women. His highly imaginative mind imagines too much and hovers in dilemmas and is assailed by "the habit of communicating on two planes—audibly and inaudibly at the same time" (8), offering more occasions for verbal irony. His sex-obsession leads him to comical but complicated situation when he attempts to force himself upon Daisy imagining her to be his future wife, and Daisy threatens to register a complaint of attempt of rape against him. But life takes a pleasant turn and Daisy comes back volunteering for a relationship with Raman. Raman's earlier attempts for sex-suppression ends in sex-gratification. The two modern lovers indulge in pre-marital sex, but their marriage never takes place.

Besides situational irony the novel is full of ironic contrasts of characters. Daisy, for example, stands in contrast to Raman in temperament and attitude to life. She is traditional and gentle in her looks and manners. But her unlikely name stands for something unusual in her. She is a family planning zealot. Her hard-edged zeal towards her work and her mysterious independence of spirit, firm resolution in all matters concerning herself negates all that Raman stands for—indecision, shaky resolution, readiness to surrender himself completely to her way of thinking with the excuse that as a husband he would not be left in the plight of Shantanu of the *Mahabharata*. The novel bristles with such contradictions and this mode of writing is described by J.M.Q. Davies as "the reflective mode of Schlegel's notion of Romantic irony, conceived not merely as prismatic complexity of point of view but as a philosophical awareness of the existential ironies and ambiguity of life" (McLeod 1994: 39).

The World of Nagaraj exposes, in an arresting style, both the author's ironic view on Nagaraj, a typical Malgudian hero, and Nagaraj's own comic and ironic view of the world. Like other Narayan heroes such as Nataraj, Srinivas, Sriram and Raman, Nagaraj is an ordinary man living in an ordinary world. Narayan delineates the everyday life of Nagaraj—a life of inaction, indecision and procrastination. He is a typical Malgudian who has a hundred and one excuses for delay. He is content and comfortable in his uneventful life. His only pastime is to let his introspective state of mind respond to the pressures of the external world by switching its reveries on. Yet in the midst of all ordinariness of life, he has his grand plans, his 'life's aim,' to write the saga of the celestial sage 'Narada,' a mission which he hopes would lift the ordinariness of his existence. The task is daunting because there is no authoritative source on the life and history of the sage to be utilized as instructive basis. Moreover, whatever is available is written in Sanskrit, a language he is not at all conversant with. But these cannot dampen his determination to take on this ambitious project commanded by a voice in a dream. He waits for the auspicious moment to begin his composition. He resolves to start his ambitious project the next day at seven o' clock, 'even if the heavens fall.' "This is a matter in which I alone can have a voice' (181), he says. He thinks further, "You must never listen to women. They will not let you do anything worthwhile, nothing more important than buying brinjals and cucumber, and mustard and rice, and caressing whenever a chance occurs. One who is out to make a mark in any walk of life will have no chance" (181-82). But this new resolve of Nagaraj ends fruitlessly and his mission is aborted before it could start. Ironically, what ruins his prospect is a series of farcical events and situations taking place in his family life. One of the farcical events is the arrival of his nephew Tim in his house. The intrusion intensifies when Tim marries and brings home his harmonium playing wife Saroja. Nagaraj is perturbed by her singing to the accompaniment of a blaring harmonium. His reactions to these situations are funny and farcical. On the one side he has his comfort in his ordinariness and monotony and on the other his pathetic struggle to break out of his circle of mediocrity. Totally powerless to act, he postpones his ambitious project indefinitely. "With the capacity only to watch life flow by Nagaraj will go on being a willing victim of destiny."[24] "'I can have no hope of writing any more. You could as well take the notebook back to the old room, where at least white ants may relish my notes on Narada'" (184-85), he tells his wife. Sharmani Patricia Gabriel puts it rightly, "Out of this Chekhovian mould of ordinary characters with their purposeless lives and overreaching ambitions Narayan demonstrates that he is a master of comedy who is not unaware of the tragedy of the human situation"[25].

The real strength and comedy of this novel comes from the remarkable use of the narrative device of the wonderful double-speech Nagaraj has developed. Nagaraj assumes two voices—one is the silent inner voice that indulges in tough straight talking and the other, the ever compliant voice of an unself-confident, uncertain and bullied man. He lacks the assertive presence and firmness necessary to meet his duties and responsibilities as an uncle. He is unable to assert himself even when dealing with his wife, brother, sister-in-law and all others who he comes across. He resorts to half-lies and deception or to an assortment of quotable lines, when he finds the 'terrible' responsibilities of life too overwhelming to be handled. In case he is face to face with unmanageable reality, his well-rehearsed lines vanish and he resorts to 'pregnant silence" or mutters a few inane remarks. In order to corner Tim and to know why he is staying out late in night, he has his lines well-rehearsed—"His opening lines would have been, as soon as Tim appeared at the door, 'Tim, don't you go away before I have a word with you,' in a firm, unambiguous tone" (67). But the moment Tim appears, he is lost—". . . . One cannot fling such a sentence at another just waking up. . . . One should allow a decent margin of time for such things" (67). Half an hour later when Tim returns to his room, after a wash or coffee, and finding his uncle still in the hall, asks 'Not gone out, Uncle?,' Nagaraj, instead of taking the right cue from his rehearsed sentence 'I'm only waiting for you,' replies 'Just for a change, that's all, I'll start out later, perhaps' (67). As he is hesitating, the boy is gone. The ironic juxtaposition of the characters of Gopu and Nagaraj with their oddities and angularities also results in the comic in the novel. Gopu is hardy, earthy, practical and selfish whereas Nagaraj is acquiescent, deferential and passive. The latter's Lakshmana-like obeisance to his elder brother causes much of the humour. His association with Tim and Saroja further exposes his character for comic viewing.

Waiting for the Mahatma has no narrator as such and the story is narrated in straightforward third person. The story is about Sriram through whose point of view life is seen. Sriram is entangled in the affairs of the nation being led by Gandhi, but not out of any nationalistic zeal or ideological conviction but due to his love at first sight for Bharati though he subsequently wakes up from his somnolence of ages. The author maintains an ironic distance from him and gives no direct comments on any matters relating to him or others. The tone of the novel is down to earth, comical, quite opposite of the serious and idealistic tone of *Kanthapura*, another Gandhi novel. Narayan's credit lies in the rendering of the Mahatma with an amused and tolerant humour simultaneously retaining his historical authenticity. In Narayan the Mahatma is not a remote and supernatural presence but a warm human being who touches two young lives. The novel, thus, presents two actions—one comic and another serious and tragic. And Bharati establishes the link between the two. The serious action is about the freedom struggle led by Gandhiji, and his assassination at the end. The comic part is played by Sriram, an ordinary average Malgudian and the pursuit of his love interest in Bharati, Gandhiji's disciple and an active soldier of his army of freedom fighters. Narayan shows how Gandhiji exerted different influences on different sections of Indian society. Conscious efforts are made by many persons—the Municipal Chairman, for example—to earn Gandhiji's approval but with vested interests. Narayan's good humoured irony brings such real aspects of Indian sensibility into focus.

Gandhiji's words of love and non-violence have a ludicrous effect on Sriram. When Gandhi advises people to clear their hearts and minds to make sure that only love resides there, Sriram, completely preoccupied by the sight of Bharati, says to himself, "Definitely it's not bitterness, I love her" (32). Though he grows in awareness and experience due to his association with Gandhiji and his freedom movement, his aim remains the same as ever—the aim of winning Bharati for marriage. That is why when Gandhiji asks him, "Do you like each other so much," he bursts out saying, "I've waited for five years thinking of nothing else" (252).

In the portrayal of the Municipality Chairman, Narayan, with his characteristic irony and humour, uncovers the hypocrisy, self-deception, corrupt and lavish ways of life of such people who proclaim themselves as Gandhi's admirers but in reality follow practices opposite to his ideology. Sriram's granny is ignorant about the issues agitating the politicians and is unwilling to be a part of all this as she has a difference of opinion. According to her Gandhiji is a trouble-maker who disrupts age-old social systems like casteism. There is the village teacher who thinks that India is not ready for self-rule and so he does not want to see Britain go. There is the carter who has no time to spare from his daily routine to think of all these. To him, "These politicians, Gandhi folk, they won't leave anyone in peace." So he says, "Why do you come and trouble us here?" (106). The characters of fiery Gopal and Jagdish are also delineated comically. In a comic situation Sriram's Granny rises from the funeral pyre fooling the doctor but is prohibited by the priest to go back to her village to avoid the possibility of any catastrophe as indicated through this unusual incident. She is sent on pilgrimage. Narayan's satire is directed towards the priests who spread such superstitions and religious fear to control a typical Indian psyche. A simple reason like a possible mistake in diagnosis on the doctor's part never crosses their minds.

The Guide is technically Narayan's most advanced novel. It displays a virtuosity which any great writer can be credited with. The novel reveals that he is not just conscious of his craft but also a willing one to make experiments with techniques, though he is not an experimenter like Joseph Conrad or James Joyce. *The Guide* is, in fact, the best in the genre of Narayan's sad comedy. It is the most innovative and sophisticated stylistically. Manipulating all his regular techniques—flashback, flash forward, interior monologue, stream-of-consciousness technique—Narayan smoothly creates an atmosphere of suspense and anticipation. He, then, adds to it a mixed narration and a braided time-scheme. First person and third person narrations come alternately. In the first person Raju describes his own experiences through his life's journey till he meets Velan, and in the third person, the omniscient narrator comes in between to show Raju's experiences with Velan and the villagers after he is back from jail. When Raju's own account of the different phases of his life comes to an end, the omniscient narrator takes the sole charge. In other words, while Raju narrates his past, the omniscient narrator narrates the present. According to Stephen Ignatius Hemenway, "the mixed narration is an intriguing device because the third person narrator takes over in many of the situations in which Raju becomes what others want him to be, and the first-person narrator provides the personal insight and idiosyncratic background information which prepare the reader to accept his transformation and ultimate submergence of individuality."[26]

Indeed, the complicated narrative is the most suitable to delineate the complicated human emotions involved. According to Iyengar, "This zigzag narration gives a piquancy to the novel without quite confusing the reader" (1983: 379). More significant is the open-ended conclusion of the novel. Whether it actually rains at the end or it is only Raju's optical delusion, whether he dies or merely sinks due to fasting—all this is left for the readers to infer. The note of suggestiveness and ambiguity that marks the conclusion of the novel is the master-stroke of the narrative technique in Narayan. The narrative technique is consistent with his deep, penetrative ironic vision. It is used to unfold the mystery of the working consciousness of his characters. Narayan recognizes the strength and reality of many paradoxes and conflicts of attitudes and motivations that arise, in the novel, from two sets of values and aspirations, two modes of living, even perhaps two kinds of human beings. Raju, Rosie, Marco, Velan, the Adjournment Lawyer and all others, who are the different faces of these conflicts, are the subject of Narayan's ironic perception.

Raju is by nature a public man and therefore, feels an instinctive and irresistible drive to mould his life in accordance with public demand and succeeds in his attempt. With the twists and turns of circumstances things go beyond his control, but he is no less responsible for his plight. For him there lie the little ironies of life. He is content as a shop-owner, and then as a railway guide. His acquaintance with Rosie and Marco changes the directions of his life. He ignores the warning of his mother and friend both of whom desert him at a later point of time. While playing the role of Rosie's impresario he lands up in jail, and after his release from there, he arrives at the village, Mangala, where he is mistaken for a saint. With some inane but seemingly profound statements he mesmerizes the credulous, illiterate, ignorant religious-minded people. Whatever he says begins to be treated as gems of thought. It is sharply ironic that Raju begins to take the spiritual status thrust upon him seriously. The theme of illusion and reality operates all through the novel that explains Raju's responses to life. Sometimes when the thin separating line between reality and illusion vanishes Raju falls prey to illusion.

In a leisurely moment during his sainthood Raju starts counting the stars; he is driven by a strong desire to do something different and be known for it.

> He said to himself, 'I shall be rewarded for this profound service to humanity.' People will say, 'Here is the man who knows the exact number of stars in the sky. If you have any trouble on that account, you had better consult him. He will be your night guide for the skies.' He told himself: 'The thing to do is to start from a corner and go on patch by patch. Never work from the top to the horizon, but always the other way.' (15)

He evolves a theory for counting the stars: "He started the count from above a fringe of palmyra trees on his left hand side, up the course of the river, over to the other side. One-two . . . fifty-five." (15-16) He suddenly realizes that looking deeper a new cluster of stars comes into view. This ironic rendering throws light on his proneness to praise-worthy achievements and explains why he is enamoured with the illusion Velan and other villagers create with their faith. He begins to think that his personality radiates glory (94). Reluctant at first, he gradually takes a fancy to his new 'spiritual status,' conferred upon him.

But Raju knows the reality and cares for it. It is curious to note that as he is observing fast, he is expected to be undergoing a transformation of soul. Yet, at the sight of Velan he feels irritated for having brought him to this state: "This single man was responsible for his present plight. Why would he not go away and leave him alone? What a wise plan it would have been if the crocodile had got him while he crossed the river!" (212)

Raju sees the irony in the fact that it is his story about the man who could bring rain by undertaking a fast that initiates the villagers to apply pressure on him to save them from the severe drought through fasting. Raju regrets having given them the idea. He even thinks that ". . . . if he had known that it would be applied to him, he might probably have given a different formula: That all villages should combine to help him eat *bonda* for fifteen days without a break. . . . And then the saintly man would stand in the river for two minutes a day; and it should bring down the rain sooner or later" (97). When all his attempts to escape the situation fail he realizes the enormous task he has to take upon his frail shoulders. Even his admission of the truth about himself is of no avail. The cause of the ordeal is linked to another ironic situation. The drought in the village brings great distress for, and creates mistrust among the villagers. This further leads to fights and feuds among different sections. Velan is injured in the fights. Raju comes to know of it from Velan's brother. He couldn't care less though he feels sorry for Velan. However, he is eager to see that for no reasons policemen and reporters arrive at the village and his true identity is disclosed. So through Velan's moron brother he sends the message to stop fighting or else he would stop eating. The moron is at first unable to connect the fight and Raju's food. Then he feels reluctant to tell the truth before an assembly of people that he has washed their dirty linen in front of the Swami"[27], and invites thrashing for it. So he deliberately misrepresents the message, that is, the Swami would not eat until it rains. Ironically, the supply of food for which Raju gets linked to the villagers is stopped, though the link is never fully severed. Moreover, it is ironic that his fast arouses public interest and draws men and women, reporters and government officials from far and wide, which he was earlier so keen to avoid. It is also ironic that Raju gives a thorough account of his shady past to convince Velan that he is no saint. But Velan's response to it comes as a surprise. He takes his words for the confession of a saint to clear his conscience before taking up such a big task. The verbal irony in the following lines of the omniscient narrator is discernible.

> After profound thought, the judge rose in his seat. 'I'll go back to the village to do my morning duties. I will come back later. And I'll never speak a word of what I have heard to anyone. He dramatically thumped his chest. 'It has gone down there, and there it will remain.' (209)

Raju realizes that he is doomed. Knowing fully well the reality, he makes an effort to believe in the illusion they all together have created—"If by avoiding food I shall help the trees bloom, and the grass grow, why not do it thoroughly' (213). He finds a new strength to go through the ordeal. Through Raju's final act of sacrifice Narayan hints at the way saints are born in India. First, there is the simple but total and collective faith wrongly conferred upon Raju. The faith itself is treated with a mild satire along with Raju's put-on act to fit him to the situation. Later the blind faith is seen leading to the instinctive wisdom of the man who realizes that it is the quality of his own faith that matters, not the quality of the object of that faith.

There is an ironical account of the efforts of the villagers to make an artificial basin in sand as there is no water in the river due to drought and when it does not fill up, they fetch water from distant wells and fill it so that there is knee-deep water for the

Swami to stand in and offer his prayers—a prerequisite to make the Swami's fast a success. It is more incongruous that people show an apathy towards the suffering of the saint who is dying for their cause. They try to make money, because with a huge gathering around there are plenty of opportunities for it. They frolic about without minding the gravity of the situation.

There is Malone, the American correspondent at Mangla. Drawn almost fifty years ago his portrayal is found to be the most relevant even today. The presence of a correspondent or a reporter is a very common and natural sight during any news-worthy occasion of the modern metropolitan society. From his entry into the scene to his exit, Malone is presented superbly with amazing authenticity. The omniscient narrator observes:

> Finally when he (Malone) had the lights ready, he brought in his camera and took pictures of the people, the temple and the Swami from various angles and distances. . . . when he had finished with the pictures, he brought in a microphone, put it near Swami's face and said, 'Let us chat. O.K.? Tell me how do you like it here?' (218)

The absurd questions Narayan puts to his mouth are not at all imaginary; one finds reporters asking such questions in real life—How long have you been without food now? Do you feel weak? When will you break your fast? Do you expect to have rains by then? Can fasting abolish all wars and bring in world peace? Do you champion fasting for everyone? What about the caste system? Is it going? Will you say something about your early life? . . . for instance have you always been a Yogi? (218-219). These are ironies of life that cannot escape notice. It is important that both the narrative voices—one of the omniscient narrator and the other of Raju himself—are bestowed with deep ironic tones. Raju's account of himself bears a tone of self-mockery; it is his wisdom acquired from real experiences of life.

The third person omniscient narrative shares Narayan's comic vision of life.

There is no doubt that Narayan's art is crafted carefully; he employs narrative techniques according to the demands of his theme and his comic vision of life. His narrative style is enlivened by his humour which is often equated with that of Jerome K. Jerome and P.G. Wodehouse; a perfect blending of humour and irony makes his narration attractive. The seriousness of the themes—the exposure of the corruption in high places, the deceitful nature of human beings and such others—being juxtaposed with humorous descriptions of characters and incidents, the stories and the novels have gained in popularity as entertaining pieces. Although he practices pre-Modernist notions of narrative, he has developed his own set of self-reflexive techniques with which detachment and attachment are finally balanced in his fiction.

NOTES

1. M.N. Srinivas, *Frontline*, October 18, 1996.
2. Ved Mehta, 'The Train Had Just Arrived at Malgudi Station,' *The New Yorker, Digital Edition*, September 15, 1962: 51.
3. H.M. Williams, *Indo-Anglian Literature: A Survey*, 1976: 50.
4. Uma Parameswaran, *A Study of Representative Indo-English Novelists*, 1976: 46.
5. R.M. Varma says, "R.K. Narayan needs no introduction to an average reader. Widely acclaimed as a novelist who has few equals among the fiction writers of India today, Narayan's art as a novelist is largely limited to storytelling, for the story is the distinguishing characteristic of his fiction. As a genial storyteller, Narayan holds his listeners simply spellbound" (1993:12).
6. Only the Story Matters: An Interview, *India Today* 7:3, 1-15 Feb., 1982: 61.
7. Ved Mehta, 'The Train Had Just Arrived at Malgudi Station,' *The New Yorker, Digital Edition*, September 15, 1962: 78.

8. Stephen Graubard in an Interview with R.K. Narayan, *Another India*, U.S.A.: American Academy of Arts and Science, 1989: 235.
9. Narayan says, "My focus is all on character. If his personality comes alive, the rest is easy for me." R.E. Wolseley, 'Narayan of India,' *The Nation* XVII, 4, 3 October, 1953: 273.
10. An interview to Naseem Khan, *The Guardian*, Nov. 2, 1973.
11. Susan E. Croft, 'An Interview with R.K. Narayan,' *R.K. Narayan: A Critical Spectrum*, Bhagwat S. Goyal, Meerut: Shalabh: 30.
12. Rama Kundu, 'Myth, Ritual and Demonology,' *Critical Response to R.K. Narayan*, ed. A.N. Prasad, Sarup, 2003: 131-46.
13. Meena Sodhi, 'R.K. Narayan: His Life into Art, *Swami and Friends*, *The English Teacher* and *My Days*,' *R.K. Narayan: An Anthology of Recent Criticism*, ed. C.N. Srinath, New Delhi: Pen-craft International, 2000: 91-92.
14. K.R.S. Iyengar, 'Sunday World,' *The Hindustan Times*, Delhi, February 10, 1974.
15. Cynthia vanden Driesen, 'The Novels of R.K. Narayan,' Research Paper No. 6, Centre for South and South-East Asia Studies, Perth: University of Western Australia, 1986: 63, qtd. in the Preface to *R.K. Narayan, Critical Perspectives*, 1994 by A.L. McLeod.
16. Keith Garebian, "Strategy and Theme in the Art of R.K. Narayan," *Ariel*, Vol. 5, No. 4, Oct, 1974.
17. R.K. Narayan, *Gods, Demons and Others*, New York: Bantam, 1986: xi-xii.
18. Stephen R. Graubard, 'An Interview with R.K. Narayan,' *Another India*, U.S.A: American Academy of Arts and Science, 1989: 234-35.
19. Susan E. Croft, 'An Interview with R.K. Narayan,' 26.
20. Indeed, "Malgudi is a diminutive world with diminutive characters whose *dharma* seems to involve the endless deferral of tasks, inconclusive armchair discourses, excursive "whinges" about everything from Nehru to aerated drinks, and an attitude of inaction and lethargy whereby things are allowed to take their course, regardless of their long-term implications." Sudesh Mishra, 'R.K. Narayan: The Malgudisation of Reality,' *R.K. Narayan-Critical Perspectives*, ed. A.L. McLeod, 1994: 91.

21. Keith Garebian, 'Strategy and Theme in the Art of R.K. Narayan,' *Ariel*, Vol. 5, No. 4, Oct, 1974: 80.
22. J.K. Biswal, *A Critical Study of The Novels of R.K. Narayan*, 1987: 80. According to Biswal, "Narayan sets himself as a pioneer in the tradition of ironic realism in Indo-Anglian fiction. In his novels irony is not only ingrained in occasional episodes of the narrative, but is a built-in phenomenon in plot, character and style" (1987: 78).
23. M.K. Naik, *The Ironic Vision*, 1983: 77.
24. Sharmani Patricia Gabriel, '"Of Snakes and Sages." Rev. of *The World of Nagaraj'*, *CRNLE Reviews Journal*, No.1, 1991: 18.
25. *Ibid.*, 18.
26. Stephen Ignatius Hemenway, *The Novel of India Vol. II*, 1975: 24.
27. C.D. Narasimhaiah, 'R.K. Narayan's *The Guide*'; *Aspects of Indian Writings in English*, ed. M.K. Naik, Delhi: Macmillan India, 2007: 189.

Language and Style: Diction of the Common Man

This chapter raises the issue of using English, a foreign language, for expressing Indian reality. R.K. Narayan's remodeling of imperial English for this purpose is discussed with reference to that of his contemporaries. William Walsh starts his book on Narayan with his comment, "In writing of R.K. Narayan. . . . one must begin with the language. Literature in the end is only—only! the most powerful, the most human, the subtlest and the most inclusive use of the language" (1992; 1). Language breathes life into literature. Language and literature share an inseparable and interpenetrating relationship. English being a colonial legacy of the Indians, who have however accepted the language as an Indian language in the post-colonial period, there has been serious scope for debates on the authenticity of English in expressing Indian sensibilities. Indian English literature as a separate entity began to evolve during the late nineteenth century. This new and exotic literature came to be known as 'Indo-Anglian literature' and later, was renamed as 'Indian writing in English.' Now, it is more than 150 years old, says C.D. Narasimhaiah, It "has to date a long line of distinguished poets, novelists, essayists and others whose mental and spiritual make-up is Indian but whose expression is English. It is not the English, that 'Shakespeare spake or Milton writ,' but English which the English themselves might not willingly let die."[1]

In the second half of the nineteenth century—the post-Macaulay period—the novel, as a literary genre, began to appear in India. Novels in India began to be written both in 'vernaculars' and in English. Many early novelists wrote even in two languages. Novels written in 'vernaculars' (or in regional languages) of India consolidated their strengths and initiated literary traditions that continue to this day. But English novels written in considerable numbers in the late nineteenth and early twentieth century are virtually forgotten now.[2] The early novelists writing in English experimented with different styles in their writing. They borrowed both from English novels and from novels in regional languages. The language of oratory was also the style that came readily to them. They wrote weighty ponderous sentences imitating journalists and orators, or wrote sentimental prose imitating poets. Mulk Raj Anand called it 'King-Emperor's English' by which he meant 'the copious prose (and verse) written in the erstwhile Indian Empire of His Britannic Majesty.'[3] This was also known as the Babu English of the Indian clerk. Anand put the blame for the use of such a language on the commercial and official English that was taught in the Universities and that students learnt to get employment rather than education.[4]

After the 1930s, however, trends began to change recognizably. The novelists who wrote during the 30s consciously attempted for a breakaway from the traditions followed earlier. They were genuinely interested in the form and dared experiment with it and with the language they used. The most prominent among them were Mulk Raj Anand, Raja Rao and R.K. Narayan. They attempted to convey the particular and the specific reality through their novels, in a language they refashioned with their experiments. They took the liberties with the accepted diction and syntax of English language which they had learnt from childhood. They treated English not as an alien language but as one of India's many languages. Through personal experiments they forged the styles that best suited their needs. Incidentally their styles were called Indian for being markedly different from the British or the American English styles. As writers they had to keep constantly in mind that they were dealing with non-English speaking people in non-English speaking situations, and that they were conveying in English the vast range of expressions and observations whose natural vehicle was an Indian language. They were to apply their experimentation while writing dialogues and presenting conversations, rendering modes of thinking, manners of observations and instinctive responses of Indian people. The areas they experimented with were diction, syntax and imagery of their respective writings.

Mulk Raj Anand experimented largely with the diction he used for his novels. For this purpose he chose literal translation of idioms, phrases or even a number of sentences following each other, from Hindi or colloquial Hindi or from Punjabi. The pages of his novels are crowded with such expressions as—'eating the air' (to take a stroll), 'counterfeit luck' (rotten luck), 'breaking the vessel' (to expose a secret), 'black in the pulse' (something wrong) or 'Is this any talk?' and many more like these. Anand also makes excessive use of swear-words which occur in the Hindi or the Punjabi speech of common people. They undergo literal translation and are expressed as 'rape daughter,' 'rape mother,' 'the illegally begotten' and the like. Proverbs play an important part in Punjabi speech in particular, and in Indian speech in general. Indian writers writing in English, therefore, show a tendency to render Indian proverbs in English. Anand, too, used the same device in his style and there appear north-Indian proverbs like "your own calf's teeth seem golden" ('The Road' 24), or "a goat in hand is better than a buffalo in the distance" ('The Road' 22), "If they see an ant they will make it an elephant in the village" (*Gauri* 66), "You talk like your half-baked vessels" (*Gauri* 42) etc.

Another stylistic device used by Anand is transliteration—words or letters written in the letters of different alphabets. Thus, he renders Hindi or Punjabi words directly in English, usually as nouns like 'angrez-log,' 'yaar,' 'khaichal' etc; and sometimes strangely and daringly as verbs like 'sisking' with cold, 'bur-burred' in sleep or 'thak-thakking' at a cauldron etc. To use 'ham' for yes, 'acha' for very well, and 'nanhi' for no, 'ao' for come, 'chalo, chalo' for let us go, is a common feature in Anand. Exclamatory words like 'Bale, Bale,' 'Are, are,' 'wah, wah,' 'Hain,' and swear words like 'Vay, ja, ja,' 'Shut up saley!' etc. which cannot be rendered in English, are also transliterated. Addresses like 'huzoor,' 'beti,' 'Daktarji,' 'Sardarji' are recurrent too. Another device used by him is to misspell English words to show the pronunciation of an illiterate Indian—like 'yus' for 'yes,' 'notus' for 'notice,' 'Amrika' for 'America' etc. One interesting aspect of Anand's style is that when he directly speaks to the reader he uses passages of ornate conventional prose cluttered with adjectives and adverbs, but when the characters speak to each other he forges for them through translation or transliteration dialogues in racy peasant speech. Thus, the latter serves as a device of his art of characterization. Anand advocates in favour of an even pitch of writing without purple patch or deliberate use of lovely words. He dislikes any showing off of one's mastery over the alien tongue. Yet he himself has followed it at some places and punctuates his writing with sentences that are heavy, complex and laden with excessive imagery. Instances of all these can be found in any randomly opened page in any one of his works.

Excessive use of transliteration or literal translation, even when used in the name of attaining realism or truthful characterization, is very likely to make English appear unusual and strange. It distorts the character of the language altogether. Even for Indians belonging to different other parts of India the language becomes unintelligible. Use of too many proverbs is not a common or desirable practice in English. When too many of them in translated form are used they impart a jarring note, particularly when they are neither relevant nor indispensable. Only when relevant and functional, such use seems more appropriate than the use of their actual substitutes in English. Misspelling English words to indicate the illiteracy of the speaker also gives out a sense of falsehood, artificiality and unreality as it is clear from the beginning that the writer is only recreating the speech of the characters in English. So it has nothing to contribute to the effect of verisimilitude. Rather when overfilled with such uses, reading a story or a novel becomes cumbersome. Anand, however, justifies the effort that goes into his creative process and that of his contemporaries, in his essay, 'Pigeon-Indian: Some Notes.' According to him, "it is a natural expression of a bilingual talent, nourished mostly on the mother-tongue, and seeking communion, beyond communication, on certain levels which had not entered into English literature until the beginning of the twentieth century."[5] Though Anand's effort to echo proletariat speech has received disapproval from some quarters, his unconventional diction and racial experiments were appreciated by certain other quarters.

Raja Rao, on the other hand, is vastly different from Anand in his experiment with style. Unlike Anand's, his experiment is not limited to the dialogue of his characters. Rather it permeates his entire style. He develops a special kind of rhetoric to indicate a different ethos, to convey the philosophical nature of his novels. He does not pick up words from his mother-tongue, Kannada, to use them directly in his English novels. He uses words which are of Sanskrit origin (like kumkum, arathi) and therefore intelligible to most Indian readers. He coins new compound words to match their counterparts in Kannada, like 'that-house,' 'next-house' etc. The flavour of the Kannada in his novel is not imparted through literal translations or transliteration but through the unobtrusive use of Kannada figures of speech and terms of reference. His major experiment has been however, with the syntax; he changes the normal structures and rhythm of English sentences in his novels. The change, in fact, imparts an archaic or even Biblical effect to the tone of his novel. The device has suited the metaphysical nature of his vision of life. His natural mode of expression is through the use of images, metaphors and similes, which abound in his novels. They are genuinely Indian and come naturally to him. According to Raja Rao, "One has to convey in a language that is not one's own the spirit that is one's own. One has to convey the various shades and omissions of a certain thought movement that look maltreated in an alien language. I use the word alien. Yet English is not really an alien language to us. We are all instinctively bilingual, many of us writing in our own language and in English. We cannot write like the English. We should not. We cannot write only as Indians. We have grown to look at the large world as part of us."[6]

Thus Raja Rao justifies his choice of language—the language which would convey the 'spirit' that is his own but will be in tune with English language. He finds a different kind of sentence structure, a different kind of imagery, and even, a different kind of thought movement for this purpose. For his *Kanthapura* he uses the *harikatha* tradition of storytelling which is popular in Mysore. The tradition makes stories of gods or saints, or uses portions of the two great epics, the *Ramayana* and the *Mahabharata*, to be told in contemporary terms. Raja Rao adopts many devices from this tradition—strings of rhyming names, repetitions and chorus like answers, and passages of elevated prose. Essentially, this is a discursive spoken style, and the digressions are carried back to the central story of the novel. A passage describing the coming of 'Kartik' (autumn) in *Kanthapura* runs as follows:

> Karthik has come to Kanthapura, sisters—Kartik has come with the glow of lights and the unpressed footsteps of the wandering gods; white lights from clay trays and red lights from copper stands, and diamond lights that glow from the bowers of entrance leaves; lights that glow from banana trunks and mango twigs, yellow light behind white leaves, and green light behind yellow leaves and white light behind green leaves; and night curls through the

> shadowed streets, and hissing over bellied boulders and hurrying through dallying drains, night curls through the Brahmin Street and the Pariah Street, and the Potters' Street and the Weavers' Street and flapping through the mango grove, hangs clawed for one moment to the giant pipal, and then shooting across the broken fields, dies quietly into the river—and gods walk by lighted streets, blue gods and quiet gods and bright-eyed gods, and even as they walk in transparent flush the dust gently sinks back to the earth.

Raja Rao followed the movement of Sanskrit syntax as the mode of his linguistic expression because he thought it expressed best the rhythms and sensibilities of Indian psyche.

David McCutchion dismisses Raja Rao's special rhetoric as 'dubious rhetoric' and "an irritating trick . . . presumably to strike a profound note."[7] S. Nagarajan on the other hand supports his style on the basis of the close relationship he finds, between Raja Rao's English prose, the rhythm of Sanskrit and Indian psyche[8]. Meenakshi Mukherjee speaks of a third possibility that these devices are intended to create a distance between the reader and the happenings of the novel and give the impression of timelessness (2001: 169). But she is doubtful of the impact it must be having on readers. According to her, either "to throw the book away in exasperation, convinced that the author is exploiting the credulity of the reader with pseudo-profundity," or "to go along with the author believing that truth itself is complex, and what he wants to convey here could not have been conveyed in simpler language, in which case style becomes inseparable from the content" (2001: 170).

Narayan's use of language in his fictional writing is quite distinct when compared to that of his contemporaries. Even when dealing with the most complex theme, he uses the simplest language. Simplicity and naturalness are unquestionably the two significant qualities of his style which are the greatest achievements of his experiment with diction and syntax. This makes his style completely different from that of Anand and Raja Rao. In his childhood Narayan was initiated into the letters in Tamil and Sanskrit—one being his mother tongue and the other, the classical Indian language. But his actual learning in classrooms took place in English. Hence, from a very early stage he got acquainted with the language and developed a liking for it. But he did not find his early acquaintance with English to be the reason for his fascination for the language. Rather, he found in the language certain qualities that drew him towards it. While speaking to Susan E. Croft, he attributes the credit for his success with English to the inherent qualities of the language itself: "I like the English language; I think it's a good language for its own sake. I owe my interest in it to the educational system of course, but even without that I probably would have stumbled on it. Even if I were an illiterate person, I would still be fascinated by the possibilities of the English language."[9]

The qualities that attracted him most towards English are its malleability and flexibility and its capacity to communicate any experience; "it can absorb anything, and you can do anything with it"[10], he says. However, having begun his learning in English from an early age and having done most of his reading in English language, Narayan mastered it adequately to make the alien language his own. So in his BBC interview given to William Walsh, he says, "Until you mentioned another tongue, I never had any idea that I was writing in another tongue. . . . I was never aware that I was using a different, a foreign language when I wrote in English because it came to me very easily. I can't explain how. English is a very adaptable language. And so it's so transparent it can take on the tint of any country."[11]

So he takes up English for painting the many shades and colours of Indian life. He conveys in English the essence of his thought and vision, the intricate social patterns of life with ease and comfort. According to Susan E. Croft, his mild, unpretentious, simple and authentic style is a result of his own innate simplicity and sincerity: "Personally uncomplicated and direct he is without affectation in conversation, and a natural sincerity comes across. Similarly in his writing he tells a story clearly in a straightforward manner avoiding convoluted sentences and elaborate vocabulary. True to the style he admires, his stories read easily and naturally. The effect is effortlessness. His novels transport readers into a different world, with no self-conscious style to bar the way. It was into this uncomplicated, almost casual atmosphere of simplicity that Malgudi is born."[12]

Narayan owes his success as a novelist much to the remodeling of the Imperial English in his own way to accommodate Indian thought and Indian sensibility. And he does so without showing any self-conscious attempt to sound Indian. Marked by straightforward manner, simplicity and lucidity, his style has grown unique, avoiding elaborate, exhaustive wordiness, extravagant rhetoric and cheap ornamentation. His narrative style maintains an even tenor, and without purple passages, almost escapes attention. Therefore, the style he forged either appears non-existent or seems no great achievement. There is rather a semblance of artlessness in his style. But the artlessness conceals real art. As Narayan claims, this is rather a deliberate attempt on his part: "I'm very unconscious of style, and I wish to make the style as unnoticed as possible—style should not be noticed. The idea must be more prominent than the style in which it is written. That is a very difficult style you know—you have the kind of thing only in the Bible. It means you have to remove things which are extraneous; an ornament here and there. You have to have a watchful eye to make your sentences just right. It's very hard. That's what I try to do. I'm aware of this style which is one that abolishes style."[13]

David Lodge, too, asserts that style should not be "a decorative embellishment upon subject-matter, but the very medium in which the subject is turned into art."[14] According to Meenakshi Mukherjee, if style is added to the material, like icing on a cake or embroidery on a sari, if it is not integral to the author's point of view, it is a false style (2001: 184). Narayan avoided everything that seemed false and the language he used is thus devoid of ornamentation. True to the demand of good art, Narayan's style is never separated from the theme of a given piece of writing. It is integral to his vision, his comic vision which explores comic possibilities in every common place, day-to-day things of life in Malgudi. A blending of seriousness and levity is discernible in the social, psychological and even the philosophical awareness of the people of Malgudi. The elements of irony, humour and satire add a liveliness and charm to his style.

In *Swami and Friends* it is the delightfully naïve world of a few juvenile characters—Swami, Somu, Sankar, Rajan, Mani, Samuel et al.—drawn to be set in ironic contrast with the artful and pseudo-serious world of the adults. Narayan had to be extra careful in choosing words that would express children's psychology and would also reveal the contrast between the children's world and the adult's world. See n through Swami's eyes, every character and every incident acquires comic proportions. In Chapter XV, *Before the Match*, Swami encounters the wrath of the headmaster for not attending the drill classes for three consecutive days. In his attempt to arrange for a medical certificate he convinces the doctor to speak to the headmaster in his favour. But standing face to face with the headmaster he realizes that the doctor has not kept his words. With the headmaster determined to punish him and Swami anxious to escape punishment, the situation reaches a comic state. Narayan's language does not miss the tempo and the tenor of the situation:

> The headmaster gave the full benefit of his wizened face to the class. His owl-like eyes were fixed upon Swaminathan, and he said: 'Get up.'
>
> Swaminathan got up.
>
> 'Come here.'
>
> Swaminathan 'came' there promptly.
>
> 'Show your shameless face to the class fully.'

> Swaminathan now tried to hide his face. The headmaster threw out his arm and twisted Swaminathan's neck to make him face the class, and said: 'This great man is too busy to bother about such trivial matters as drill and scouting, and has not honoured these classes with his presence since last Monday.' His lips twisted in a wry smile. The class considered it safer to take the cue, and gently giggled. Even on the geography master's face there appeared a polite smile.
>
> 'Sir, have you any explanation to give?' the headmaster asked.
>
> With difficulty Swaminathan found his voice and answered: 'It was the doctor—didn't the doctor talk to you about me, Sir?'
>
> 'What doctor talks about what?' . . .
>
> Swaminathan realized that the doctor had deceived him. He remembered the genial smile with which the doctor had said that he would see the headmaster. Swaminathan shuddered as he realized what a deep dyed villain Dr. Kesavan was behind that genial smile. He would teach that villain a lesson, put a snake into his table-drawer; he would not allow that villain to feel his pulse even if he (Swaminathan) should be dying of fever. (146-47)

The comic effect of the passage quoted above solely depends on the twists of the language used by the author.

In *The Bachelor of Arts* Chandran's life as a student, a romantic lover, a 'sanyasi' and a married man is brought to ironic focus; Narayan's language etches out every aspect distinctly and effectively. Chandran is a typical college student. Narayan draws his experiences as a student convincingly treating them with his sharp ironic perception. The part describing Chandran's elaborate plans of preparations for his forthcoming examinations and his dilemma while implementing his plans reveals Narayan's keenness of observation, and truthful delineation of the life of a student, in a language that is most fitting and highly expressive. Chandran gets up early one day and sitting at his study table strengthens him with several resolutions. Then taking out a sheet of paper he notes down all his subjects and calculates the total number of preparation hours that would be available from November the first to March. "He had before him over a thousand hours, including the twelve hour preparation on holidays."

> He then drew up a very complicated time-table, which would enable one to pay equal attention to all subjects. Balance in preparation was everything. What was the use of being able to score a hundred percent in Modern History if Shakespeare was going to drag you in the mire? (18)

Amusingly, as he starts with his plans innumerable difficulties pose before him. He is confused about how to start the study of the Modern Period in Indian History, and this confusion is articulated in a mock serious tone.

> The texts on the subject were many, the notes of class lectures were bulky. Moreover, if he went on studying the Modern Period, what was to happen to the Medieval Period and the Ancient? He could not afford to neglect these two sections of Indian History. . . . Chandran sat for nearly half an hour lost in this problem. (19)

Narayan's language does not also fall short in expressing the experiences of a young, romantically inclined man who falls rashly in love and creates for himself an amusing situation. Frustration in love leads him to become a sanyasi and make a fool of himself. Even at the end, his eagerness to know more about Susila, the prospective bride, the anxiety to express before long his willingness to marry the girl are rendered with comic effect. To a question of his mother, "Do you like the girl?," he says 'yes' with fervour. Then asks

> "Did you tell them that?"
>
> "We can't tell them anything till they come and ask us."
>
> Chandran made a gesture of despair and said: "Oh, these formalities. I loathe them. All this means unnecessary delay. Why shouldn't we send them a wire to-morrow?"
>
> "Be patient. Be patient. All in its time, Chandra."
>
> "But supposing they don't ask us?"

> "They will. In two or three days they will come to us or write."
>
> "I ought to have told Mr. Jayarama Iyer that I liked his girl," Chandran said regretfully. (161)

Even after marriage his romantic inclinations—his monologues on Susila and his ecstasy at getting letters from her—are described in a familiar language.

> His talks to Mohan were usually on the subject of these letters. "She has written a wonderful letter to me to-day, and has addressed me as 'My Own Darling' for the first time; she has sent me twenty thousand kisses though I sent her only fifteen thousand in my last letter." (165)

The adolescent romanticism, the youthful display of knowledge with vain seriousness unfold the irony, and as J.K. Biswal says, "From a sentimental lover to a world-renouncing sanyasi donning an ochre robe and then again to a devoted husband—these are the successive somersaults of the comic hero" (1987:79). Narayan's language holds his perception of reality and his comic vision in perfect balance.

The Financial Expert—the comic story of the sad, ambitious and absurd financier Margayya and his morbid passion for money exposing the modern materialism—is full of sharp verbal irony. Margayya who believes he can buy everything with money and dreams that his son would be a doctor does not lose hope even after seeing his son's S.S.L.C. Register:

> (His) marks in almost all subjects were in single digits. The highest mark he had obtained was twelve out of a hundred in hygiene. . . . Margayya hoped that perhaps he was destined to be a doctor, and that was why his inclination was so marked for hygiene. What a wonderful opening seemed to be before him as a doctor! Doctor Balu—it would be nice indeed. If only he could get through the wretched S.S.L.C. barrier, he'd achieve great things in life. (117)

Narayan's irony and humour aimed at absurd ambitions of an eccentric man are couched in very simple language.

The Guide reveals Narayan's maturity in using language in a very simple but effective manner. The illusion created by the villagers with their faith and the way Raju is enamoured by it, is described in an innocent way that explains Narayan's success in revealing his comic-ironic vision.

> There was so much warmth in their approach that he began to feel it was but right they should touch his feet; as a matter of fact, it seemed possible that he himself might bow low, take the dust of his own feet, and press it to his eyes. He began to think that his personality radiated a glory. . . . (94)

His language has enough force to maintain and balance the intricate and inseparable alliance between the serious and the comic.

Though Narayan does not follow the ornamental prose of the Victorian writers, sometimes he creates situations in which his fictional characters write in the heavy and serious toned Victorian prose. For example, Swami's father writes a letter to the headmaster of the Mission School raising objections against the teaching of scriptures. He writes,

> I beg to inform you that my son Swaminathan of the First Form, A Section, was assaulted by his scripture master yesterday in a fanatical rage. I hear that he is always most insulting and provoking in his references to the Hindu religion. It is bound to have a bad effect upon the boys.

When a letter from Messrs Binns arrives, Swami and his friends feel excited. But the content of it is beyond their comprehension.

> The letter informed the captain that Messrs Binns thanked him for his letter and would be much obliged to him if he would kindly remit 25 cent with the order and the balance could be paid against the V.P.P. of the railway receipt. (119)

It is Macaulay's English taught in Indian schools and colleges at the time which undergoes Narayan's ironic treatment.

In his own style Narayan gives distinct impressions not only of the spatial setting but also of the conversations and thoughts, emotions and instinctive reactions of those who inhabit his fifteen novels and innumerable short stories. For depicting those people and their life it is natural that he chooses a language that is simple, lucid, limpid, and even bare at times. It is plain, unaffected prose which is 'not far from talk, and not too near'[15], something that F.L. Lucas considers it essential for a style of simplicity. In its simplicity it is highly communicative. In *The Guide* Raju presents a close authentic picture of himself as a reluctant school student, and presents his father as a stern disciplinarian, in a simple but realistic manner. Narayan's language does not at all fail to demarcate the roles of a father, a mother and a child in a close-knit family in India:

> A tremendous fuss was made before I started for my school each day. My mother fed me early and filled up a little aluminium vessel with tiffin for the afternoon. She carefully put my books and slate into a bag and slung it across my shoulder. I was dressed in clean shorts and shirt; my hair was combed back from the forehead, with all the curls falling on my nape. For the first few days I enjoyed all this attention, but soon developed a normal aversion; I preferred to be neglected and stay at home than to be fussed over and sent to a school. But my father was a stern disciplinarian; perhaps he was a snob who wanted to brag before others that his son was going to a school. He kept an eye on my movements till I was safely on the road each morning. He sat in his shop, and kept calling every few minutes, 'Boy, have you left?' (23)

But Raju 'walked endlessly' to reach his school. There is objectivity in the details and these details bring out a close and concrete picture of life. With reference to *The Guide* C.D. Narasimhaiah explains how language serves to bring to life Narayan's characters and the plots of his stories. He says, "Narayan hasn't evoked that atmosphere as an exploiting commentator but by presenting a series of characters, by the rendering of personality, its 'reactions and vibrations.' But it must be said at once that his concern is not the mere 'creation of characters.' His characters have a representative function in the plot. But what is admirable about his characterization is the fidelity and penetration with which he brings them to life. A sentence, a phrase, a word would often suffice to bring a character to life."[16]

Another quality of Narayan's style is its precision. Short and brief statements speak volumes to create a concentrated effect. Certain things are better when left unsaid. This way either suspense is maintained or a truth is just hinted at giving his writing an enriching effect. The beginning of the illicit relationship of Rosie and Raju is said in a single sentence in *The Guide*—"But on an impulse I gently pushed her out of the way, and stepped in and locked the door on the world" (78). Later it is said that they "were a married couple to all appearances. . . . All day long she danced and sang," and he "made love to her constantly and was steeped in all-absorbing romanticism," until he woke up to the fact that "she was really getting tired of it all" (155). Narayan's treatment of sex, though restrained in the characteristic Indian way, is fairly pronounced in such statements.

H.M. Williams ascribes Narayan's confident ease and simplicity, clarity and precision to his journalistic training[17]. Speaking about the same journalistic flavour in Narayan, S. Rama Chander says, "Minimal use of exaggeration, and keeping well away from worn out cliché's as well as flowery words are the signs of sureness of touch, which journalists in particular could emulate" [18]. Similarly, according to V.Y. Kantak, "If we must seek affinities we may have to admit even that it is closest to the language of the newspaper and the Sunday Weekly and the common use an Indian makes of it for conversation among educated Indians of different language groups. But with an important reservation. From these scrappy sources Narayan has fashioned for himself a kind of 'diction of common life' for his Indian scene—a medium which is at once casual and convincing and used with such utter confidence. It can always subtly convey the flavour of Indian speech in an Indian setting without any awkwardness of translation."[19]

Truly, it is due to Narayan's love for precision that his novels and short stories are not big in volumes though he creates a world of innumerable characters, real and genuine who are found in real and authentic situations of life.

So far as speech is concerned, Anand experimented mostly with the diction and Raja Rao with the syntax, Narayan made a moderate experiment with both diction and syntax. Narayan's aim was to facilitate smooth reading of his novels or short stories. As a step towards it he avoided excessive use of Tamil words in his writing, unless or otherwise its use was inevitable to convey something very particularly Indian. Names of festivals like 'Navaratri, Deepavali, Pongal'; items of dress like 'saree, dhoti, jibba, khaddar, khaadi'; names of food items like 'badam halwa, barfi, bonda, chapati, dosai, idli, jilebi, pulav, sambar'; or names of vehicles like 'jutka, tonga' are used directly, for these words don't have their corresponding substitutes in English. Sometimes, though, he uses Indian words which can be translated into English. Words like 'ahimsa, himsa, bhojan, goonda, karma, mantra, puja, sadhu, rakshasa, shastras, zamindar, swargaloka, darshan, vasana, samadhi' are transliterated into the pages of his novels and short stories, though most of these words can very well be translated into English. However, the use of these words does not give the impression of labour or artificiality. Like Raja Rao, Narayan too coins compound words corresponding to their use in Tamil. Innumerable such words like nose-led, line-cleared, eating-stuff, one-roomed house, deep-dyed villain, monkey-faced, low-roofed dingy house, worm-eaten bellows, servant-maids, tiffin-business, well-proportioned features, housing difficulties occur frequently which are, in fact, translated from Tamil idioms.

Narayan's language has the vitality of a living speech. He successfully captures the rhythm of life peculiar to Malgudi and its people. In conversation his sentences are short and immensely communicative. More importantly, the straight-forward and matter-of-fact style does not fail to convey the sharp ironic tone in conversations. Narayan's characters don't speak English in real life. So he does not attempt to put into their mouth English that would ring false and absurd, and which will not be in its character, and finally, would fail to convey unambiguously the thoughts and acts of personalities who flourish in a small town in a far off corner of India. His concern is not to reveal the nuances of their native language but to convey a sense of the syntax of the native language. In this he is close to Raja Rao. In *The World of Nagaraj* Sita asks Nagaraj, "You didn't ask for breakfast; have an early lunch?" (155). Gopu says, "When I meet Tim and talk to him, you don't talk. Why? asked Nagaraj. It is so."

Narayan solves the problem of how to report in English a conversation which takes place in another language without affecting the spirit of what is said in the native language. Firstly, he seldom tells us directly which language his characters speak, but it is clear from the internal evidence that the conversations are obviously not in English but Tamil. Secondly, most of the time it runs so smoothly that one does not pause to think of the language the speaker speaks. In writing dialogues Narayan's approach is ingenuous. The conversations in English never read like a translation from Tamil, nor do they follow English colloquialism. The Malgudians speak as any ordinary Indian having a basic knowledge in the language would speak. The long and funny conversation between the ascetic and the inebriated Alphonse in *A Tiger for Malgudi*, is one of the best examples of Narayan's style used in conversations:

> My Master, who had stayed back unobtrusively came forward to ask him, "Whom were you talking to?"

> "You," said Alphonse, "I knew you were here. I knew you'd not go. I saw you—you obstinate devil. . . . So, I thought, what did I 'thought'? I don't know. I have forgotten. No, no, if the beast comes out and swallows you, it'll serve you right. . . . that's what I thought. Don't look at me like that. . . . I'm not drunk. . . . It's only watery rum . . . less than ten percent proof. . . . I'll deal with that cheat yet . . . that bastard."
>
> . . . . And then my Master asked, "What about the tiger?"
>
> "What about what?"

The character of Alphonse is a caricature of foolish foreign-returned Indians.

The language in which intimate conversations between different members of a family are couched shows great naturalness, ease and intimacy. *Swami and Friends* is full of such instances—conversations among friends, between father and son, grandmother and grandson, husband and wife. In one such conversation Narayan's humour and his enchanting way of presenting a real picture of father-son relationship in an Indian family is revealed. The fun-loving and easy-going son detests his father's tyranny and is insensitive towards his mood. His father stops him from going to his friends.

> 'Where are you going?'
>
> 'Nowhere.'
>
> 'Where were you yesterday at this time?'
>
> 'Here.'
>
> 'You are lying. You were not here yesterday. And you are not going out now.'
>
> 'That is right,' Mother added, just appearing from somewhere,' 'there is no limit to his loafing in the sun. He will die of sunstroke if he keeps on like this. .' . . .
>
> 'How many days is it since you have touched your books?'
>
> . . . . 'Should I read even when I have no school?'
>
> 'Do you think you have passed the B.A.?' father asked.
>
> 'I mean, father, when the school is closed, when there is no examination, even then should I read?'

> 'What a question! You must read.'
>
> 'But father, you said before the examinations that I needn't read after they were over.' (83-84)

Unlike Anand, Narayan very rarely uses swear-words—neither Indian nor English. Sometimes vernacular phrases, idioms and proverbs are translated into the pages of his stories which add to the Indianness of his characters and the milieu in which they live. Ponni shows Savitri, in *The Dark Room*, the way to control man, "Keep the men under the rod, and they will be alright. Show them that you care for them and they will tie you up and treat you like a dog" (105). At another place, she consoles Savitri, "God will protect you. The difficulty that has risen before you like a mountain will soon vanish like the dew" (122). In *The Vendor of Sweets*, Jagan muses to hear the lawyer who claims to be knowing more about America, "That was the limit. How presumptuous of the man to talk of America, while he was there to provide first hand information! People's notions were fixed. Stupid fellows. Frogs in the well!" (53). In *The Dark Room*, again, the servant uses idioms and phrases in English that are close to Tamil conversations. As he says, 'only a battered son will grow into a sound man,' 'what should a father do?,' 'But it is a proper thing to do, after having her in the house for five years?' and a straight translation like, 'The fire in a mother's belly when her child is suffering' and 'a dinner which a dog wouldn't touch' etc. Raman's aunt expresses a typical orthodox Indian view when she says—"One cannot forever flourish and fatten in a father's house, especially one born woman" (20). In *The Man-Eater of Malgudi*, Nataraj's wife wonders, "You may close the mouth of an oven, but how can you close the mouth of a town?" (177). There appear English proverbs too but in a way that ensures authenticity. For example, Raju cites one wittily to Velan, a poor illiterate man: "Have you not heard the saying—an empty vessel makes much noise?" (212). Velan, though fails to comprehend the implications of his words, accepts them with admiration as his 'good sentiments and philosophies.' In the discussion between Jagadish and Sriram about an English proverb, it is deliberately made clear that two non-English speaking Indians are quoting English idiom in a relevant situation. Jagadish says,

> "I suppose I'd better take it back with me and repair it. As a soldier I will not cry over spilt milk?"
>
> "Is it spilt milk?" Sriram asked nervously.
>
> "Of course it is," asserted Jagadish. "When milk goes bad it splits into water and solid, you know. It's no use crying over spilt milk," he repeated. (152)

Narayan writes a language almost devoid of imagery, for, imagery is not the vehicle of his perception. He does not generally use figures of speech, similes or metaphor. But when he uses these devices he is apt and suggestive. In *The English Teacher* Narayan suggests intense grief and vacuum caused by the death of a dear one in the course of depicting the indifference of the world and the numbness at heart that Krishna experiences at the time of observing funeral rites.

> The priest and the carriers ceaselessly shout for someo. . . .
>
> We are on our homeward march, a silent and benumbed gang. As we cross Nallappa's Groove once again, I cannot resist the impulse to turn and look back. Flames appear over the wall. . . . It leaves a curiously dull pain at heart. There are no more surprises and shocks in life, so t hat I watch the flame without agitation. For me the greatest reality is this and nothing else. . . . Nothing else will worry or interest me in life hereafter. (96)

Rare moments of beauty arise in the lines describing the intense joy felt at the mystic experience of having a union with his dead wife's spirit:

> A cock crew. The first purple of the dawn came through our window, and faintly touched the walls of our room. "Dawn!" she whispered and rose to her feet.

> We stood at the window, gazing on a slender, red streak over the eastern rim of the earth. A cool breeze lapped our faces. The boundaries of our personalities suddenly dissolved. It was a moment of rare, immutable joy—a moment for which one feels grateful to Life and Death. (184)

The highly emotional language of *The English Teacher*, full of similes, metaphors, audio-visual images make it different from the language used in his other works. Laxmi Holmstrom correctly points to the deliberately blurred, deliberately imprecise adjectives used in *The English Teacher* in contrast to the single, precise and clear images used in other novels, citing such examples as 'Why have you splashed all the water on yourself like an elephant on the river edge?' (*Mr. Sampath*), 'A complexion, not white, but dusky, which made her only half visible as if you saw her through a film of tender coconut juice' (*The Guide*). Holmstrom shows the use of common, not exotic, material for his imagery, the novelty of which arrests attention.[20] As an example of Narayan's suggestive and lyrical style can be cited the last lines of *The Painter of Signs*:

> Raman took out his bicycle, waited till the Chevrolet turned around the fountain and disappeared in smoke in the direction of New Extension and on to the mountain road. He looked at the key in his hand. "To hell with it," he said, and slung it into the dry fountain—an act which somehow produced the great satisfaction of having his own way at last. He mounted his cycle and turned towards the Boardless—that solid, real world of sublime souls who minded their own business. (183)

These lines describe Narayan's recurrent references to Malgudi order. A similar suggestive reference to Malgudi order has been made in *The Man-Eater of Malgudi*:

> Now an unusual thing happened. The curtain stirred, an edge of it lifted, and the monosyllabic poet's head peeped through. An extraordinary situation must have arisen to make him do that. His eyes bulged. 'Someone to see you,' he whispered. (15)

After order is restored the curtain is drawn again, and Sastri vanishes behind it saying—"We must deliver K.J.'s labels this week. I will set up everything. If you will paint the first colour" (182). With this Narayan announces the arrival of Vasu—the symbol of disorder. In *The Painter of Signs*, Narayan suggests the fragile, volatile nature of the relationship between Raman and Daisy, of which Raman is fully aware and always apprehensive;

> After all we are a married couple." He avoided the words "husband and wife." Such a precaution seemed to please her, and she nestled close to him and let him caress her body. She shut her eyes and remained still. It was a moment of profound harmony between them. One part of him was afraid to speak for fear of it might tear the gossamer-texture of this moment, but the practical part of his mind urged. (174)

Narayan's English remains free from any blemish of gimmickry or mannerisms. It remains clear and smooth while expressing a variety of moods and manners. Extracts from Indian scriptures like the *Gita*, the *Ramayana*, the *Mahabharata* are translated in his stories to focus Indian religious ethos in more concrete terms. Jagan refers to the wisdom he has derived from the *Gita*—"We are blinded by our attachments. Every attachment creates a delusion and we are carried away by it" (138). Puzzled by Mali's many faces, Jagan is reminded of the concept of *Viswarupa* he has read about in the Bhagavad Gita, "When the warrior Arjuna hesitated to perform his duty on the battlefield, God came to him in the guise of his charioteer and then revealed Himself in all His immensity. On one side He was thousand faced" (147). Narayan quotes the exact lines in translation, "I behold you, infinite in forms on all sides, with countless arms, stomachs, mouths, and eyes; neither your end or middle nor beginning do I see." (147)

The short passages of digressive nature which Narayan uses as narrative devices to depict the inner wanderings of his characters,—the states of their mind, their metaphysical attitudes, philosophic awareness or inner responses to outer events—speak immensely of Narayan's linguistic achievement. In *The Financial Expert*, for example, when Margayya is sitting before the image of the Goddess and worshipping, the thoughts of Dr. Pal and his works force into his mind. He feels 'an unholy thrill at the memory of Pal's book.' He thinks of the pictures of Dr. Pal, the wicked man, the 'awful rake,' and then of the chapters of the book. "He realized with shock what line his thoughts were pursuing, and he pulled them back to the verse." Then his mind is diverted to think of the fruits of the penance he is undertaking. "How was wealth going to flow in? When he became rich, suppose he bought from his brother the next house too, tempting him with a handsome cash offer. . . . He realized that this was his major concern in life. He would be a victorious man if he could bring his brother to his knees and make him part with his portion of the house; and then he would knock down the partition wall." From this his mind moves to the thought of food, 'Since he had to fast completely while praying' (56). The stream of thoughts flows on.

The simple, uncomplicated voice of Narayan, the voice that so successfully evokes the common kaleidoscopic rhythm of life as lived in India, or in particular, in south India—has earned him immense admiration and applause. Graham Greene is charmed by Narayan's "light vivid style" which, with its sense of time passing, of the unrealized beauty of human relationships so often recalls Tchekhov."[21] Walsh finds his language beautifully adapted to communicate a different, an "Indian sensibility" (1992: 16). Narasimhaiah discusses Narayan's capacity to "appeal to the sensuous imagination" and to "charge the colloquial element in his prose style with the literary." He finds Narayan's prose—sometimes glowing, glittering or sometimes silent. He also appreciates his capacity to create "a riot of colour without making it in the least appear excessive or decorative". For example he quotes 'purple play of colour in the northern skies,' 'the tops of the trees lit up by stray red rays' etc. from *The Guide*. He lauds his prose—'fluent, flexible, vigorous with words properly and naturally massed.'[22] Critics like V.Y. Kantak and Shashi Tharoor point at certain shortcomings of his style. Kantak compares it with 'the one-stringed instrument'[23] which cannot emulate the feats of the Veena or the Sitar. According to him Narayan's style lacks the range and amplitude to satisfy readers equally all the time and on all occasions. His language does not show the same appositeness and the power in all his works. Shashi Tharoor, commenting on the inadequacies of his language, compares it with the familiar bullock-cart: 'a vehicle that seems able to move in one gear, is unable to turn, accelerate or reverse, and remains yoked to traditional creatures who have long since been overtaken but know no better'[24]. He finds his style inadequate in intense and potentially charged situations. According to him, Narayan does not take care of the nuances of the English language and shows an apparent unconcern for the wider connotations of words and phrases used to tell his stories. Yet these critics too agree that notwithstanding these shortcomings Narayan's modest language used with honesty and confidence has worked miracle. Referring to Kantak's comparison of Narayan's style with a one-stringed instrument, Meenakshi Mukherjee says, "no other instrument would have better suited the simple honesty of Narayan's vision" (2001: 185). In no sophisticated mode can Narayan's feat be replicated.

NOTES

1. C.D. Narasimhaiah, 'R.K. Narayan's *The Guide*,' *Aspects of Indian Writing in English*, ed. M.K. Naik, New Delhi: Macmillan India, 2007: 172.
2. There are many factors responsible for this fate of Indian English novels of the time. For example, as Meenakshi Mukherjee says, "Literary texts get canonized in different and invidious ways—by being discussed and praised by influential critics, by being mentioned in histories of literature, by being taught in classrooms and

through an accretion of commentary around them. Indian English novels of the nineteenth century have not been subjected to any of these canonizing processes, and have as a result been denied literary, historical or even archival value." *The Perishable Empire*, 2002: 13.

3. M.R. Anand, *King Emperor's English*: A paper read to the Second All India Writers' Conference at Benaras in 1947 as quoted in Lakshmi Holmstorm's 'The English Language in India,' *The Novels of R.K. Narayan*, 1973: 34.
4. English remained mostly functional. Perhaps that is why, as Meenakshi Mukherjee says, "Even during the heyday of imperial rule, despite the overwhelming presence of English literature in the curriculum of higher education; the English language remained quite peripheral to the literary agenda of the country." *The Perishable Empire*, 2002: 23-24.
5. M.R. Anand, 'Pigeon-India: Some Notes,' in M.K. Naik, 40.
6. Raja Rao; Foreword, *Kanthapura*, Delhi: OUP, 1989.
7. David McCutchion, 'The Novel as Sastra' *Writers Workshop Miscellany*, No.8, 1961: 93.
8. S. Nagarajan, 'An Indian Novel' (Rev. of Raja Rao's *The Serpent and the Rope*), *Sewanee Review*, LXXII, 1964: 516.
9. Susan E. Croft, Interview with R.K. Narayan, *R.K. Narayan: A Critical Spectrum*, Bhagwat S. Goyal, Meerut: Shalabh: 29.
10. *Ibid.*, 29.
11. William Walsh, *R.K. Narayan*, London: Longman Green, 1971: 7.
12. Susan E. Croft, 30.
13. *Ibid.*, 29-30.
14. David Lodge, *Language of Fiction*, London: Routledge and Kegan Paul, 1970.
15. F.L. Lucas, *Style*, London: Casell, 1964: 124.
16. C.D. Narasimhaiah, 179-80.
17. H.M. Williams, *Indo-Anglian Literature 1800-1970: A Survey*, 1976: 50.
18. S. Rama Chander, 'Tribute, The English Teacher,' *The Hindu*, Sunday, January 14, 2007.

19. V.Y. Kantak, 'The language of Indian Fiction in English,' *Critical Essay on Indian Writing in English*, ed. M.K. Naik, S.K. Desai, G.S. Amur, Dharwar: Karnatak University, 1972: 213.
20. Laxmi Holmstrom, *The Novels of R.K. Narayan*, 1973: 97.
21. Qtd. V.Y. Kantak, 218.
22. C.D. Narasimhaiah says, "Thus the prose *The Guide* establishes for written prose the virtues of educated Indian's speech—now colloquial and racy, now literary and refined. . . . (Narayan) has evolved an altogether new genre of English, Indian English in the best sense of the term. It is the kind of English which has grown out of the Indian soil during the past 150 years. Its virtue is its freedom and flexibility. It is simple, direct, fluent and reflects the intonations of the speaking voice, the rank and station of the characters who speak it. That brings us to an astonishing achievement of Narayan. When his half-literate and illiterate characters speak English, we are not even aware that they can't speak English: we seem to accept it and take it for granted. Such is the naturalness of their dialogue and of the words which suit their thoughts. (196)
23. V.Y. Kantak, 212.
24. Shashi Tharoor, 'Revisiting R.K. Narayan,' *Indian Review of Books*, Vol. 4, No. I Oct-Dec, 1994: 22.

Narayan as a Realist: Artist par excellence

So far R.K. Narayan's approach to reality in the context of various approaches to reality in fictional writings has been discussed. The view that realism in fiction is a mode of writing that gives an impression of a faithful reflection of an actual life has been reasserted. Narayan's concern for reality in Indian life is often underestimated by critics, as the world he portrays appears free from the agonizing political conflicts and terrible socio-economic oppression which are found in abundance, say, in Anand's India. Narayan's novels between 1930 and 1945, a period of global turmoil and of intense political activity in colonial India, are surprisingly devoid of political themes. His post-Independence writings take up an ironic attitude, exposing the corrupt practices in Government offices and among the politicians, along with the passivity of the common people. *Waiting for the Mahatma (*1955), the only novel where Narayan deals directly with Gandhiji's *Satyagraha* and his assassination, fails to satisfy the critics who expect a lifelike sketch of Gandhiji and the details of his movement. The critics are disappointed with the comic caricatures and the apparently fantastic incidents in his novels and praise him nonetheless as a plain storyteller. However, here the myth of 'plain story-teller' has been broken and the concerns of a social realist beneath the comic rendering of life has been explored

The term realism, in fact, refers both to a literary method, and to a more general attitude that rejects idealization, extravagant qualities of romance and recognizes soberly the actual problems of life. Broadly speaking, the term 'realistic novel' is most applicable to works which are realistic both in subject and in manner, and throughout the whole rather than parts—like the novels of William Dean Howells or Arnold Bennet. Yet Daniel Defoe (1660-1731), who selects extraordinary adventures as his theme is regarded as the first realist because of his circumstantial and matter-of-fact presentation. Similarly, Fielding (1707-1754) and Jane Austen (1775-1817) who shape their plots in tightly wrought ironic patterns are also realists because they render common people and their life in a very convincing way. Realism as an element is found in the literary works of all genres—in Chaucer's poetry, Shaw's plays as well as in Defoe's novels. But as a dominant literary trend it is associated chiefly with the fiction produced in Europe and the United States from about 1840s till 1890s. In fact, the growth of novels in nineteenth century England is associated with the rendering of the problems of ordinary people belonging to the middle or lower-class. Close attention to the details of physical setting and to the complexities of social life was the distinguishing mark of those realistic novels.

Realism began in France in the novels of Balzac (1799-1850), Gustave Flaubert (1821-1880) and short stories of Maupassant (1850-1893). In Russia realism was represented in the plays and short stories of Anton Chekhov (1860-1904). George Eliot (1819-1880) introduced realism into English fiction to give a faithful representation of commonplace things. Mark Twain (1835-1910) and William Dean Howells (1837-1920) were pioneers of realism in the United States. Anglo-American realist, Henry James (1843-1916), drew his inspiration from his mentors George Eliot and Howells. Howells, however, while opposing idealization, made a comic criticism of society. His aim was to show how life is 'more good' than evil, and, in return, through his work he tried to inspire 'more good.' Arnold Bennet (1867-1931), the master realist, recorded with exact detail the nature of provincial life where every little event has a public dimension and is taken up for scrutiny by the active and conscious citizen.

Naturalism, often called extreme realism, is another movement that influenced the nineteenth century novel. Naturalism believes that man belongs entirely to nature, and his character and fortune are determined by two natural factors, heredity and environment. Naturalism presents man with an objective scientific attitude with elaborate documentation about activities and bodily function, not known earlier. Initiated by Jules Goncourt (1830-1870) and Edmond Goncourt (1822-1896) in France it came to be led by Emily Zola (1840-1902). Among other well-known novelists Maupassant (1850-1893) in France, Theodore Dreiser (1871-1945) and Frank Noris (1870-1902) in America, George Moore (1852-1933) and George Gissing (1857-1903) in England are associated with Naturalism.

A realist's emphasis on external reality was challenged in the first few decades of the twentieth century by 'modernism' and, to be specific, by the movements of Symbolism, Imagism, Expressionism and Surrealism etc. The novelists like Franz Kafka (1833-1924), Joseph Conrad (1857-1924), Marcel Proust (1871-1922) and William Faulkner (1897-1962) abandoned the conventions of realism to adopt complex and difficult forms and styles. James Joyce (1882-1941) brought about change both in style and content of fiction. They attempted new ways of tracing the flow of characters' thoughts and devised stream-of-consciousness techniques to capture the sense of time as it actually operates in the human consciousness. Modernism often expresses a sense of urban cultural dislocation, along with an awareness of new anthropological and psychological theories. In America modernism was ushered in by writers, who shattered conventional taboos of expressing physical and psychological actuality. These writers felt the need to control and document the social condition of post World-War I—the isolationist fears, corruption, disenchantment, dehumanization, social and moral confusions caused by war etc. With the use of symbolism they tried to explore the spiritual nature of men and the value of their society and institutions. Writers like Hemingway (1899-1961), Faulkner and Francis Scott Fitzgerald (1896-1940) spearheaded the modern renaissance by employing both realistic and naturalistic techniques.

It is interesting to note that Surrealism—a 1920s revolutionary movement launched in France and America—violated all that realism stood for, namely, conventional modes of artistic organization, syntax, chronological order etc. It went for an expression of free functioning of the human mind in dreamlike and nightmarish sequences, and juxtaposition of the bizarre, shocking or seemingly unrelated images. A further development of the twentieth century was the use of magic realism in novels. Magic realism leads to a kind of fiction in which fabulous and fantastical events are included while simultaneously maintaining the reliable tone of objective realist report. The term was first applied to a trend in German fiction of the early 1950s and is now associated chiefly with certain leading novelists of Central and South America, notably Miguel Angel Asturias (1899-1974), Alejo Carpentier (1904-1980) and Gabriel Garcia Marquez (1927). Marquez's *One Hundred Years of Solitude (*1967) is a leading example of the kind. The term magic realism is also extended to works from very different cultures, designating a tendency of modern novels to reach beyond the confines of realism. For that it draws upon the energies of fable, folk tale and myth while retaining a strong contemporary relevance. The fantastic attributes given to characters in such novels—levitation, flight, telepathy, and telekinesis—are adopted to encompass the phantasmagoric political realities of the twentieth century.

Though realism and modernism are two different movements to emerge within a gap of twenty years, they are not poles apart as long as they focus on detailing the internal and external problems of the individuals. Modernism could not remove the trend of putting emphasis on external reality altogether; writers of the late twentieth century often felt an urge to expound their social preoccupation through the traditional mode of realism. Take for example works of Evelyn Waugh (1903-1966), Graham Greene (1904-1991), L.P. Hartley (1895-1972), C.P. Snow (1905-1980) and Anthony Powel (1905-2000). The contribution of Joyce Cary (1888-1967) to the realistic trend is no less important. William Golding (1911-1993) and Lawrence Durell (1912-1990) however have reasserted the experimental tendency.

As far as Indian novel in English is concerned, realistic novel has reigned supreme till the 1970s. Critics divide the Indian novel in English written from 1930s to the end of the twentieth century into two phases, Modernist (1930s to 1980s) and Post-Modernist (1980s to the end of twentieth century). Novelists like Mulk Raj Anand, R.K. Narayan and Raja Rao started writing during the 1930s and continued to write till the end of the twentieth century. They continued the tradition they had established without much change all through their careers. The modernist phase in Indian literature may, however, be traced to nineteen twenties when Indian society faced a change, the depth and magnitude of which were not felt earlier. The First World War and India's Freedom Struggle aroused nationalistic feeling and spread a social and political awareness. Literature became valuable to the nationalists and revolutionaries as a convenient way to dramatize and popularize their cause. As a result, the setting of the novel was shifted to the contemporary battles and agitations. Even the purely social reform novels were influenced by the politics of the time. Indian novelists writing in English became determinedly more realistic and less idealized like their counterparts in the regional languages, and sought a more earthy presentation of India. Yet, they could not keep themselves detached from the technique of the literature of revolt fashionable in Europe and America at that time. Commenting on the impact of these influences on the Indian novelists of the same period, H.M. Williams observes that ". . . . Indo-Anglian literature can be consistently viewed in two ways: as a more or less faithful reflection of Indian consciousness reacting to the experienced world; and as part of the world of English-speaking literature, sharing with England and America, trends and genres and attitude that suggest a certain degree of literary uniformity stemming from the shared language and its literary traditions"1. The Indian English novel based on the theme of social reality and revolution—from Venkantaramani's *Murugan the Tiller (*1927) and *Kandan the Patriot* (1932) to Anand's passionate progressivism and Raja Rao's emotional zeal for Gandhian ideas—supports H.M. Williams's view. R.K. Narayan's novels are not much different from those novels of the main body of English Novel which treat common men as the centre of the human drama. Narayan is ordinarily faithful to the original bourgeois inspiration of the English realistic novel. Yet he is different, and the difference lies not in his concern with the middle-class but rather in his concern with the unique cultural character of this class. A thorough reading of his novels brings out a candid and concrete picture of this unique cultural character. Narayan's choice of setting in his fiction, the characters and situations selected by him, his ironic presentations of life as well as his use of language offer a full picture of Narayan the realist.

Malgudi, the south Indian town in which Narayan places his characters is apparently different from Anand's India of distress and suffering caused by political conflicts and social inequality, and also from Raja Rao's India of metaphysical concern. Yet it is a faithful reflection of an India as real as Anand's or Raja Rao's. The difference lies, in fact, in Narayan's angle of observation—in his comic vision that sees a comic propensity in every small or big event and character. Malgudi gives him the necessary fixity of background against which he sets his comedy of deviation and disturbance of the normal. But the presentation of the normal itself is richly ambiguous because it is an odd mixture of the opposites. The ambiguities of the Malgudi world are seen and reflected through Narayan's comic vision of life. Narayan uses all the weapons of the comic—irony, humour and satire—and presents a subtle and delightful portrait of middle-class life in India. Narayan's Malgudi serves an important purpose by fulfilling the tradition of realistic novels—of placing its characters in a definite location—in temporal and spatial reality. The small town gives the novels a unity of existence. The town grows and changes in the same way as a small and conservative town in any part of India would do. It is linked to Madras and to the surrounding villages such as Mangala and Talapur. Notwithstanding the superficial influence of western and modern forces, Malgudi retains and displays the characteristic of an older and more human way of life. That is why once in Madras, Chandran wishes that "people of Madras were more human; they were so mechanical and impersonal; the porter at the station had behaved as if he were blind, deaf and mute; now this hotel men would not even look at his guest; these fellows simply did not care what happened to you after they had received your money" (*The Bachelor of Arts*: 95). In contrast to life in Madras, a big town with modern culture, Malgudi stands for community living. A concrete picture of the town emerges as the old and new landmarks—the river, the forests, the eternal gutters, the municipality, the schools, college, lanes, streets, saloon, studio, club etc.—are repeatedly introduced in Narayan's novels.

It comes out of Narayan's novels that he has avoided presenting the nuances of Indian life. The theme and situations he has chosen have validity for the entire pan-Indian heterogeneous audience. The regional variations in social structure, values and customs of India have not been incorporated into the theme of his novels. But the theme of common social change like the disintegration of the old hierarchical and agrarian society, and the collapse of the joint-family system are treated with care. Narayan's own life has also been a major theme of his novels. His own experiences, his encounters with people around him, the major events of his life, the kind of world he grew up in, have all gone into his work. But one can very well see how these bits and pieces of his life do not exist there like mere autobiographical statements. Narayan's greatness lies in his serious and superb craftsmanship with which he turns facts into fiction, moulds them to fit them into the particular framework and ambience of the stories, and successfully universalizes his personal experiences. S.C. Harrex says rightly that the transformation of 'Reality' by 'Imagination' in his works reveals the "maturing novelist discovering, experimenting with, and defining certain shaping principles which have become hallmarks of his narrative art"[2].

Usually, the centre of life in Narayan is domestic life, the authenticity of which is hardly questioned. Narayan earnestly maintains this position, accurately describing middle-class domestic life. Swami's relationship with his new-born brother, his mother, father and grandmother is revealed distinctly and vividly. Chandran's relationship with his parents and brother, Krishna's with his wife and daughter, even the relationship between Mali and Jagan, Nagaraj and his wife and brother are drawn with similar dexterity and authenticity. The portrayal of the enduring loyalty and deep sense of obligation of a brother shown to an old sister fallen on evil days, as depicted in *The Guide*, may be rare in life, but not unreal. The dark side of small agricultural communities is also revealed with subtle details. For example the picture of drought, the cattle without fodder and human beings wrangling for drinking water, is drawn realistically in *The Guide*. The topic of gradual collapse of the joint family system, an important factor behind the social changes in postcolonial India, finds a place in Narayan's novels too. The topic raises a number of related issues to be encompassed in the theme of the concerned novel. Group behaviour, complicated human relationship, conflict between different values, force of orthodoxy, helplessness of the individual and similar other issues well up encircling a joint family. Narayan's heroes and heroines, while experiencing nostalgia for the gradually collapsing extended family system, seek their own identity consciously by breaking away from the kind of life found in it. The story of Daisy's childhood days and Jagan's youth (as described respectively in *The Painter of Signs* and *The Vendor of Sweets*) can be cited as instances. The vast arena of the unconscious, a much discussed topic in twentieth century psychology, a topic that occupied an important place in twentieth century literature, too, can be discovered in Narayan's introspective concerns with the individuals in his later novels. His later novels deal successfully with the non-urban, indigenous but inward-looking situations and characters. The fact that Narayan's later novels tend to focus more on individuals and their personal stories becomes apparent in *The Financial Expert*, *The Guide*, *The Vendor of Sweets*, *The Man-Eater of Malgudi*, *The Painter of Signs* and *The World of Nagaraj*. *The World of Nagaraj* is about the fancy, disillusionment and pathos of a traditional middle-class, day-dreaming protagonist who is driven adrift by circumstances. In an attempt to get at harsh realities Narayan depicts human predicament and disillusionment in a realistic manner.

Fancy and imagination are included in Narayan's world as the reality of human consciousness, not as elements to reduce harsh reality. It is also noteworthy that in Narayan's work one does not find ideologies like Marxism, positivism or existentialism being propounded. *The Dark Room* which seems to have an echo of modern feminism has no theory to propound but to show the actuality of the status of women in middle-class Indian society. Narayan deliberately shuns the subject of abject poverty, suffering, bloodshed, death, romantic love and lust in his novels. He is a comic realist whose creative vision renders human predicament in terms of comedy of affirmation. Human follies and failures, which fail to cloud his dispassionate mind and embitter his compassionate heart, create the comic disorder and comic tension in his novels. The comic in Narayan is found blended with sadness—the sadness that comes from the most intimate experience, namely the painful experience of dismantling the routine self and the reconstitution of another personality. Narayan is a detached observer of this reality.

In his short stories, Narayan finds enough scope to deal with a variety of subjects. As he says, "the short story is the best medium for utilizing the wealth of subjects available. A novel is a different proposition altogether, centralized as it is on a major theme, leaving out, necessarily, a great deal of the available material on the periphery. Short stories, on the other hand, can cover a wider field by presenting concentrated miniatures of human experience in all its opulence" (Introduction, *Under the Banyan Tree*). He found his material for the stories in the open-air, the market-place, and the streets of Mysore. He watched the crowds at the market for the sheer pleasure of watching people from which however his stories took root. That is why, unlike his novels, the stories reveal "the crowded jostling life of the Indian bazaar and the short and simple annals of the Indian poor" (P.S. Sundaram 1988: 122). Even when the place of occurrence is a well-to-do family, the central character is either a servant or a child. His sympathy for characters in his stories sometimes extends to birds and animals too. Most importantly, sly irony and thread of melancholy are the stamps of a Narayan story, as they are in his novels.

Though Narayan has often been criticized for neglecting the political scenario of the time he portrayed, the story of British invasion of India or the achievement of Indian Freedom remain in the background of his novels. He also touches upon the cultural problems created by the colonial presence, at least on certain levels of life. The unique cultural Indian character of Malgudi comes in contact with the British—their polity and educational policy—which in turn gives it a new and peculiar identity. On one side it has its members who are rigidly and spontaneously religious, god-fearing, orthodox and superstitious. On the other, there are the mission school boys, the Bachelors of Arts, the English teachers, the printers and editors of English weeklies, the railway stall-holders and guides, and above all, a host of English knowing clerks in the background who owe their existence to the impact of the British. From the odd mixture of the two arises the comic world of Malgudi. One or two marginal English or American characters—Mr. Brown in *The Bachelor of Arts* and *The English Teacher*, Grace in *The Vendor of Sweets*—appear in his novels. In fact, the vast majority of Indians hardly ever came across or talked to Englishmen or Americans. It is Narayan's fidelity to his subject that he lets his Malgudians be talked about them rather than talk to them, with the exception of the conversation between Muni and the American in 'A Horse and two Goats.' A colonial presence is very much felt in *Swami and Friends*, *The Bachelor of Arts* and *The English Teacher*. Swami, ignorant of the cause and consequence, takes part in the agitation against the British that suddenly breaks out in Malgudi. The situation is delineated as a comic one with no one actually knowing the meaning or the seriousness of it. But Jagan, the self-proclaimed Gandhian, recollects "how as a volunteer over twenty-years ago he had rushed into the British Collector's Bungalow and climbed the roof in order to bring down the Union Jack and plant the Indian flag in its place" (*The Vendor of Sweets*: 132). He got beaten by the police and was put in prison. He was a 'satyagrahi' meant to practice truth in all matters—personal and others, in all sorts of things. Generally however, the people in Malgudi are indifferent to the pressures of the world outside and remain complacent and sleepy. Nothing momentous happens in their life, and life is pleasant without major achievements. As ordinary men living in an ordinary world, Malgudians suffer defeat and accept it gallantly, and yet enjoy triumphs that occasionally come their way.

Another significant theme, common to all Indian novels in English and recurrent in Narayan, is the place of faith in the socio-cultural life of India. People in India are religious. Their religious ethos conforms to the age-old Hindu philosophy of Karma,

Rebirth etc. A rational mind does not fail to see that religious ethos here is blended with blind faith, superstition, fear of punishment and above all, a fatalistic attitude leading to inertia and the lack of a sense of responsibility. Narayan's Malgudi is a fundamentally conservative Hindu society, under the impact of the west, industrialization and modern ideas. The Malgudians are simple and naïve, but are no different from the vast Indian majority. As long as things go on normally, the Malgudi life remains unruffled. When a crisis arises, the true nature of the credo surfaces. It is to this that Narayan directs his irony. But his irony is directed as much towards the modern rebels as towards the old conformists. The modern rebels with their materialistic attitude are devoid of ethics. The power of scientific knowledge is misused for domination and destruction. Hence, traditional Indian values and resources on one hand, modern ideas and attitudes on the other—the conflict between the two turns out to be the basis of Narayan's ironic comedy. The incident concerning the fake 'sanyasi' in ochre robe and Chandran's recourse to 'sanyasi hood' as a solution to his problem in *The Bachelor of Arts*; Margayya's attempt to propitiate Goddess Laxmi with a view to getting rich; the blind faith of Velan and his fellow villagers that Raju is the saint who could induce rain for their drought hit village; and the belief of Nataraj and others that Vasu, as a demon, carries the seeds of his own destruction; these are all parts of the kind of faith that prevail among the Malgudians. Narayan's keen observation of life around him made it clear to him that most of the Indians adopt 'sanyasi hood' as an escape from real life. They adore God only for material benefit. Their fear to take up responsibility explains their inclination to the old scriptures where demons are supposed to have carried the seeds of their own fall much to the relief of the commoners who can very well choose the cosy corner of fatalism. Narayan also found that a few persons who challenge the passivity of the average Indian are extreme representatives of a secular world—like Vasu, Mali,

Raman and Daisy in his novels. They are lacking in moral values and principles to effect a positive change in society.

Narayan's detection of ambivalence in human nature and action also accounts for his success as a realist. In *The Vendor of Sweets*, for example, Jagan's renunciation is charmingly freckled with an appealing human flaw. He leaves for the forest carrying his bank book with him, and the key to the backdoor of the house as well. He, in fact, runs away from what he can no longer cope with—the exorbitant financial demand of his son and the immoral way of life he leads with Grace. His escape may turn out to be a real renunciation of worldly attachment in future but it is not so at that moment. The same ambivalence can be noticed in Raju's attitude in *The Guide* who thinks of escaping even after he has fasted for two days. That Raju has not yet attained spiritual growth is suggested by Narayan who is always faithful to life. Raju is far too self-centered to be humble about his own importance whereas humility is the essence of sainthood. Narayan traces the growth of his character with its pulls and stresses from all directions. What at first reconciles Raju to his new role as a holy man is his habit of seeking success and offering guidance; and secondly, the thought of his own survival. His success with Velan and other villagers secures his requirement of food and shelter. He then begins to feel that he has grown wings. Narayan also focuses on the urgency of the villagers to find a saint who could solve their problems, and so he gives an ironical account of the people making an artificial basin in sand, and fetching water from distant wells to fill it so that the Swami can stand in knee-deep water and pray for rain.

Critics often fail to see the incongruity of the situation and the humour that lurks beneath. These are the master strokes used by Narayan for delineating the real nature of the Indian mass. In Narayan's world there are people who make a business of religion exploiting the gullibility of others. There are some others who with their blind adherence to rituals and innocent faith in the myth of superior wisdom of a guru seek 'sanyasis' around turning to them for support in the time of crisis. All of these people are ironically exposed in Narayan's novels. From the counterfeit 'sanyasi' of *The Bachelor of Arts* to the centenarian priest of *The Painter of Signs*, from the enforced sainthood of *The Guide* to the true asceticism of *A Tiger for Malgudi*, Narayan's theme of the faith in India covers a wide area and leaves many questions unanswered. Yet to say that Narayan suggests his religious philosophy in his novels is to claim too much from an ironic realist.

Another aspect of Indian attitude to religion is that Indians display a mythical consciousness even amidst the day-to-day actuality of their lives. In every crisis they draw mythical parallels, feel fated and avoid responsibility. Raman finds in his situation as regards Daisy a concurrence with the situation of Santhanu of *The Mahabharata*. Jagan's reference to Arjuna's *Vishwaroopa Darshan* while brooding on the many faces of Mali, the reference of the ascetic in *The Tiger for Malgudi* to Gautama Buddha's renunciation of the world, and in *The Grandmother's Tale* the allusion of Narayan's Granny to Savitri's adventure with Yama to justify her mother's recourse to deceitful means to fulfil her objective are instances of the myth-steeped minds of the Malgudians. But Sastri's frequent allusion to myths, particularly the myth of Bhasmasura attracts the critics' attention more than anything else. Most of the critics ignore the ironic implication of these myths—the Bhasmasura myth in particular—and are tempted to explain Narayan's use of myths in terms of his inclination to believe things as he finds in Hindu scriptures. William Walsh's comment in this context is used in support of the view that Narayan has firm faith in the tenets of Hinduism. Walsh says, "The religious sense of Indian myth is part of Narayan's grip of reality, of the particular view of human life and his individual way of placing and ordering human feeling and experience" (1992:166-67).

Narayan's use of myth in his fiction is a part of his ironic scheme. For example, in the actual myth Bhasmasura is outmaneuvered by Lord Vishnu Himself and order is restored after his death. In *The Man-Eater of Malgudi* Vasu kills himself while slapping the mosquitoes sitting on his forehead. This self-annihilation is accidental and ludicrous. Moreover, peace is not restored to Malgudi immediately after Vasu's death; the Malgudians are opposed to murder and they fail to accept Vasu's death as a relief because they suspect Nataraj to be Vasu's murderer. Only after the truth is explained by Sastri, the Malgudians are relieved as everything has occurred as per myth. An intelligent reader is not expected to overlook the discrepancy between the sublime realm of the myth and the ludicrous realm of the novel. The symbolic use of the blue curtain drawn again at the end in Nataraj's press suggests that the Malgudians return to a pre-Vasuan world. With the pre-Vasuan Malgudi, its corruption and discrepancies, being ruthlessly exposed by Narayan, it is not proper to say that Narayan's imagination was shaped by myth. Rather, through an ironic treatment of the myth he has exposed the common Indians' inability to face the evil and their habit of shifting responsibility to the divine order. Narayan has exposed the incapacity of the common people who are unaware that they have their own responsibility to fight evil forces. These people are in what Jean Paul Sartre called 'bad faith' [3].

The style Narayan developed for his realistic novels is not a simple or easy achievement. He evolved an altogether new genre of English to describe unique Indian situations and Indian sensibilities. Its virtue is its freedom and flexibility without the loss of its original character. He uses the same ordinary spoken English for all characters—peasants, petty shopkeepers, illiterate persons as well as the educated middle-class Indians. A whole range of character, personality and temperament emerge out of the unique use of language. The naturalness of their dialogues and the effortless ease in the use of language to express the actuality of daily speech contribute to a part of the loveliness and flavour of his novels.

In its long journey through the twentieth century and early 21st century, Indian writing in English—Indian fiction in English in particular—has reached a stage where it can now be placed in its proper historical and cultural context. With the burst of activity in this literature and the global proliferation of interest for it, Indian English literature has come of age. It now successfully meets the challenges of Bhasha literatures at home and Post-Colonial literature and Anglo-American literature abroad. Amidst these Narayan stands as a class of his own. He shows India to the world in a way no other writer does. His genius lies in his capacity to show the extraordinary ordinariness of most human experiences, and to convince readers that the lives and characters of his fictional writings represent substantial human nature. With its range and depth his fictional writings will undoubtedly stand the test of time.

NOTES

1. H.M. Williams, *Indo-Anglian Literature 1800-1970: A Survey*, 1976: 35-36.
2. S.C. Harrex, 'Celebrating Malgudi's Golden Jubilee: Review of *Talkative Man*,' *CRNLE Reviews Journal* No. 1 & 2, 1988: 8.
3. Sartre described 'bad faith' as 'lying to oneself.' "To be sure, the one who practices bad faith is hiding a displeasing truth or presenting as truth a pleasing untruth. Bad faith then has in appearance the structure of falsehood. Only what changes everything is the fact that in bad faith it is from myself that I am hiding the truth." *Being and Nothingness* (trans. Hazel E. Barnes), 1972: 49.

R.K. Narayan in the 21st Century

Age cannot wither her,
nor custom stale
Her infinite variety.

Shakespeare: *Antony and Cleopatra*

This statement of Shakespeare can be aptly applied to the perennial appeal of R.K Narayan in the present century. Let us examine the history of Indian fiction and contextualize his place in the annals of Indian English literature. By the time R.K. Narayan, M.R. Anand and Raja Rao emerged on the literary scene, Indian English Literature was just more than a century old. But it had not produced any significant novelist with substantial output or any significant novel of an enduring interest. The three grand masters broke new grounds on their arrival, and continued to dominate it for more than five decades. Of course, there were powerful writers like G.V. Desani, Ahmed Ali and Kamala Markandaya during that phase, making marks of their own, but no one could surpass the popularity of the three masters.

Let us look at the contemporary scene. The period of globalization and that of Post-globalization witnessed remarkable changes. This is true of Indian literature as well. Salman Rushdie's *Midnight's*Children heralded a new generation of writers. The output by this new generation is remarkably high. The new young Indian novelists are winning literary awards, prizes and distinctions all over the world. The new writers appear to be influenced by Camus, Kafka or Gabriel Garcia and the like, and doing experimentation with narrative techniques. Thus, they are becoming more globalized than ever before. The array of talents encourages critics to critically examine their works. The east and west encounter becomes the major theme of scrutiny.

For this generation of readers, new writers are plentily available and the choice is manifold. The western influence on readers is unavoidable. There is electronic media, the internet that makes everything available on finger tips. Harry Potter and comic series like Batman and Avengers easily catch the imagination of the youth. An upsurge of interest in the new literature is occurring. This interest is evident in academic, newspaper, and lending library circles and combines a taste for random general viewing with a growing specialization of critical attention. These literatures tend to be in fashion nowadays, and are deservingly in need of responsible criticism from the west as well as locally.

However, all these cannot wane the charm of a writer of Narayan's stature. In fact, the old masters have not at all outgrown the interest of the new generation. Narayan's short and long fictions have not lost a bit of their popularity. For a long time, critics and scholars of India and overseas have established Narayan as the most popular of the founding fathers of the modern Indian novel in English. Perhaps there are more than a thousand publications on R.K. Narayan—monographs, essay collections, contributions to learned journals and magazines, reviews of single works in diverse media and filmed versions of a few of his works which stand witness to it. Narayan's books are still available in book shops, are seen on the stalls in exhibitions, and on the bookshelves of many at home. Among the readers he is still the same old Narayan, the creator of Swami. To meet that demand, Penguin and Vintage have published all his works and they are widely available. He is still prescribed in the curriculum of schools, colleges and universities.

It is time we evaluate the position of R.K. Narayan in terms of world literature. How do we grade the great literature? For instance, Classical European literature—the literature of ancient

Greece and Rome—has not only stood the test of time but has also influenced various literatures of the world, down the ages. For students of literature, this literature will never become obsolete: rather it will provoke intense thought and arouse deep interest, and thereby become the basis of all literary and critical theories. Similarly, Indian Literature which has become an integral part of literary studies at different levels cannot survive without the literature produced by writers like R.K. Narayan and his contemporaries, who have laid the foundation to a genre—widely known as Indian Literature in English. So reading this literature without R.K. Narayan is simply unimaginable. The time has arrived to recognize his works as the classics of Indian literature in English or even global literature.

There has been a sustained interest in Narayan's fictional art all through the six decades in the twentieth century. And astonishingly it continues to flow into the twenty-first century. He is still very relevant. His novels deal essentially with human psychology that never changes—human emotions that never stale. He is lucid and down to earth. He has a timeless appeal. Any reader would identify himself or herself with any of the characters of Narayan. Beginners love to begin novel reading with Narayan. The reason being: his writings feature simplicity of ordinary life, with a good dose of humour. His realistic portrayal of characters with relaxed lifestyles, simple human emotions, living in the fictional town of Malgudi brings nostalgia to the readers.

Narayan is a writer who has covered the whole cycle of the human seasons, from boyhood to old age. He has populated his imagined world of Malgudi with an amazing variety of characters, viewing the landscape of human existence from a rich diversity of perspectives ranging from adolescent fantasy to renunciatory philosophy over a period of about 70 years.

R.K. Narayan has brought to the Indian novel a profound sense of vocation and a high degree of sensitivity and refinement as a literary form responsive to human situation. M.K. Naik considers him as a serious artist preoccupied with what man can make of himself and of the entire human condition. He tries to trace the growth of his irony from merely a weapon into a vision. He also observes 'Narayan's novels belong to a difficult genre, the serious comedy.'

R K Narayan seems to have borrowed from Henry Fielding and Jane Austen the technique of realism in the fictional craft, for like them the Indian novelist does not lead his reader to fairy lands forlorn; his heroes are down to earth and do not allow their creator to make his imagination run wild. The realist sets out to write a fiction which will give the illusion that it reflects life as it seems to the common reader. . . . The realist, in other words, is deliberately selective in his material and prefers the average, the commonplace and the everyday over the rarer aspects of the contemporary scene. His characters, therefore, are usually of the middle class or (less frequently) the working class—people without highly exceptional endowments, who live through ordinary experiences of childhood, adolescence, love, marriage, parenthood, infidelity, and death; who find life rather dull and often unhappy, though it may be brightened by touches of beauty and joy; but who may, under special circumstances, display something akin to heroism.

A thoroughgoing realism involves not only a selection of subject matter, but more importantly, a special literary manner as well: the subject is represented, or "rendered" in such a way as to give the reader the illusion of actual experience.

R.K. Narayan's popularity has received further recognition because of a shift in the fast-changing material world. This has been quite advantageous to the third-world writers, for their books reach the world over in no time. It is no longer uncommon to see a book on the day of its release selling at different places in different counties. Books are now being treated as revenue-generating products. There are several reasons for the popularity of the novels published by Indian writers in India and abroad. Of the several qualities a book needs to have, is its capacity to capture the imagination of the reader. In other words, the most pertinent question is whether a book is 'readable'? The fiction of R.K. Narayan has caught the attention of the audience for one or the other reason. At the turn of the century—in the post-Narayan era, a new trend seems to be emerging. Marketing strategies are now as important as the contents of a book or its author. Modern technology, especially the media and the Internet, has played a significant role in promoting new at need, apart from other ingredients, an author who has promotion potential and a publisher with a wide marketing network.

This development has helped an Indian writer in English much more than a regional Indian writer. Works of writers like R.K Narayan have been re-published by international book companies. Quality production, effective cost structure and easy mobility have given a boost to sales; books are treated as products of a corpus culture, to be bought and sold with frenzied efforts. For example, *The Idea of India*, a diasporic book by Indian-born, Oxford Professor Sunil Khilnani, was listed by The *Guardian* among the best ten world books, published in 1998.

Many of the regional writers too have been quite visible through translations. The translation phenomenon has become prominent, thanks to the efforts made by the Sahitya Akademi, Katha and other organizations. It has brought into cosmopolitan reckoning some of the brilliant writers in the regional languages. Indeed, one of the most popular novels of recent times is U.R. Anantha Murthy's *Samskara,*written originally in Kannada. The English translation by eminent poet A.K. Ramanujan may be considered a contribution both to traditional Indian literature as well to Indian English literature. The novel won the author many prestigious awards including the Sahitya Akademi and the Jnanpith Award. The works of R.K. Narayan can be placed in this category which, though modern, conform to India's tradition and culture.

India has contributed significantly to world literature. This contribution of India has been chiefly through the Indian Writing in English, novelists being in the forefront in this respect. A good number of novelists on the contemporary scene have given expression to their creative urge in no other language than English and have brought credit to the Indian English fiction as a distinctive force in world fiction.

To attempt creative expression on a national scale in an alien medium has seldom happened in human history; and it speaks of the prolific quality of the Indian mind to assimilate the newly confronting situations and the complex dilemmas of the modern world.

While life today is highly complex and frustrating, Narayan's fiction acts as soothing balm to the readers. His adept handling of the comic is his distinguishing mark as a writer of fiction. It is something benign and softly tickles the mind of the readers. Narayan's sense of the comic never laughs all the way, nor does it depend upon the merely satirical which manifests in the exposure of folly to ridicule, accompanied by indignation or laughter. Indignation of any kind is just not known to Narayan, the writer.

Narayan's popularity rests on the themes he selects—which are simple, both by nature and design. The tone of his novels is quiet and subdued. He is not essentially a moralizer, but his works are drawn out of a moral temperament that gently contemplates the incongruities of human action and behaviour. His 'norms of morality are traditional and conventional' in action and performance, but universal in importance and significance. Narayan feels that the essential quality he wants the writer to develop is artistic integrity. His stories thus do not overtly deal with morals, nor do they attempt to philosophize in the abstract. A perspective study of his novels reveals an aesthetic objectivity, which seems to depict an adult view of life with a subdued tone and temperament.

Narayan's work can be considered as a cornerstone of popular literature as it finds favour with a large audience. It at the same time sets the canon as it is representative of society, providing a snapshot of a given point in time. His work is worthy of examination and study, and worthy enough to help us to retain it as a true embodiment of India's cultural norms and mores. And by studying canonical works of the past, we can glean new appreciation for them in a modern perspective. In 2004, Pier Paolo Piciucco edited a book entitled *ACompanion to Indian Fiction in English*. In this book there is a single chapter by Geoffrey Kain who says it is impossible to think of Indian Literature in English without recognizing the central place of Narayan's tales of life in and around the fictional South Indian town of Malgudi.

An article in the *Hindu* on 7 November 2019 says, "Renowned Indian authors like R.K. Narayan, Arundhati Roy, Salman Rushdie and Vikram Seth are among 100 writers who have featured on a list of the most inspiring novels chosen by a panel of experts and revealed by the BBC. The list has been collated by a panel of writers, curators and critics to select the 100 English language—'Novels that Shaped our World.'"

In the *NewYork Times,* Barbara Crosstte writes a tribute to Narayan on his death, "R.K. Narayan, the literary chronicler of small-town life in South India and one of the first Indian writers in English to achieve international acclaim, died yesterday in Madras, India. He was 94". From Graham Greene, his mentor and friend, instrumental in his rise as a writer of international repute to the criticism of William Walsh and H.M. Williams to the critics of the twenty-first century—it is an imperishable saga. Narayan provides an awareness of the past, of a literary tradition. And as Eliot says, tradition has less to do with imitation and more to do with understanding and expanding upon the intellectual and literary context in which one is writing. All art is in conversation with itself, with each new generation's contributions expanding and altering the ways in which the literary canon as a whole is understood.

No wonder, Narayan's popularity has not waned even in the present century. Viewers still recall how generation of Indian audiences would tune into Doordarshan channel to catch an episode of Hindi serial 'Malgudi Days.' Their eyes were glued to the television screen and ears alert for the soft, simple flute sounds that prefaced every episode. Starring Girish Karnad in the leading role, the show followed the story of a young school boy called Swamy and his adventures in the fictional town of Malgudi.

As for as the general readers and common people are concerned, Narayan achieved the zenith of his popularity with the novel *The Guide,* which was adapted by veteran actor and producer Dev Anand into a film, with the same name in 1965. Even in the modern era of science and reasoning, the film won accolades because of its mystic appeal. The audiences were swayed by the ambiguous ending: the protagonist tries hard to become a saint and risks his life as he goes on a fast. He cannot let down the thousands of people who have reposed faith in him. The rain seems to have come as the man appears to be collapsing. The Indian audience finds a philosophic frame of reference with their inherent faith in intuition, magic and mystery. But what makes Narayan's fiction truly enduring and compelling is its pure aesthetic appeal—the appeal for life, truth and beauty. And to quote John Keats,

> A thing of beauty is joy for ever
> Its loveliness increases; it will not
> Pass into nothingness.